GROWING UP TRANSNATIONAL:
IDENTITY AND KINSHIP IN A GLOBAL ERA

Edited by May Friedman and Silvia Schultermandl

In our global era, conceptions and experiences of identity, nationality, personhood, and family are in flux, yet many of the ways that lives are lived, and the cultural imperialism and stereotypes that provide a framework for postmodern life, presume fixed characteristics that allow for an easy response to difficult questions. *Growing Up Transnational* challenges the assumptions behind this fixed framework while looking at the interconnectivity, conflict, and contradictions within current discussions of identity and kinship.

This collection offers a fresh, feminist perspective on family relations, identity politics, and cultural locations in a global era. Using an interdisciplinary approach from fields such as gender studies, queer studies, postcolonial theory, and literary theory, the volume addresses the concept of hybridity and the tangible implications of assumed identities. The rich personal narratives of the authors examine hyphenated identities, hybridized families, and the challenges and rewards of lives on and beyond borders. The result is a new transnational sensibility that explores the redefinition of the self, the family, and the nation.

MAY FRIEDMAN teaches at Ryerson University in the School of Social Work and is a doctoral candidate in the Department of Women's Studies at York University.

SILVIA SCHULTERMANDL is an assistant professor in the Department of American Studies at the University of Graz.

EDITED BY
MAY FRIEDMAN AND
SILVIA SCHULTERMANDL

Growing Up Transnational

Identity and Kinship in a Global Era

UNIVERSITY OF TORONTO PRESS
Toronto Buffalo London

©University of Toronto Press Incorporated 2011
Toronto Buffalo London
www.utppublishing.com
Printed in Canada

ISBN 978-1-4426-4297-3 (cloth)
ISBN 978-1-4426-1160-3 (paper)

Library and Archives Canada Cataloguing in Publication

Growing up transnational: identity and kinship in a global era/
edited by May Friedman and Silvia Schultermandl.

Includes bibliographical references.
ISBN 978-1-4426-4297-3 (bound).   ISBN 978-1-4426-1160-3 (pbk.)

1. Transborder ethnic groups – Social conditions.   2. Transnationalism –
Social aspects.   3. Families.   4. Identity politics.   5. Feminist theory.
I. Friedman, May, 1975–   II. Schultermandl, Silvia, 1977–   III. Title.

HM1271.G76 2011   305.8   C2011-900250-7

This book has been published with the help of grants from the Austrian
Federal Ministry of Science and Research and the University of Graz.

University of Toronto Press acknowledges the financial assistance
to its publishing program of the Canada Council for the Arts and the
Ontario Arts Council

University of Toronto Press acknowledges the financial support for its
publishing activities of the Government of Canada through the Canada
Book Fund.

To our parents and children, past, present, and future

*In loving memory of Waltraud Schultermandl (1953–2009)
and Friedrich Schultermandl (1948–2009)*

Contents

Acknowledgments   ix

Introduction   3
MAY FRIEDMAN AND SILVIA SCHULTERMANDL

PART ONE: REDEFINING SELF

1 Transnational Rio de Janeiro: (Re)visiting Geographical
Experiences   21
ALAN P. MARCUS

2 When Russia Came to Stay   36
LEA POVOZHAEV

3 'Neither the End of the World nor the Beginning': Transnational
Identity Politics in Lisa Suhair Majaj's Self-Writing   55
SILVIA SCHULTERMANDL

4 Identity and Belonging among Second-Generation Greek
and Italian Canadian Women   69
NOULA PAPAYIANNIS

5 Time and Space in the Life of Pierre S. Weiss: Autoethnographic
Engagements with Memory and Trans/Dis/Location   84
SAMUEL VEISSIÈRE

PART TWO: REDEFINING NATION

6 Contemporary Croatian Film and the New Social Economy   103
   JELENA ŠESNIĆ

7 Identity, Bodies, and Second-Generation Returnees in West
   Africa   119
   ERIN KENNY

8 What Is an Autobiographical Author? Becoming the Other   140
   JULIAN VIGO

9 Transnational Identity Mappings in Andrea Levy's Fiction   160
   ŞEBNEM TOPLU

PART THREE: REDEFINING FAMILY

10 The Personal, the Political, and the Complexity of Identity:
    Some Thoughts on Mothering   181
    MAY FRIEDMAN

11 Mothers on the Move: Experiences of Indonesian Women
    Migrant Workers   190
    THERESA W. DEVASAHAYAM AND NOOR ABDUL RAHMAN

12 From Changowitz to Bailey Wong: Mixed Heritage
    and Transnational Families in Gish Jen's Fiction   210
    LAN DONG

13 Tug of War: The Gender Dynamics of Parenting in
    a Bi/Transnational Family   222
    KATRIN KRIŽ AND UDAY MANANDHAR

Notes   233

References   243

Contributors   263

Acknowledgments

This project has been a transnational labour of love characterized by our own mobility, the dispersed and transient nature of our contributors, and the experiences we have had, and continue to have, through our changing and evolving families. The project came to fruition through the guidance and hard work of many different people. First and foremost, we would like to thank our terrific contributors for their patience and hard work. Most of all, however, we would like to thank them for their amazing insights and great wisdom. At the University of Toronto Press, our gratitude goes to Virgil Duff.

In addition, our thanks go to the Association for Research on Mothering (now the Motherhood Initiative for Research and Community Involvement), for its stellar work and for providing us with the context to begin this collaboration. It was at the association's conference 'Mothering, Race, Ethnicity, Culture, and Class' at York University in Toronto in October 2005 that our friendship and collaboration (and hence this project) began.

Silvia would like to thank in particular her colleagues in the Department for American Studies at the University of Graz, Austria, for their good cheer and encouragement during the completion of this project.

As with everything in our lives and work, this project was inspired by our families. May would especially like to thank her parents, both Dalume and Friedman, for their patience and the childcare that allowed this project to bloom. Of course, Dan, Molly, and Noah provided the inspiration for this project (albeit unwittingly); my thanks and all my love go to them. Silvia would like to thank her families, Müller and Schultermandl, for their support and patience. Especially Andi, who continues to amaze me with his endless love and support. And Aviva, who arrived in my life as this project came to completion.

GROWING UP TRANSNATIONAL:
IDENTITY AND KINSHIP IN A GLOBAL ERA

Introduction

MAY FRIEDMAN AND SILVIA SCHULTERMANDL

'Where are you from? And who are you with?' It is the impossibility of these seemingly innocuous questions that led to the creation of this anthology. In a global era, identity, nationality, personhood, and family are in flux, yet much of the stereotyping and cultural imperialism that provide a framework for postmodern life assume a fixity of characteristics that allow for an easy response to these questions. But an easy acceptance of hybridity does not acknowledge the very tangible implications of the identities we are presumed to embody. *Growing Up Transnational* does not attempt answers to this frustrating conundrum. Rather, it provokes more questions and seeks, above all, to trouble the ways in which contemporary globalization has rendered a presumption of fixity an antiquated and outmoded line of enquiry.

Many personal narratives, including those in this collection, enquire into the complicated nature of hyphenated identities, hybridized families, and both the challenges and the richness of lives on, and outside, borders. Such narratives evidence to what extent identity and kinship are not merely interconnected but often complicated, even contradictory, forces in a person's life. Within our personal lives, this project has spanned pregnancy, birth, migration, death, marriage, as well as the countless mundane and complex daily details of family in the twenty-first century. This collection is rooted in the personal, in exploring the transnational through the details of everyday life. It is with these details, then, that we begin.

May

I was very newly pregnant with my second child and engrossed in the details of parenting my first. As my son grew from baby into child, all of a sudden issues around the transmission of identity, culture, and values were foregrounded. In particular, I was struggling with the politics of living in a multicultural brown, female body while parenting a white, male child and gestating this new, unknown entity. How would our family dynamic change if this next child took after me? And how would I cope if she, as I eventually discovered, did not? While all parents want to share their values with their children, the specific multiplicity of my various identities, and in particular, the ragged edges where identities were imperfectly reconciled, became less manageable when put into the realm of family.

I attended a conference on motherhood and ethnicity at which I stumblingly asked my questions and was shocked to find that I had struck a chord. Notably, participants at the conference either viscerally understood my grappling for a way to negotiate a multifarious and imperfect self through the twin minefields of identity politics and nationalism, or they emphatically did not. While I was lucky enough to be met with many nodding heads, a few participants were outraged that I could not view existing 'easy' methods of reconciliation as effective. Ironically, by situating myself within contemporary feminist thought, I became a target for outmoded feminist ideals about the importance of singular identity and the primacy of sisterhood. The panel culminated with an illustrious second wave feminist dismissing my presentation and, after the talk, shaking my hand, fixing me with her gaze, and declaring, 'You're a good girl.' Luckily, as this ridiculous statement was still ringing in my ears, another scholar approached me. Excited by my ideas, she suggested that we continue the discussion with an eye toward eventual collaboration, and that we specifically consider the ways in which families have negotiated living in a transnational era. The product of that collaboration is before you.

Silvia

'You take so much after your mother' is a comment that I hear now more than ever, as one of the many changes in my life since my mother's very unexpected death only one month ago. Yes, I do, and I am grateful for the ways in which her memory lives in and through me, but I am of course also very critical of such comments that rely on biological and genetic discourses and that single out the nuclear family as the place that seems to give us our identities. 'Yes,' I want to reply to such comments, 'but I am also my father, my grandparents, and my mother's biological parents, whom she never met and who never entered the realm of our otherwise candid and sensitive conversations. I am also the many places in which I have lived since my college graduation; I am my friends in places such as the United States, Canada, Macedonia, France, and Austria.'

Perhaps what people are actually saying is that I look like her and that this physical resemblance – the broad smile, the confident stride, the very slim wrists and ankles – remind them of her and demarcate my belonging. In my personal context, as a child of two Austrians living in the rural South, such a comment reflects its innocence and good intentions. But for my more global self, the one that might continue to move to different countries or continents, such a comment goes against my thoughts on selfhood. What does it say about my niece, who looks more like her Nigerian father than her Austrian mother? Or one day about my own daughter, Aviva, who looks so much like me but might become more adept at performing the language and culture of wherever my Austrian husband and I end up living?

Belonging, to family and to place, is more complex than that. From my work on mother–daughter relationships in American literature, I can name a whole army of protagonists who look like their mothers but are aware of and pained by the cultural distance between them. Yes, the similarities matter, but I am most interested in the incongruities, the grey areas, the messiness of identification within the family. And even as an Austrian citizen, born of Austrian parents, currently living in Austria, and married to an Austrian, I can feel these tensions invigorate my personal and scholarly life.

And yes, in this sense I do take after my mother, who saw easy answers as the most profound problems.

A Transnational Sensibility

Growing Up Transnational does not seek answers. Rather, it explores the tensions and possibilities implied in the questioning itself. We have come to think of this process as a 'transnational sensibility.' It begins by looking at life in and on borders, yet goes beyond these inarguably contested subjects to look at the person who is looking, and can be fruitfully applied both to hybridized subjects and to those whose identities are presumed to be fixed. As such, this form of sensibility sees a lack of fixity as simultaneously inevitable and rich in possibility. It is both a methodology and a mode of enquiry: a way of seeing and deliberately *not-knowing*, a way of inhabiting the spaces between questions and answers.

This collection lives within the processes of hybridization, looking at identity, family, and nation as contested and agitated concepts. At the heart of each chapter is a commitment to subvert and deconstruct hegemonic discourses and to promote a transnational sensibility as a methodology that resists specific disciplinary constraints. The emphasis on feminism in a transnational context allows this book to investigate the various aspects of power and privilege at play in the interaction of people and nations in a global economy.

We consciously adopt the term *transnational* instead of *global* because we are convinced that the movement of people and cultures contributes to a *Weltbild* (conception of the world) in which borders and boundaries of nation, culture, race, and gender need to be reconceptualized, blurred, challenged, and, potentially, eliminated. Finally, we appreciate the tension within transnational feminism between the analytical scope of postcolonial theory and the transnational sensibilities this book displays.

The impetus for this collection was our deep conviction that globalization has a substantive impact on family structures.[1] Despite the abundant production of excellent scholarship in transnational studies, this realm has thus far been undertheorized.[2] Given the high degree of individual movement, the need for a transnational sensibility is particularly evident in contemporary families all over the world. In looking at transnational families, we also consider the shifting workforce that results from women's mobility in the new economy. In this respect, the collection strays from the mandates of many other documentations of family and personal growth and development. Books such as *Growing Up Latino: Reflections on Life in the United States* (Stavans and Augenbraum 1993), *Growing Up Catholic: The Pursuit of Truth from Tradition to Satisfaction* (Lott 2007), and even *Growing Up Empty: The Hunger Epidemic in America* (Schwartz-Nobel 2002) seek to document a specific experience and, to some extent, to fix the identity on which that experience is based. By contrast, the authors of *Growing Up Transnational* attempt not only to discuss transnational families in a traditional descriptive sense but also, in their analysis, to disrupt the very identities, nationalities, and niches that underpin many coming-of-age and family narratives. This mode of analysis borrows from transnational feminism and exemplifies a specifically transnational sensibility that should – must – in future be applied beyond subjects that explicitly bear the marks of globalization. We hope that this methodology will capitalize on the complexity of all lives, even (if not especially) those that outwardly display the hallmarks of 'a' 'stable' 'identity.'

Indeed, the very notion of stable identity seems ill conceived. It is true that much feminist scholarship has explored alternative notions of subjectivity, but those that seem to offer the most promising approach come from transgender and transnational feminist theory, those that view female subjects as open to scrutiny themselves. In *Gender Trouble*, Judith Butler, for instance, asserts, 'There is a great deal of material that ... questions the viability of "the subject" as the ultimate candidate for representation or, indeed, liberation, but there is very little agreement after all on what it is that constitutes, or ought to constitute, the category of women' (1990, 4).

Feminist criticism over the years has become sensitive to the representational fallacies Western scholarship has committed in its conceptualizations of the lives and experiences of women in the developing world (cf Grewal and Kaplan 1992, 1994; Kaplan 1992). An appropriate investigation of the category of women poses a particular challenge in an era in which global mobility and identity cannot do without a transnational sensibility. This sensibility, so we believe, is mandatory in contemporary discussion of the cross-cultural encounters that frame the transnational experience. As such, this collection establishes an impetus toward a new critical framework that engages identity from a strictly non-essentialist stance.

Where transgender meets transnational, ambiguities about both are revealed that open possibilities for a radically new response to arrangements of individualism and liberal notions of family.[3] Antiquated ways of thinking of people and families are in trouble, and in this trouble are new possibilities that we may capitalize on. Butler suggests that trouble is, in fact, an inevitability:

> To make trouble was, within the reigning discourse of my childhood, something one should never do precisely because that would get one *in* trouble. The rebellion and its reprimand seemed to be caught up in the same terms, a phenomenon that gave rise to my first critical insight into the subtle ruse of power: the prevailing law threatened one with trouble, even put one in trouble, all to keep one out of trouble. Hence, I concluded that trouble is inevitable and the task, how best to make it, what best way to be in it. (1990, xxvii)

Making trouble, as our own life stories suggest, is an indispensable part of our academic lives, of our lives in general. Receiving so many different submissions from all over the world in reply to our call for papers for this collection gave us a sense of the extent to which many scholars have similar experiences of making such trouble. Our shared aim is to revel in trouble, to take full advantage of its possibilities while in no way underestimating its pitfalls and the ways in which, in resisting fixity, we are 'restrained by the very structures of power through which emancipation is sought' (Butler 1990, 5). Indeed, the transnational sensibility that we display and advocate may very well be characterized as troublesome above all else. But at the same time, without this trouble we would have to accept nonspecific classifications, unhappy compromises, undifferentiated otherness.

Why/What Transnationalism? Why/What Feminism?

The questions 'Where are you from?' and 'Who are you with?' are of course not new. But in a world that becomes smaller as more and more sophisticated technological advances triumph, these questions take on a different form. In an era of hypermobility, more people than ever encounter these questions. And perhaps more than ever, it becomes clear that they are far from being innocent small talk; on the contrary, such questions often imply assumptions of belonging and legitimacy.[4] A trend that emerged in the immediate decades before and after the millennium, global mobility describes the degree to which people increasingly live in more than one nation and the ease with which persons, goods, and knowledge can now travel.[5] Transnationalism defines the experiences we are assumed to share in this era of global mobility, regardless of our race, class, gender, and citizenship. And in this sense, transnationalism has become an umbrella term for global linkages and the diversity and contradictions of these exchanges. For example, Alejandro Portes, Luis Eduardo Guarnizo, and Patricia Landolt, who have investigated the potential of transnationalism as an emergent research field, define the term as 'occupations and activities that require regular and sustained social contacts over time across national borders for their implementation' (1999, 219). That not all people are equally affected by the 'occupations and activities' that Portes mentions is clear. But it is the people who see their lives affected by this emergence of new global linkages who tell new and important stories: their stories, (and the ones in this collection are no exception) present the human face of this global era.

Transnationalism and globalization are thus linked, but they are not synonymous.[6] This becomes especially evident from current developments

in feminist theory and practice, where scholars draw a clear line between global and transnational feminist approaches. Shirley Geok-lin
Lim, for instance, observes that global feminism often tends to be confused with 'an international feminism coming out of the West' (2004, 8).
Lim uncovers the imperialist and racist nature of projects that apply
Western feminist thought in their investigations of non-Western cultural
phenomena. Chandra Talpade Mohanty's seminal essay 'Under Western
Eyes: Feminist Scholarship and Colonial Discourses' offers an avid critique of feminist enquiries that, in their investigations of the feminist
practices of women in the Third World, end up producing 'the '"Third
World Woman" as a singular, monolithic subject' (2003, 17), thus promoting 'an image that appears arbitrarily constructed but nevertheless carries with it the authorizing signature of Western humanism' (19).[7] Unlike
global feminism, which was characterized by 'its tendency to essential-
ize, homogenize, and centralize Western social and cultural concepts of
women' (Lim 2004, 8), transnational feminism offers a more dynamic set
of parameters, language, and frameworks for a contemporary discussion of experiences of migration across times and places. Such feminist
practices recognize that the attempt to analyse both global inequalities
and the specific detrimental factors in people's experience of culture
emerge from a world order in which borders constituted by space and
time are being held fast more easily than are ideological borders that
dictate where we belong and who we can be with.

It is through an investigation into ideological borders, and not only
into the physical border crossings generated and augmented by globalization, that transnational feminist practices offer new insights into that
microcosm of globalization, the transnational family. Through a new
conceptualization of the postmodern world order (such as by uncov-
ering the artificiality of national borders and, in fact, of the nation-state
altogether) many categories of identity, including race, class, and
gender, are being investigated in new contexts. Transnational adoption,
transnational sex work, and transnational labour markets, for instance,
do not obliterate the impact of 'race' as a shaping force on social power
structures; on the contrary, they put it into sharper focus.[8] At its best,
transnational feminism tilts common perceptions of identity, nationhood, and family: perceptions that in the past operated along essentialist criteria and thus failed to offer meaningful and satisfactory
definitions of lives that are marked by increased global flow and the
new challenges it poses for society. Transnational feminism operates
within an 'antiracist and anti-imperialist' ideological framework and a

vocabulary that 'articulates differences in power and location as accurately as possible' (Kaplan 1992, 116).

To this end, transnational feminist theory draws from contemporary feminism, which blends postmodern analysis with acknowledgment of the systemic nature of privilege and oppression. Such a theory can succeed in disrupting both systems and identities; it can also succeed in seriously destabilizing the subject by considering what emergent and valuable ideas may come from this disruption. It furthermore involves an acknowledgment of the very real ascendancy of the nation-state, and of static notions of self and family, on the lives on individual subjects. This acknowledgment, however, exposes these 'truths' as simply working types of knowledge and relishes the potential found in instability and hybridization. *Growing Up Transnational* exists in this grey space.

Emergent Themes

The thirteen chapters of this collection are divided into three thematic sections. Part One, Redefining Self, investigates constructions and representations of identity by individuals who grew up positioning themselves within multiple national contexts. Part Two, Redefining Nation, deconstructs ideas of a homogenized nationhood based on an investigation of narratives that lay bare the dis-congruencies between cultural and national identity; and finally Part Three, Redefining Family, builds on the earlier sections in applying the ambiguities and inconsistencies of nation and self to the specific realm of family. The individual chapters in each section espouse three types of enquiry: a predominantly anthropological approach, a predominantly auto/biographical approach, and a predominantly textual/literary approach. By using different critical enquiries into the same thematic field, each section facilitates a stratified picture of the intricacy of transnational feminist theory and practice.

While some of the contributors begin from an anthropological perspective, they understand that anthropological investigation does not produce knowledge per se, but rather offers an entry point into various 'modes of knowing.' Mani asserts that these modes are defined through their 'questions of positionality and location and their relation to the production of knowledge as well as its reception' (2003, 365). As such, anthropologically specific terminology is itself re- (or de-)codified. The language of kinship, which has a specific reading within the disciplinary boundaries of anthropology, is resurrected and then resisted within chapters that look at the impact of commerce and race on arrangements that withdraw from an easy characterization as kin or non-kin.

Likewise, the notion of 'growing up' in our title refers as much to the emergence of an ongoing field of enquiry within transnational sensibility as it does to the individuals it describes. To this end, anthropological enquiry into family is a way of determining how the social patterns of power and privilege manifest themselves in the familiar realm, and to what extent they shape projects of identity formation (such as those implicit in parenting strategies and courtship practices).

A similar potential emerges from the kind of auto/biographical enquiry into selfhood that operates with a transnational sensibility. Written through this lens, autobiography, whose capacity to communicate a feminist heuristics some scholars have come to question, can indeed be redeemed.[9] In *De/Colonizing the Subject: The Politics of Gender and in Women's Autobiography*, Sidonie Smith and Julia Watson remind us that the very genre of the autobiography is a Western literary form, one that, in the post-Enlightenment tradition, 'sees its destiny in a teleological narrative enshrining the "individual" and "his" "uniqueness"' (1992, xvii). Smith and Watson argue that 'autobiographical practices can be productive in that … the subject, articulating problems of identity and identification, struggles against coercive calls to a "universal humanity"' (xix). Autobiography may transgress through a careful consideration of the author's 'politics of location,' a term coined by Adrienne Rich (1986, 225) that denotes the deconstruction of any hierarchical use of 'gender.' This idea reminds us that there is no such thing as a universal global sisterhood at the root of all women's experiences of gender, but that attempts to subvert gender hegemonies always operate within a specific cultural and political space. To assume that all subjects write from similar positions of selfhood is thus equally problematic. By extension, there cannot be a linear autobiographical discourse but perhaps a 'discourse of situation' (Kaplan 1992, 117), one that emerges from specific experiences of power and privilege. Such a discourse is sensitive to the innate contradiction implied in the autobiographical project as a means of presenting a sense of selfhood rather than as a project that performs, through a variety of literary gestures, the processes that shape identity formation.[10]

The auto/biographical chapters within this text thus exemplify Sidonie Smith and Julia Watson's call for 'perspectival adjustments' (1992, xvii) to produce a successful decolonization of the subject in autobiography and other forms of life writing. Smith and Watson place their definition of a decolonization of the subject in autobiographical practices in opposition to the questions that Foucault, Lacan, and Spivak raise about the possibility of a decolonization in the face of the multiple power structures in which the subject is embedded: Foucault (1980b) about social; Lacan (1993) about patriarchal; and Spivak (1988) about postcolonial power structures. In this sense, Smith and Watson's take on decolonization is a more optimistic one, precisely because it takes into consideration the 'perspectival adjustments' necessary for an analysis of life writing beyond the Eurocentric literary tradition.

Such perspectival adjustments are also at play in much literary scholarship on the transnational production and reception of feminist literature. In *Going Global: The Transnational Reception of Third World Women Writers,* for instance, Amal Amireh and Lisa Majaj emphasize the ideological expectations that textual productions meet, such as their appropriation of sociological data for the purpose of presenting evidence of cultural practices possibly foreign to the reader (2000, 7). This foreignness between reader and text locates the narrative in a specific critical context in which the implied ideology of the author confronts the ideology of the recipient.[11]

In keeping with this appropriation of texts as discursive situations, the authors of this section show a deep awareness of the many complex dynamics that shape the reception of literary texts in a transnational world. This discursive construction of Western superiority also contributes to a Eurocentric appropriation of the Third World in which the practices and values of the West serve as indicators for the degree of advancement of the entire world (Shohat and Stam 1994, 2–3). Unlike the practice that Ella Shohat and Robert Stam critique, such textual readings do not seek out the 'West' in order to apply it to 'the Rest' but offer insights not only into ways in which West/Rest boundaries are blurred but in which the West needs to reimagine itself after confrontation with the Rest, in which the West ultimately becomes part of the rest of the world.

The authors in the textual/literary chapters of this collection apply a critical self-consciousness in their investigation of the mode of enunciation and the reception of the texts they study. Like the auto/biographical chapters, the textual/literary ones recognize transnational families as complex modalities and engage that complexity in order to interpret postmodernity in a new light. In addition to the sensitivity to issues of power and privilege that the previously discussed approaches display, these chapters investigate the incorporation of transnational feminist theory into the literary/textual representation of issues of globalization. To various degrees, the authors read examples of transnational identities beyond the 'master narrative of the generational conflict' (Lowe 1991, 26), between different generations that experience the world, differently, as a transnational place. Not only do the individual authors highlight heterogeneous conceptualizations of identity but they also question the parameters on which these conceptualizations are founded. In this endeavour, so we believe, lies one of the book's strengths.

Redefining Self

Critical attention to the impetus to renegotiate structures of identity needs to embrace a concept of identity that provides room for the contradictions generated by the multiple locations and positionings that transnational subjects experience. In other words, in a global era, perhaps more than ever before, identities are constantly in flux. In this context, Stuart Hall's (1996, 608) concept of 'identification' as a conglomeration of the ways in which we position ourselves and in which we are positioned by others gains additional importance: no longer does it suffice to look into specific locations, such as within a nation-state, to determine identities. We must also look into how these locations confine, interfere with, and contradict individual projects of selfhood.

In critical discourses on multiculturalism such as the ones that invigorated academic departments and reading canons in American universities in the 1980s and 1990s, investigations of such fluid boundaries hardly went beyond the nation-state as conceptual framework. Multi-ethnic American identities and their representations in literature and other media, for instance, were often regarded as colourful addenda to American culture, but did not sufficiently disrupt the solidified concept of what 'American' meant as a cultural category assigned to a specific nation-state. Dominating discussions of American diversity during this meek foray into 'multiculturalism' was the concept of hyphenation, a suggestion that everybody had, in addition to his or her American identity, an ethnic identity that complemented the national.[12] The limitations of such an assumption become particularly evident once we consider ethnicity not only as a defining adjective of national identity but also as a global vector that expresses migratory movements and patterns.

The forces of globalization shape identities in transnational families. Therefore, the individual life narratives of people who live on and across national borders underscore the need for a conceptualization of identity beyond hyphenation and, by extension, beyond national borders. Alan P. Marcus opens the discussion of identity by resisting a traditional autobiographical approach to his story of growing up in Rio de Janeiro within a transnational family. Marcus coins the term *autobiogeography* to guide his history of geographic knowledge framed as the spirit of place of Rio de Janeiro – experienced through different periods and spatial perspectives. Lea Povozhaev writes about a Protestant American woman and an orthodox Russian man who achieve a union across cultural differences as they fall in love, in faith, in place, tacitly taking into account Kaplan's (1994) charge to consider the dynamics of power and location within geographies both global and minute, in this case a small house shared by disparate families. What becomes of the very concept of identity in a transnational context is also the question at the heart of Silvia Schultermandl's chapter on Lisa Suhair Majaj's writing. Schultermandl reads Majaj's life and literary production as an example of rhetorical strategies and textual performances that do not seek to recover a sense of selfhood but instead present selfhood as a communicative project between the text and the reader, and between the individual and her onlooker. The tensions of such transnational encounters within the family shape Noula Papayiannis's analysis of the shifting meanings of otherness and Canadian-ness for second-generation Italian and Greek Canadian women like herself. A similar communal project between the individual and his or her social environment characterizes Samuel Veissière's chapter. Veissière's performance of the transnational persona of Pierre S. Weiss challenges the traditional form and content of selfhood. Together, the chapters of this section narrate, rewrite, and scrutinize the partly fluid and partly disembodying experience of being located within multiple cultures.

Redefining Nation

The shift from multicultural and national to diasporic and transnational projects coincides with a deep commitment to dismantle the concept of the nation-state itself. At the same time, recent scholarship in transnational feminism has understood that nationhood cannot be addressed without looking at the implications of gender in the formation of national identities. In the introduction to *Between Woman and Nation: Nationalisms, Transnational Feminisms, and the State*, Norma Alarcón, Caren Kaplan, and Minoo Moallem argue that 'the nation-state sharpens the defining lines of citizenship for women, racialized ethnicities, and sexualities in the construction of a socially stratified society' (1999, 1). Such definition of the nation-state and its impact on communities draws upon Benedict Anderson's concept of imagined communities (1983, 7) and Homi K. Bhabha's discussion of nationalist discourses (1994). In *The Location of Culture*, Bhabha contends that the complex strategies of cultural identification and discursive address that function in the name of 'the people' or 'the nation' make them the immanent subjects of a range of social and literary narratives (140). Bhabha's definition of counter-narratives of the nation, argue Alarcón, Kaplan, and Moallem, 'evoke and disturb those ideological maneuvers through which "imagined communities" are given essentialist definitions' (7).

Women maintain a special position within this social formation of nationhood. As Alarcón, Kaplan, and Moallem specify, 'Women are both of and not of the nation. Between woman and nation is, perhaps, the space or zone where we can deconstruct these monoliths and render them more historically nuanced and accountable to politics' (12). In this contestation, Alarcón and her co-editors follow a general determination in transnational feminist studies to point out the limitations of modernity, whose formation was largely overshadowed by the 'naturalization and essentialization of nation and woman' (13). Instead, volumes like this one underscore the discursive constructedness of woman and nation, arguing that the cathexis of the two formed the discourses of normativity that coined the modern nation-state.

This critical stance unites the chapters in this section. Jelena Šesnić's article offers a discussion of three contemporary Croatian movies and analyses their depiction of the tension between traditional patriarchal family models and anti-traditional family dispensations. Erin Kenny's chapter follows with an investigation of the experience of foreign-born children who return to their sending communities in Guinea, paying specific attention to the issue of female genital mutilation. As Šesnić does with regard to film, Julian Vigo does with regard to autobiography by deconstructing the narrative representation of nation and identity in analysing the boundaries between textual medium and social reality. Vigo offers a critique of monolithic constructions of race, sexuality, and national identity in biographical and autobiographical narratives of and about AIDS. By paying special attention to the metatextual elements embedded in the texts they discuss, Vigo and Šesnić expose the mechanisms at play in the hegemony prevalent in contemporary identity narratives. The essay by Şebnem Toplu adopts transnationalism as a reading practice of texts that depict multiculturalism in Britain and the United States. Toplu discusses the work of Andrea Levy with emphasis on the narrative voices of second-generation Caribbean British protagonists who experience both internal conflicts with their diasporic parents and external tension created by the host society.

Redefining Family

If identity and nationhood are in flux and are both discursive constructs, then the family itself is perhaps the place where such construction happens. For instance, how to define the culturally 'traditional' is a recurring question, which the authors in this collection meet with their adherence to a deconstructionist approach. What constitutes the 'traditional,' they assert, depends upon the disjunctures that emerge from the specific rhetorical situations that construct other cultures as 'other.' Not only is the personal political but the domestic exhibits issues of power and privilege as well.

The family thus is, as Patricia Hill Collins has already pointed out successfully, located at the intersection of nationhood, gender, race, and class (1998). It is also the place that mirrors social tensions and patterns, as many projects that seek to reconceptualize the family have exemplified.[13] And in much anthropological scholarship, kinship operates within similar parameters. Linda Stone for instance, defines kinship as 'an ideology of human relationships; it involves cultural ideas about how humans are created and the nature and meaning of their biological and moral connections with others' (2000, 5–6).

In transnational families the ongoing negotiations of family identity mirror global linkages and movements. If gender inequality, as Judith Lorber emphasizes, 'is not an individual matter but is deeply engrained in the structure of societies' (2005, 7), it is also symptomatic of the global inequalities that separate the global North from the global South. Inequalities between men and women thus often undergo drastic shifts when the global workforce offers more potential for transnational mobility to women. This is a phenomenon that Barbara Ehrenreich and Arlie Russell Hochschild have called the 'feminization of migration' (2002, 5), referring to the dominance of women in global care economies, holding jobs in fields such as child care, cleaning services, and sex work, which are meant draw on the qualities that women are thought to possess to a greater degree than men.

Many scholars have observed gender inequalities not primarily between geographic and geopolitical entities such as 'global North and

South' but between individual members of the same family and their extended kin. Access to global mobility, for instance, can vary for individual family members. Such differences within the family are not always negative; on the contrary, they provide space for the trouble that Butler (1990) places at the heart of innovative feminist thought. Rhacel Salazar Parreñas describes transnational families and the economic and structural choices they make on a daily basis – equipped with the potential to call into question established gender boundaries – as watershed moments in the deconstruction of 'cultural parameters and institutional norms marked by material inequalities between men and women as well as ideology' (2005, 1).

The essays in this section demonstrate a keen awareness of the interrelatedness of the particular issues their personal accounts raise and the general discussions within which they are located. They relate observations about the cultural encounters within a person's homeplace to prevalent issues in society at large.[14] In particular, May Friedman explores the challenges of parenting children while attempting to blend multiple, seemingly incongruous identities. Similarly, Theresa W. Devasahayam and Noor Abdul Rahman's study of female foreign domestic workers in Singapore explores the challenges these workers face as they juggle life away from their families and their traditional roles as mothers. Lan Dong analyses the female characters in Gish Jen's depictions of transnational Chinese American families and their attempts to reshape ethnic identities and to redefine whiteness through interracial and transnational encounters. Dong investigates Jen's formulations of whiteness, which emerge from an alternative rationale as the Eurocentric paradigm of engaging the West as a centre of modernity and thus elevating it ideologically over the rest of the world. Finally, Katrin Križ and Uday Manandhar investigate the gender dynamics of parenting in middle-class, dual-earner transnational families in the United States.

Growing Up Transnational

The chapters in this collection successfully interrogate and reject static notions of kinship and nationality and present a compelling and disquieting portrait of family within an era of intensifying globalization. As much as they concur with the general impact of transnational feminism on identity politics in a global era, the contributing essays also exemplify, in the variety of the physical and metaphorical areas they investigate, that 'transnational processes are situated cultural practices'

(Ong 1999, 17) and that the specific cultural practices connected to a specific location determine the conditions and modalities with which transnational identities emerge. In short, no unified theory of trans- nationalism can be applied to the numerous situations in which in- creasing mobility and immense cultural exchanges occur.

Given the vast range of ideas it contains, this book demonstrates in- consistencies in the degree to which the authors embrace transnational practice as a philosophy. Indeed, some are rather critical of its potential whereas others see in it the solution to the world's malaise, as becomes apparent from the subtext of their discussions. In our process of selec- tion, we considered Kobena Mercer's valuable reminder: 'Solidarity does not mean that everyone thinks the same way; it begins when people have the confidence to disagree over issues of fundamental im- portance precisely because they "care" about constructing common ground' (1990, 66). But this diversity of thought – and we see it evi- denced also in the choice of genres and modes of enquiry that the indi- vidual chapters exhibit – is a driving force that constitutes the potential of transnational feminism to function as a new way of conceiving of this global era. As Sanjeev Khagram and Peggy Levitt astutely observe, a transnational perspective is 'a way of understanding the world, a shared set of questions and puzzles, and a different expectation about what constitutes an acceptable answer' (2008, 5).

Growing Up Transnational: Identity and Kinship in a Global Era invites readers to take a close look at the contested territory of kinship and identity within a transnational context. The thirteen chapters tackle dif- ficult questions about the fluidity of identity and the potential pitfalls and opportunities found within hybridized locations and kinship ar- rangements. What makes the collection so exciting, however, is its po- tential to push the boundaries of transnational scholarship by extending the analysis of identity and nationality into the intimate quarters of the family. Thus the authors, using anthropological, autobiographical, and literary techniques through the lens of transnational sensibility, view transnational subjects and families, and the connections between the two, as a profoundly important site of praxis. The moments of political and personal synthesis unearthed here reveal the limitations of trad- itional notions of identity and identification and highlight the variety of textures of transnational families. We hope that range of experience as well as miles travelled in this collection will allow readers to react on both emotional and scholarly levels, in much the same way that the chapters themselves were written.

PART ONE

Redefining Self

1 Transnational Rio de Janeiro: (Re)visiting Geographical Experiences

ALAN P. MARCUS

> The sun was setting, and a gentle southerly breeze, striking against the
> southern side of the rock, mingled its current with the colder air above;
> and the vapour was thus condensed; but as the light wreaths of cloud
> passed over the ridge; and came within the influence of the warmer atmos-
> phere of the northern sloping bank, they were immediately re-dissolved.
>
> (Darwin [1909] 2000, 39)

My transnational understanding of Rio de Janeiro, Brazil, through different periods and various spatial and experiential perspectives draws
on theoretical concepts applied in humanistic geography. The conceptual premise of my investigation of Rio is in line with geographer
Anne Buttimer's observation: 'It is time we discovered that humanistic and scientific enquiry are not inevitably opposed' (1976, 290).
Transnational sensibilities were formed and passed to me through my
family, where the *experiencing* of Rio de Janeiro was constructed within
a transnational sensibility. I am most interested in the multidimensional geographies of Rio de Janeiro viewed as complex and multi-
layered human experiences, keeping in line with René Dubos's
observation that 'Nations exist not as geological, climatic, or "racial"
entities, but as human experiences' (1972, 100). The histories of geographic knowledge of Rio de Janeiro are constructed within an autobiogeographical perspective and framed as sense of place. I use the
term *autobiogeography* as a fundamental aspect to the greater understanding of self in the context of transnationalism, sense of place, and
humanistic geography.[1]

Rethinking Rio as a Sacred Place

This portrayal of my experiences of Rio de Janeiro is meant to act as a foil to views of Rio as the site of a well-known, sensationalized, and unruly Carnival, a generalized joie de vivre, and an 'unbridled' sexuality – all of which bear clichéd perceptions that have reached mythic proportions in universal popular imagery. I perceive, describe, and (re) visit the Rio de Janeiro of my childhood in a very different light – as a sacred place, a place of memories represented through writers, artists, naturalists, family homes, oral histories, and direct transnational experiences – surrounded by ambiguous and contradictory experiences of warmth and elation yet at the same time of isolation and apathy.

I do without the more commonly discussed aspects of Rio, the political, social, racial, and economic dilemmas that Brazil currently faces. I must make it clear that although I do not address these dilemmas at this particular moment, this absence should not be seen as indifference or callousness to the fundamentally chronic political and social malaise that afflicts Rio, and Brazil more generally. To look at Rio's cultural and physical landscapes is to look into my family's background, and hence to look inside myself, to revisit and experience *self*, and to investigate the transnational component in attachment to place, or to use humanistic geographer Yi-Fu Tuan's coined term, *topophilia* (1974).[2]

For such an enquiry, two approaches to knowing sense of place are in line: the gaze from *the outside in*, and the gaze from *the inside out*. European navigators and naturalists who first viewed Rio de Janeiro (re)produced vivid literatures and imagery, but they were not merely passive actors. They were part of a very embodied experience (see, for example, Driver and Martins 2002). However, they were also engaged in a contradictory experience, coming from both the inside out and from the outside in. Their representations and experiences fed each other, as they were a part of the sociocultural outcome of previous imaginative geographies[3] and at the same time, these navigators were genuinely producing original representations from their own direct, embodied experiences. Although imaginative geographies have historically produced negative consequences within colonial and postcolonial political and social systems (Livingstone 2003; Martins 1998; Moffitt and Sebastian 1998; Smith 1999), this does not necessarily mean that we should dismiss them as entirely irrelevant to our understanding of sense of place, nor discard them as merely endeavours of imperialist histories. Rather, we should take a step back for a moment from a critical thinking stance and reposition ourselves to recognize such representations through a sort of 'postcritical thinking' approach in order to fully understand the historical context and multidimensionality of transnational experience. In other words, we should remain aware of the detrimental consequences of colonial and postcolonial imaginative geographies and at the same time allow ourselves to dwell deeper on such representations and their emblematic significance over time.

Moving beyond imaginative geographies to an autobiogeographical standpoint, I examine *place* through family oral histories, former family homes, and personal experiences. As Buttimer states, 'To dwell implies more than to inhabit, to cultivate, or to organize space. It means to live in a manner which is attuned to the rhythms of nature, to see one's life as anchored in human history' (1976, 277).

The active and direct narratives conveyed here emanate from my personal experiences, conveyed through memories of growing up in Rio with its vibrant cultural and physical landscapes. Pioneer humanistic geographer John Kirtland Wright aptly noted the imagination found within conceptions of place: 'The imagination not only projects itself into *terrae incognitae* and suggests routes for us to follow, but also plays upon those things that we discover and out of them makes imaginative conceptions which we seek to share with others' ([1947] 1966, 73).

I (re)visit the autobiogeography of my maternal grandparents,' my parents,' and myself as a way to convey the *genius loci*, or spirit of place, of Rio. My grandmother arrived with her family in Rio from Cairo, Egypt, and, my grandfather arrived from London, England. My father also arrived in Rio from London, and met and eventually married my Brazilian-born and -raised mother. I recollect my childhood in Rio – the repository of experiences and memories of place. Geographer Richard W. Wilkie states, 'For many people the discovery of special places through one's explorations can be nearly as powerful as revisiting one's own pantheon of sacred places' (2003, 31). It is through revisiting my own sacred memories of place that I evoke my attachment to Rio de Janeiro and its sense of place.

Place as Memory

Buttimer observes that space is 'construed as a mosaic of special places, each stamped by human intention, value, and memory' (1976, 283). She describes experience as filtered socially and proposes that space exists as a context, not as an expression. We may apply Buttimer's approach to the experiential context of Rio as a transnational mosaic of intentions, values, and memories.

Wright pointed out in his presidential address to the Association of American Geographers in 1946 that a geographer may portray a place or region with aesthetic subjectivity and that can may lead to illusion and error. However, there is a fundamental difference between illusion and delusion, as 'we are not deluded by all of our illusions ... and an illusion only becomes a delusion when it is either designed to deceive or unskillfully employed' ([1947] 1966, 77). In this sense there is legitimacy to the concept of illusion. The gaze and the reservoir of past visual and literary imagery thus legitimize the geographer's work by adding colour, vividness, and aesthetic devices to the idea of place.

Kazuo Matsubayashi states that 'attachment is both a physiological and a psychological interaction with the environment ... [It] is an existential and phenomenological experience' (1991, 341). In this context of 'attachment,' eminent English naturalist Charles Darwin experienced Rio de Janeiro. His diary, written from 1831 to 1836 and entitled *The Voyage of the Beagle* ([1909] 2000), describes his experience within the majestic visual surroundings, describing Botafogo, where I was born:

> Everyone has heard of the beauty of the scenery near Botafogo. The house in which I lived was seated close beneath the well-known mountain of the Corcovado. It has been remarked, with much truth, that abruptly conical hills are characteristic of the formation which Humboldt designates as gneiss-granite. Nothing can be more striking than the effect of these huge rounded masses of naked rock rising out of the most luxuriant vegetation. ([1909] 2000, 39)

Darwin was so enamoured of Rio's landscape that his language transcends the standpoint of positivistic science to almost echo the articulations of a 'subjective' poet or artist (in line with the vernacular used by naturalists of his day), suggesting emotional attachment to the land (i.e., topophilia) and capturing the sense of place. Darwin also describes the difficulty Europeans face in expressing their feelings, which might shed light on his overwhelming experience in the tropics as an Englishman:

> I entered a noble forest, and from a height of five or six hundred feet, one of those splendid views was presented, which are so common on every side of Rio. At this elevation the landscape attains its most brilliant tint;

and every form, every shade, so completely surpasses in magnificence all that the European has ever beheld in his own country, that he knows not how to express his feelings. ([1909] 2000, 43)

The histories of geographical knowledge of Brazil were constructed from visual and literary imagery in books and paintings. European botanists, geographers, and naturalists who first visited Brazilian landscapes produced works of art and science that were widely disseminated in Europe (Martins 1998, 2001). The result was that Europeans saw these imaginative geographies of Brazil as the 'wild tropics,' a place of 'exotic' human and physical landscapes. These literary and visual representations were constructed and conveyed in interrelated, complex, and often contradictory ways from *the inside out* and at the same time, within a specific cultural and historic context, from *the outside in* because the writers and painters were also reflecting and representing their own cultural world view.

These representations of Brazil were inherently transnational. European navigation was generally safer after the end of the Napoleonic Wars in 1815. As a result, Brazilian ports saw an increase in arrivals of French, British, Russian, German, and Dutch naturalists and artists, who came to collect plants, birds, and insects, as well as to paint landscapes. Through the representations created by these visitors iconic images of tropical landscapes were disseminated (Martins 2001).

British botanists and gardeners such as Alan Cunningham from the Royal Horticultural Society and John Forbes from Kew Gardens; painters such as Charles Browne, Augustus Earle, William Havell; and naturalists such as William Burchell and Charles Darwin brought back to Europe a new iconography of the tropics (Martins 2001, 19). Ideas of tropicality that originated in Europe and the notion of infinite natural resources were assimilated by the Brazilian intellectual elite and rearticulated for national interests (15). Through the narratives and visual representations that were (re)created and brought back to Europe, it is possible to speculate about the expectations of a voyage to Brazil. For example, the smell of the tropical beaches and warm sea breeze, the sight of a landscape of palm trees jutting from the hills into the horizon, especially Pão de Açucar (Mount Sugarloaf), which stands over Guanabara Bay. As geographers Felix Driver and Luciana Martins maintain, 'The Sugar Loaf would have been familiar sight to thousands of British sailors during this period, as Rio de Janeiro was a significant location in the global geography of British maritime power' (2002, 145).

These iconic images allow for a better understanding and interpretation of what I assume my grandparents and my father also felt when first arriving in Rio de Janeiro. Moreover, it is especially through the understanding of how these family members responded, interacted, and adapted to both the cultural and the physical landscape that I gain insight into my later personal experiences within the context of place and transnationalism.

A Model for Experiencing Sense of Place

I propose an approach to experiencing place that is conveyed through two types of gaze.[4] The indirect gaze from the past, the gaze from the outside in, conveys an indirect experience of place through the (re)production of literary and visual images by virtue of not being present at the time of these (re)productions. The direct gaze from personal experience, the gaze from the inside out, articulates an autobiogeography of place through direct experiences and recollections. In this case, the position of being inside allows a different dimension to perspective and experience of place.

These two frameworks are used to examine and illustrate the relationships among three main themes: personal experiences; oral histories and family homes; and literature, art, and photographs. This model provides a theoretical conjuncture of these themes and forms a basis for understanding sense of place.

The Indirect Gaze: Memories through My Grandparents

Yi-Fu Tuan's approach to the human cultural disposition combines three themes: biological facts, the relations of space and place, and the range of experience or knowledge (1977, 6). Tuan notes that the first environment an infant explores is his parent (22), and as a starting point I shall accordingly begin the indirect gaze by looking at my parents and grandparents as the first environmental and transnational experience that helped shape my childhood memories. To think of Rio is to think of my grandmother, grandfather, mother, father, greataunts, and aunt (and more recently my cousin, Barbara Andersen, who lives in Rio with her family). To think of Rio evokes memories of family, memories of home, and memories of place. It evokes the smells of the ocean breeze, of the hot afternoons, of the hills of Gávea, and of the omnipresent *Cristo Redentor* statue (Christ the Redeemer) on the Corcovado hills.

My maternal grandmother, Yolanda Imbruglia, was born in 1908 in Cairo and came to Rio in 1927 with her family of two sisters (Natalina and Maria Grazia) and two brothers (Alfonso and Salvatore). They settled in a house in Ipanema. Yolanda's parents, Alessandro (born in 1871) and Egizia (born in 1876), were born in Milazzo, Italy, and met each other in Alexandria, where they married in 1894. They later moved to Cairo, and lived on Soliman Pasha Street, in the downtown area. Although all the Imbruglia children were born and raised in Egypt, the family's ethnic identity was Italian (the entire family had Italian passports) and they were all practising Roman Catholics.

A 1912 map of Cairo reveals the presence of German, Italian, Jewish, French, and British communities, schools, hospitals, and a busy international community that added a cosmopolitan flair. These same international, religious, diplomatic, and ethnic communities existed in Rio at the time of Yolanda's eventual move, and, Rio, like Cairo, was a capital city. Cairo's culturally diverse diplomatic and business environment included the German and British hospitals, the French Institute of Archeology, the Ottoman Bank, the Anglo-Egyptian Bank, an opera house, an international tribunal, and a native tribunal. Alongside mosques were several churches: Roman Catholic, Anglican, Syriac Christian, Coptic Catholic, Coptic Jacobite, Armenian Catholic, Greek Catholic, and Maronite. Cairo's cultural and multireligious diversity, as well as its status as a diplomatic, business, and trading hub, probably translated easily into Yolanda's new geographical understanding of Rio.

Yolanda eventually met an Englishman, Edward Hughes, working in Rio. They married in 1931 and had two daughters, Josette (my mother) and Jane (my aunt). Jane later moved to São Paulo (a city south of Rio) with her husband, Robert Martin, and they had four daughters. Sadly, Jane died unexpectedly in March 2005.

Alessandro Imbruglia's house in Ipanema was eventually demolished, and today a tall skyscraper stands in its place. I remember visiting that house in the 1970s, while one of my greataunts, Maria Grazia Imbruglia, still lived there. The house was always cool, and it seemed like an old bastion of elegant 1920s belle époque resistance among the surrounding ungraceful contemporary buildings. It is helpful to emphasize the dwelling aspect of my great-grandfather's old house in the context of Buttimer's remark that 'to dwell implies more than to inhabit' (1976, 277).

My grandparents moved to Petrópolis (a city near Rio) in 1940 and lived there until 1955. In 1955, after raising Jane and Josette in Petrópolis, they moved back to Rio, to a very small apartment by Lagoa Rodrigo de Freitas, where they lived until the mid-1980s. This new phase of their life reflected the polar opposite of the chic 1920s, when Yolanda had first lived in Rio. She spent all her adulthood in Brazil, dying in São Paulo in 1999. My memories of her are as sacred as my memories of Rio.

'Your Letter has just reached me this minute. I wish I could reply with the Pacific in front of me, or any other ocean for that matter, as I can only see the sky through the window, at a level somewhat above my head.' These words were written by my maternal grandfather, Edward Hughes, to his Australian cousin, Robert Collins, in 1918 while he was detained in Ruhleben, a British internment camp near Berlin. It was specifically designed for British civilians living in Germany at the time of the First World War, and Edward was detained there from 1914 to 1918. Ironically, only two years later, he would indeed be living by the ocean: on Guanabara Bay in Rio, opening into the Atlantic. The gaze from the outside in expressed within this letter would eventually lead him to new geographies that once belonged to the imagination – the *terrae incognitae* that Wright ([1947] 1966) so eloquently talked about – across the ocean from Europe. Brazil was a place unlike the back-to-back monotonous brick buildings of London or of the ghastly barracks of Ruhleben. The irony of his letter is found in the discriminating imagery of ocean and how the imagination manifested itself as Rio de Janeiro, eventually a 'real place' of livelihood and family for my grandfather.

Edward Hughes was born in London in 1895 and raised in Seven Oaks, Kent. After the First World War, he was released from Ruhleben and returned to England. He then took a job as a clerk and moved to Rio in 1920, working for the British-owned Leopoldina Railway Company. He died in 1986 and is buried in the British Cemetery of Gamboa in Rio.

Along with the social networks available to European foreigners in Brazil, in this case the British, came acceptance into traditional British social clubs such as the Paissandú Athletic Club, the Rio Cricket Club in Niterói, the São Paulo Athletic Club, and the São Paulo Yacht Club. Edward represented the values and norms of a quintessential Victorian Englishman. He was an active participant within the British community in Rio – he organized a formal dinner in 1921 to honour Anglo-Irish explorer Sir Ernest Shackleton when he visited Rio before leaving for his famous last Antarctic expedition – and his favourite hobbies were playing tennis at the English club and sailing.

I will make an imaginative leap and take the liberty of establishing a figuratively antithetical relationship between the cultural and physical landscapes of England and Brazil, between Victorian London and tropical Rio, at the time when Edward Hughes arrived in Brazil. London featured tight, close spaces, nondescript residential and commercial brick buildings, and the harsh smells and dim colours of Victorian industrial London. This contrasted starkly with the vastness, fresh air, spectacularly vivid colours, magnificent hills, and open spaces of Rio. In contrast to the brick mills and factories that covered England's urban landscapes, Brazil enjoyed overwhelmingly lush and tall vegetation, with tropical palm and coconut trees lining the Atlantic coast. Rio shared in the sheer enormity of the country, the warm climate, and the sandy beaches.

Expressing the geographies of England and Brazil as conceptually opposite suggests other differences: northern and southern hemisphere nations; temperate and tropical climates; a staunchly 'white' society and a loosely 'miscegenated' population; and a dull and dreary landscape versus a vibrant and dramatic one.

Like most Englishmen who moved to Brazil, Edward Hughes was already employed before leaving England and had signed a temporary contract to work in Rio for a predetermined time with the Leopoldina Railway Company. The terminology involved with this particular type of transnational labour force has a curious aspect. In general, British foreigners in Brazil have preferred to call themselves 'ex-pats' (i.e., expatriates) rather than 'immigrants,' 'migrants,' or 'sojourners.' The British have shied away from the socially loaded semantics of these terms for reasons that reveal much about their deeply embedded notions of imperialism, ethnocentrism, and colonialism. The British saw themselves as individuals who had merely taken temporary positions 'overseas' and had then decided to continue residing in the host country. They considered themselves 'settlers' and the conveyors of presumptuous British cultural propriety, regardless of their prior social status in Britain. This insular mode of interaction in Brazil led to an equally insular collective mentality.

Furthermore, social class and colour are inseparable in Brazil: the darker the skin colour of an individual the more likely they are to belong to a lower socio-economic status. Hence British foreigners were automatically and artificially elevated in social status regardless of prior socioeconomic background. What mattered most to the British in Brazil was their national identity; they (re)created a type of self based on merely 'being British' and not necessarily stemming from income, education, regional, or social background.

The most common ways to fraternize within the British community in Brazil were to spend time in social clubs and to send one's children to British schools such as Escola Britânica, located in Botafogo, Rio, or St. Paul's School, located in the Jardins, São Paulo. I was a student at the British school in Rio de Janeiro in the early 1970s, where my mother had been a primary teacher in the mid-1950s and early '60s. After my family moved to São Paulo, I attended St. Paul's, from 1977 to 1982.[5] My childhood was slanted to a certain degree toward experiences revolving around the Anglo-Brazilian community, and these experiences were marked by indifference.

The gaze from the perspectives and autobiogeographies of Edward Hughes and Yolanda Imbruglia are intrinsically linked to the gaze from the outside in and from the inside out. It is highly unlikely that in their youth, before moving to Brazil, either Edward Hughes or Yolanda Imbruglia would have imagined that one day their grandson would swim in the ocean at Ipanema or Copacabana Beach and, speak fluent Portuguese. However, it is through their stories and my own memories of them that I have attempted to piece together a more complete understanding of sense of place of Rio de Janeiro.

Experiencing Place through My Father's Gaze

Now that I have explained my grandparents' trajectories to Rio, I will briefly explore what I call my parents' *spirit in Rio*. My father, Derrick Marcus, was born in Cork, Ireland, in 1937, two years before his sister, Helen (who currently lives with her husband, Ray Bona, in Dover, England). His own cultural and national identity is embedded in complex and fluid transnational processes. My paternal grandfather, Bill Marcus (born in Cork), and his wife, my grandmother, Mona Marcus (born in London) – both now deceased – moved the family from Ireland to England in 1949, when my father was twelve years old. My father arrived in Rio in 1963, a year before the military dictatorship took over Brazil.[6]

He had left London as a chartered accountant contracted for a British company. Before leaving for Rio he was offered a position in South Africa but he selected Brazil without any qualms. As a young boy he had been fascinated with Brazil on several levels: 'I think my move was influenced by an imagined perception of the Brazilian lifestyle and friendliness. It seemed like a country of adventure. My love of soccer, and the Brazilian team in particular, had a small part in my decision' (personal communication, 2006). Although my father's decision to move to Brazil was only partially because of soccer, this sport should stand out when one speaks of Brazil. Famous for its unique style of soccer (better known as the *jogo bonito*, Portuguese for 'beautiful game'), Brazil's national team was made famous by players during the 1950s and 1960s such as Pelé, Garrincha, and Gilmar. My father's interest in Brazilian soccer was such that in London in the early 1950s he wrote a short story about a fictitious soccer match between Santos and Bahia, two Brazilian soccer clubs. The piece won second prize in a competition sponsored by the London Federation of Boys Club.

While my father became involved in the Anglo-Brazilian and British community activities, my mother worked as a primary teacher at the British school in Rio. My parents met through the British community in Rio and through tennis games, marrying in 1964. There exist several photos of my parents when they first met, showing the Gávea hills in the background and Ipanema Beach, a recurring image.

My father was very much involved with Clube de Regatas Flamengo (Flamengo Rowing Club), a major rowing and athletic club, but better known as a major national soccer team. Through the club my father met several major athletic and sports personalities, and in the 1970s became a part-time athletic correspondent for *Athletics Weekly*, a British magazine. His civic contribution to Brazil was through sport. He was sport director for the national and Rio state federations, team manager for the World Cup of Race Walking and Pan American Race Walking Championships, and the only civilian foreigner to be invited to organize the World Military Race Walking Championship, held in Brazil during the military dictatorship. Later, he was actively involved with British community charity work in Brazil and in 2002 was awarded the Order of the British Empire to acknowledge his work.

Rio is a place of passion for soccer equalling my father's, and the sport is a reflection of the sense of place par excellence. My father has asserted that it is 'impossible to separate soccer from Brazil.' During a major game between the two main soccer teams of Rio, for example, Flamengo and Fluminense, all townsfolk gather in and outside bars, called *botecos*, to watch the game on television. The love of soccer is such that when the World Cup is televised, businesses close and people leave work early to watch the games.

My father's commitment to Rio is expressed likewise in his marriage to my mother, Josette, who was born and raised in Rio – a *carioca*.[7] My mother and her late sister, Jane, grew up in Rio in the 1930s and '40s, when cordiality was more than just good manners; it was synonymous with being Brazilian. Josette and Jane attended a Catholic school run by French nuns. The school, in Petrópolis, was called Colégio Sion. At that time, Rio was widely influenced by French culture, and French language was taught in Brazilian schools and spoken by most 'upper-' and 'middle-class' *cariocas*. Memories of my mother are also deeply embedded within my *sense of place* in Rio, although she now lives in São Paulo.

My grandparents' and parents' autobiogeographical trajectories leading to Rio have constituted the main part of my indirect gaze of Rio. Their experiences and perceptions reflect the notion of Rio as a sacred place. My family's religious, cultural, and national hybridity – Roman Catholic, Anglican, Italian, Egyptian, French, British, and Brazilian – reflect the syncretism of transnational autobiogeographical complexities, emanating from the concept of place.

Personal Experience: The Direct Gaze from the Inside Out

My fondest memories have always been of the ocean. The reason for this sense of the sacredness of the ocean is perhaps because it was a conspicuous locale where I was born and raised. I was born in the São José Hospital in Botafogo, Rio de Janeiro, in 1967, three years before Brazil won its third and legendary World Cup Jules Rimet trophy in 1970, and seven years after the capital of Brazil was transferred from Rio to the newly constructed city of Brasília. My sister, Susan Marcus, was also born in Rio, two years after me. My family lived in Leblon, a continuation of Ipanema Beach. We then moved to an apartment on Avenida Atlântica on Copacabana Beach, facing the ocean and a block or two away from the Copacabana Palace Hotel, whose guests over the years included celebrities such as Brigitte Bardot and Catherine Deneuve. No matter where I looked I could always see the ocean.

My engagement with sense of place is represented both from the inside out and from the outside in. First, I experienced Rio as a place of rhythm and movement, as a place of crowds, sound, colour, and transnationalism. Second, I experienced Rio as a place of opposites and contradictions, of dangerous encounters, of the 'unknown or bizarre,' and of social apathy, yet at the same time as a place of affection, sensuality, and warmth.

My experience of always being able to see the ocean and the horizon from home was thwarted when my family moved to São Paulo. I was unable to see more than a few blocks ahead of me, let alone the horizon. The spatial, physical, and cultural differences between São Paulo and Rio were enormous to me at the time and remain so today. The effect of seeing the open horizon over the ocean carried a sense of continuity and freedom for me as a child, whereas the effect of looking at the outside from behind bars on a window in my own house in São Paulo, for protection against crime, conveyed symbolic notions of constraint and limitation.

For a better understanding of place and period, I have listed in chronological order the places of my experiential perspectives:

1967   My first home in Rio was on Rua Ataúlfo de Paiva in Leblon, only two blocks from the ocean.
1969   My second home in Rio was on Rua Gomes Carneiro, in Ipanema.
1969   My third home was on Delfim Moreira, Leblon.
1971–2 My fourth home was in São Paulo.
1972–6 My fifth home was on Copacabana Beach, an ocean-front apartment on the sixth floor, on Avenida Atlântica in Rio.
1976   My sixth home was a house on Rua Quintino Bocaiúva, now changed to Rua Pirandello, in a neighbourhood called Brooklin in São Paulo.

The ocean provided a place of peace, warmth and comfort for me – a place away from loneliness and aspects of my life that were vexatious to my spirit. I could always see, touch, and smell the ocean water and, more important, I could always see a horizon hovering over a blue landscape. For elucidation of my experience in Rio, I turn to Tuan's observations about the understanding and expression of experience in the context of one of the three themes he explores:

> Experience can be direct and intimate, or it can be indirect and conceptual, mediated by symbols. We know our home intimately ... It is possible to articulate subtle human experiences. Artists have tried – often with success. In works of literature as well as in humanistic psychology, philosophy, anthropology and geography, intricate worlds of human experience are recorded. (1977, 6–7)

Tuan continues and notes that the very word *experience* has a common root with *experiment, expert,* and *perilous.* He states, 'To experience in the active sense requires that one venture forth into the unfamiliar and experiment with the elusive and the uncertain' (1977, 9). In this context, I establish my own intimate, direct gaze of Rio. The unknown human sensuality of the beachgoers, which I saw as a young boy, the unseen dangers, the blistering sun, and tropical warmth of Rio's colourful and vibrant residents all added to the magic of the ocean. The physical landscape, such as the hills of Gávea and the Corcovado, towered over the blue Atlantic and I recall the pleasant misty breeze in the afternoons. I experienced the gaze from the inside out through my first views of Ipanema Beach from my family's apartment window: 'To see and to think are closely related processes. In English, "I see" means "I understand"' (Tuan 1977, 10). The meaning of *understanding* in this case relates to my gaze as a boy and my intimate relationship with the physical and cultural landscapes of Rio, from the mysterious to the mundane.

The second type of gaze I experienced many years later by reviewing old family photographs, literature, and art from Rio. These represent the conceptual or indirect gaze from the outside in. The geographies of Rio are thus manifold within the framework of sense of place that I have established here.

Buttimer asks whether *dwelling* is a noun or a verb, a building or a craft. She continues, 'Strange indeed sounds the language of poets and philosophers ... The humanistic geographer cannot afford to dismiss anything which may shed light on the complexities of man's relationship to the earth' (1976, 277). In this context, I provide the setting for the direct gaze within this approach to sense of place.

It is precisely the direct gaze that has made an lasting impression on me. The smell of the ocean in the afternoon, the omnipresent hills surrounding my home, the sounds of the streets, the feeling of ocean water on my skin, the heat of the beach, and the sound of the waves are just some of my warm memories of the geography of Rio. Tuan observes of childhood experiences,

> The child sees himself as the hero of the stage and is unable, or unwilling, to imagine how another actor – the little boy at the end of the road, for instance – would see him as he approaches ... The geographical horizon of a child expands as he grows ... His interest and knowledge focus first on the small local community, then the city ... To an intelligent and lively child, experience is active searching and occasional wild extrapolations beyond the given. (1977, 28, 31)

With each year and from every angle I seemed to be able to see the mountains towering over Rio on different scales. This is consistent with Tuan's note on early childhood experiences. It was as if I could never become lost because landmarks were conspicuous and the natural environment was almost impossible to ignore. This is the physical landscape that I convey within the context of the outside in but also within the inside out. I am able to experience sense of place from the outside in, as the same landscape once towered over my great-grandparents' house, my grandparents' apartment, and my parents' apartment. This is the landscape where my family's historical geography took place. Moreover, to look at the physical and cultural landscapes is to look into my family's own past: hence, to look at the geography of Rio de Janeiro is to look inside myself and to experience a profound feeling of sacredness as well as a sense of belonging.

Conclusion

The histories of geographic knowledge expressed above were framed as the sense of place, specifically of Rio de Janeiro, experienced through different periods and spatial perspectives. Perceptions of Brazil today are a far cry from the imaginative geographies portrayed by early European visitors in their paintings and descriptions 100, 200, or 300 years ago. Rio is obviously a very different place today. It is a disheartening endeavour for me to discuss from the comfortable geographic distance of the United States (where I now live) the levels of social conflict and social distress in the country where I was born and raised.

This chapter was written with the intention of restoring the memories of Rio as a sacred place, and of conveying the aesthetics of its cultural and physical landscapes as I experienced them growing up. Understanding Rio in a transnational context is part of my perspective of it as the place of experiential formations, and hence, I have an auto-biogeography. These experiences and sense of place are rooted in memory and within my own feelings of attachment to Rio.

2 When Russia Came to Stay

LEA POVOZHAEV

Memories and recollections won't give me total access to the unwritten
interior life of these people. Only the act of the imagination can help me ...
If writing is thinking and discovery and selection and order and meaning,
it is also awe and reverence and mystery and magic.

(Morrison 1998, 192).

The wind blows wherever it pleases. You hear its sound, but you cannot
tell where it comes from or where it is going. So it is with everyone born of
the Spirit.

(John 3:8)

When Russia came to stay, she nested in my heart by chance. And she
gathered there – in thin blue days, Dima's hand warming mine; in frozen awe as I tread St Petersburg's crystal snow to her ancient church; in
Grandma's thick arms spilling over the small wooden rocker, as she
rocked and sewed, rocked and sewed, our small home becoming a
deeper fold of past and future. Ours was one life, woven with disparate
strands – Dima's Russian childhood and family, my American; his
Orthodox culture, my Protestant; his restful nature, my sharp passions.
Like a bird coursing through the Ohio air, the journey became our life.
And now, I pause, look overhead, wonder where I've been and what it
means, for me and those with whom this life allows me love.

Faith is red like blood and anger, passion and fire.

'Are you seriously going to burn that entire Christmas tree? Dima!
You're freaking me out. The thing's blazing. Put the gasoline down!' A
fury of arms slapped the night crackling above the tin roof of the garage.

'You are definitely a pyromaniac,' a smile pulled the corners of my thin lips. Hugging bare legs close to my chest, I felt the fire raging against my shins. He stoked the blaze with his old hockey stick.

'I can't believe my parents and Grandma will be here in three days.' His wide eyes glowed in the firelight. 'It's going to be crazy for them to be here, especially Grandma. They might have to drug her to get her on the plane.'

'Wonder what they'll think of our neck of the woods. You think they get that the Holmeses are rich and we're not?' I said.

He looked up from the dancing fire, 'Oh yeah, they understand. They know exactly how it is for us.' Nodding my head, I doubted they could.

He had come to America at thirteen to play hockey, leaving his mother and father for nine years. Grandma was issued a visa and visited us in high school, but his parents came to the States for the first time to celebrate our wedding. His father, clad in his red- and black-checked robe softly climbing the mound of his belly, leaned a full face over Dima and cupped his large head in his hands. He breathed deeply the sweet-flesh scent of his boy's scalp. I backed out of the Holmeses' bedroom and left for home, my parents' house.

We were to be married in days. His parents' first visit, a stretch of six weeks, was almost up. The mantra repeated: savour now. Think of Dima and his family instead of yourself. It has been nine years since he saw them.

The internal argument came easily, visceral: they hang sheets over windows, slurp soup, refrigerate peanut butter. His mother, Tatyana, inhales jellybeans with wine.

'I don't know,' my voice broke. 'Mrs Holmes, I love Dima – and his parents. But. This is so hard … ' Susan squeezed a clothespin over the wet shorts, her face concentrated.

'How long did you stay at Sea World?' Always calculating.

'We were there from eleven till eight. Honestly, I was really trying to be patient. I mean, we stared at the seals for two hours! It wasn't so bad until around six. That's when I started hinting we needed to leave. But he would not speak up! He's driving me crazy.'

'Maybe he didn't see a reason to. You weren't there all that long … ' She sifted through the utility room for a clothes basket.

'Well, by eight we were. And I said so. Tatyana was mad at me. She wouldn't look at me or talk. I could tell, she was thinking I was a selfish American.'

'How do you know that? Maybe she was just tired?'

'No. When we got into the van, she was actually pouting. And when we stopped for gas and I was alone with them, I couldn't handle it. As soon as Dima got back, I made him translate. I told them I was sorry, but it was getting late and stuff.'

'It wasn't that late.'

'I know. But his mother actually said that I have childhood playing in my butt, whatever *that* means.' A subtle smile rested over Susan's plain features.

'Do you want a glass of wine?' she asked.

Five years later, Dima and I faced the back of our boxy home, sharing the last bonfire of the summer – alone. Stillness cloaked the guest room of our bungalow, where wedding pictures and pale, cylindrical candles rewrote my childhood dressers. A tall iron lamp, left as trash by the past homeowner, crowded a corner by the bed. In the thick of summer, with skin like melting wax, we would trade our bedroom upstairs for the saggy bed of the guest room. We lay naked in comfortable silence, summer pushing through old windows, open and unlocked through the night.

For three years we lived as newlyweds among warm colours and wood. We absorbed quiet moments in the crimson bedroom, dreaming of filling the 'baby's nook,' a pinched space, with bleached wood and Noah's ark. Old-fashioned Christmas lights lined the bar in the basement. A tattered plaid quilt draped the futon beneath pillows that smelled faintly of Dima's scalp and cinnamon. Knobby antiques were gifts from Aunt Caroline's house sales.

Before the family came, he watered house plants and I made coffee and oatmeal on Saturday mornings. There was always a phone call to Russia, a 500-minute calling card turning in his square fingers, long legs crossed, chords of Russian playing through the kitchen. I loved the sharp sounds spoken in his soft voice. I was transported back to my travels in Russia, reminded of the longing I had had. And had still.

It was eleven years since Dima and I first met. It was easy to return to that late spring night, facing his host family's brick mansion. It had seemed a fairytale, his Russian past hardly figuring in then. I was sixteen.

Ivy spilled over the earth and front stairwell. An American flag hung between white pillars. Waiting for the door to open, my stomach tightened, face burned. The doorbell chimed classical music; I had never heard anything but a bell before. When the door finally opened, the smell of oily Chinese vegetables wafted from the belly of the home.

'Come on in. The boys are upstairs.' Susan Holmes reminded me of Martha Stewart, except she was not quite as put together. Her face was kind but reserved. She wore little make-up and small, wire-rimmed eyeglasses. Wiping her hands over her wide apron, she motioned us upstairs. An enormous chandelier hung from the ceiling. Pink and silver wallpaper flowered behind Oriental statues of birds, monkeys, and lions. Red ribbons and orange dragons sprawled across shelves. A basket of dark walking canes rested under a dull-bronze icon of Christ.

Steam and Dove soap hovered in the hall and seeped into the three boys' rooms. Dima stood there, tall and thin, an untucked Grateful Dead t-shirt over khaki cut-offs frayed just above pale knees. His face was hidden in the shadow of a baseball cap.

We weren't supposed to meet. The odds were against it from the start. But fate has a way of turning the slickest corners, landing us where we would never expect. From then on, our lives would collect in each other's: my studies in Russia, the birth of our son, his American citizenship, the family's visit to the States. Our days would grow thick with life.

Months before we met, I stared out my bedroom window at the dulling oranges of sunset. I whispered, 'God, if you are here, if you are really part of my life, I need a sign.' Nothing changed. I barely breathed. There were no mountains to move. Only postage stamp yards, empty sidewalks curling the cul-de-sac, and silent street lamps. Across the street was a long yellow light in the shape of a cross. Just a porch light. The dark of night blanketed the earthy smells of grass and dying heat. Just the end of a day. And yet hovering inexplicably near was the sense that all of this was God. I drew my breath, still as the old tree across the street.

Telling the stories of our life swayed me to see the hand of God – to sense, again, his realness. When I travelled to Russia in college as an Evangelical Christian, visiting Orthodox churches was like visiting museums, strangely peaceful and interesting sometimes, and then, one church after the other, little more than ornate marble, antiquated wood, restored paint.

I spent twelve weeks studying in Nizhny Novgorod, compelled to return to dark, Orthodox parishes – places so unlike the many churches I had experienced growing up Protestant. I slipped behind wool coats and covered heads that mysteriously bowed. Fingers crossing chests, lips softly chanting. I stood in the shadow. I grew as quiet as melting ice drawing behind their rings of prayer candles, my eyes closing, heart slowing. There were deep, rolling prayers and the smell of baking bread. I felt the cold from a woman's coat, smelled a man's body odour. We were so close. So quiet. My nose warmed in the murky dark as I drew breath. A young girl bowed to touch the hem of the priest's vestment as he continued down the church, spreading incense in a bronze ball the size of an egg.

After years and a slip of fate, this tradition, this historic spirituality began to fill a still and quiet place within me.

I'm pregnant. I'm pregnant. I'm pregnant. The words rattled for months, even still. I always knew I wanted to be a mother and sensed there'd be complications.

'I believe it will happen, Lea. I don't know when or how. But I have faith.' I thought it was easier for Dima. After all, it had been seven months of infertility specialists prodding my flesh, drawing my blood, rushing his 'top' sperm into the cavity of my womb.

'Your chances of conceiving on your own are less than 1 per cent. Even with artificial insemination, it will be difficult. Probably a 7, 8 per cent chance,' the doctor said.

I lay back on the stiff white paper, closed my eyes to see the pain I felt. The timer, a black sperm on its face, was set for ten minutes. 'Just relax. Are you cold?'

'I'm okay.' The doctor draped my spring jacket over bare legs and left the room. Soft music, footsteps on the other side of the door, the pounding of my heart – all went quiet. Completely still and unfeeling. At first, thoughts of unfinished graduate school and the barren bank account. But then the idea of a child – the smell of soft, the touch of need, the nuance of pushing past myself. Flesh of our flesh, blood of our blood, it all seemed like the greatest ambition, the highest calling. Without knowing why, I knew I had to have a child.

Above all else, dear God, I beg your mercy. If it's your will, give us a child. I didn't sense the cross had been taken. I might have never conceived, but rare peace replaced fear.

Midway through our two weeks of waiting, I was dusting the basement and on the phone with my sister when she said, 'I'm just really tired. I, ah, don't feel that great.' My heart flushed nauseating heat to my cheeks, fingers grew icy.

'What? Are you pregnant or something?' I was half-joking.

'Well, actually, I am.' Silence. It had been so easy for her. So natural. My mind went blank, face felt stiff.

'Oh … Melanie, that's wonderful! I … I,' a sob lodged the words.

'I'm so sorry. I feel awful. Me and Mom didn't know how to tell you.'

'Oh, please don't. Please don't ever keep anything from me. It's really hard right now for us, that's all. I'm happy for you, really. A baby …'

There was anger and jealousy alternating with hope and love, and emotions moved as quickly as turning a switch on, off. On, I hoped to be pregnant too, though there was little faith, and a glimmer of natural joy met my sister's. Off, I'd ruminate, anger and self-pity drawing darkness through me.

Our mother said, 'I'm proud of yours and Dima's attitude.' I flicked the light on, almost believing I had been as positive as Dima that things were all right, that we'd conceive, too. I pushed back the hurt. Maybe it would have returned, mutated into the score of emotions that one with the inability to conceive experiences.

'You're pregnant!' I heard over and over as I slipped outside pain and longing and numbly drifted with the news. A physical sensation of sinking past myself to a tenderness just outside carried past my lips into the silent car. *Thank you, Lord.*

As our son drew from my blood, gathered in my flesh, as Dima's foreign strand of DNA joined to mine in perfect unity, we began the endless path to becoming parents. 'Lea, did you see this?' Dima entered the computer room where I was typing. He held a yellow and red paperback, tapping the cover with his forefinger. 'It's on the differences between Russian and American childrearing.'

'I haven't had time. Besides, I'm exhausted. I don't even want to think about all that.' There was graduate school, three baby showers, teaching; there were bathrooms to clean, furniture to dust, meatloaf to make at ten in the morning when I was *starving*. All piled like a blurring mound of responsibility that I might have chucked for the sake of long hours of rest. The more to do, the more I felt I had to push myself faster, harder. There was no time for patience with Dima.

'I'm telling you, it's really good. I think we should both read it before Baby comes,' he said.

'Look, after you read it, then I'll read it.' I figured it would be behind our bed collecting dust alongside his Russian war memoir, Michael Savage's *Liberalism Is a Mental Disorder*, and Tom Clancy's *The Bear and the Dragon*. He cocked his head to the side, straight-faced, and charged me. His fingers wedged under my arms as he tickled me. 'Stop! Sssstop,' I laughed.

'You have little-woman syndrome, you know that? I've said it before, and I'll say it again – Balls said the Queen! If I had them, I'd be the King!' I slipped from the office chair onto the old carpet.

'Come on. Please, stop or I'll – '

'What, what can you do?' Laughing, he pinned me down.

'You're hurting the baby.'

With the swelling of my womb, hope and possibility seemed endless, enough to swallow any differences, any obstacles.

Nana had come from Florida to visit, and we drove an hour north to Melanie's brick ranch for a pool party and cookout. The family circled the pool, while Nana reminisced.

'I remember when your mother told me that Melanie was stealing your blankey. I had said, "Surely, Diane, she's too little for such antagonistic behaviour," unable to believe it! And, sure enough, she was just seven months old and you, Lea, just nineteen months, but she'd scoot over, wiggle herself on top of your bee, and laugh. Why, I'd never seen anything like it!'

I smiled, moved my painted toenails through the cool water. Melanie and I had always been close, and being pregnant only two weeks apart seemed nothing short of a miracle.

'Are you going to come into the water?' Melanie asked.

'You're a total fish. I'm not in the mood to swim.' I felt cold, hungry, tired. Even pregnant, she seemed so carefree. She wore her plaid two piece, small belly beginning to show.

'Do I look fat?'

'Well, fatter. I mean, we are pregnant,' I said. She had always been thick. When we were little, I used to worry about her stomach sticking out. 'Suck it in,' I'd tell her when we shared baths, but she'd arch her back and let it go, not paying attention.

'Have you been taking it easy?' my mother asked me, chewing the inside of her cheek as she did when she concentrated or worried, which often went hand in hand for my mother and me.

She leaned forward, 'Nono!' She grabbed the beagle's collar and pulled him from her burger. He whined and snapped at her hand.

'Ponch! Bad dog!' Melanie lifted herself out of the pool. 'Are you okay, Mom?' Our mother just smiled, biting back any comment that might upset Melanie and her husband, Joe. Always the peacemaker.

'You have to get rid of that monster before the babies come,' I said. Joe's brown eyes met mine from across the pool, and though his face was blank, I felt his anger.

'You know, Reverend Leroy Zimkey told me you would become pregnant,' Nana said, shifting her round body, clad in golf shorts. 'He said that once you were still and relaxed it would happen.' I wanted to believe someone could tell the future.

My father sipped his bottled Budweiser and looked at me with a weak smile. His dark hair was peppered with white, but he still had a youthful body, strong and healthy like his father's. He looked on the brink of boredom and irritation. I was sure he was itching to walk the block home and paint a plaster fish.

Fish mounted his basement walls – Rainbow Trout, Small-mouth Bass, Perch. 'It's my showroom,' he'd say, pushing the old couch farther from the wall to hang a speckled fish. He was up at five and could spend full days in his faded Lincoln Electric shop coat, reading glasses half-way down his long nose, bowed over a stained table. He'd have a cup of weak coffee beside old canisters of Metamucil and Folgers Coffee refilled with plaster and paint.

'Your mother doesn't understand, and maybe I am crazy. Who knows? But you understand. It's something you just have to keep working on. You're driven like I am,' he'd tell me. And after years, my father and I would reconnect through art. And faith. In such feathery moments, I was no longer the catalyst of his irritations. My soul seemed peeled from his.

Summer fed into fall and finally winter as love took shape in a tiny poke of an elbow that rippled my taut flesh. Hope persisted in lazy evenings leaning against Dima on the futon in the basement. Boxes of baby 'necessities' collected by the bar: diaper genie, bouncy seat, high chair – most of which needed to be assembled.

'But *when* are you going to do it? We don't have that much longer, honey. I really want everything set so there's less stress when Viktor is actually here.'

'I'll do it soon, okay? This weekend.' I wondered if our son would have a still and patient nature, veering toward lazy at times, or live on the edge of his seat, jumping to the next thing. Would he be tall and quiet like his father – or small and dark like me? Would he learn Russian, sharing Saturday phone calls with Daddy? Would he be convinced that colds came from cool air against one's neck, that garlic was the cure-all, that only boiled water was safe to drink – even in America? How would

Russia separate me from my son? And how would our son change the dynamics of our family?

I had heard the stories. 'My father left home when he was fourteen, after eighth grade,' Dima would say. 'He was on his own, like me. It's in our blood, woman.' But my blood would rush stronger, harder through the sinewy fabric of our son.

His parents and Grandma returned five years after our wedding for a month of the most oppressive summer. He drove a borrowed minivan from the small suburb of Stow, Ohio, to New York City to fetch the family, flying in from St Petersburg. I couldn't sleep. Instead, I lay on squirrel sheets damp with waxy heat, mind filled with the five of us sitting at the kitchen table clinking champagne flutes.

The clock chimed 2:00 a.m. when the Povozhaev Express finally rumbled up the drive to our fifty-year-old home, the American flag flapping against the white post, waving hello in the breath of night.

Dima's father, Viktor, stepped out of the van first, hugging me tightly but careful not to press my chest against him. His face was less full than it had been five years before. He stood straight, hands down by his sides, and looked at me with a playfully serious expression, modelling his fifty-three-pound weight loss. I told him 'hodasho,' that he looked good. His chin had lost a few layers, but there was still a hearty belly to fill.

As I wiggled myself into the stuffy vehicle, past her cane and bags, Grandma's dry lips pressed my cheek. She was shaking slightly as I embraced her soft age and natural scent. Tatyana, Dima's mother, squeezed my bare arm from the back seat, 'Leea, Leea, Previet!' We strained toward each other. Grandma slowly stepped down from the van, gripping Viktor's arm. Grey slacks slid past her swollen ankles, tops of feet like pink fish. Tatyana followed, warm night moving her fuzzy hair and mismatched clothes. I approached her and cuddled against the mass of her bosom like a child.

I ran to the back of the van to help unload, but Dima and his father took all of the bags, shooing me away. I led them through the polished kitchen, past the coffee table we had salvaged from the neighbour's trash three years before, and into their bedrooms. Grandma set her plastic bags down in what had been my office. She ferreted through bags for a yellow and red tea set. 'Beautiful, Babushka. Very beautiful.'

I silently asked, What about my gift to you, Grandma? An Orthodox cross was embroidered on a thick cloth above her bed.

Before they came, my mother had asked, 'Where will they sleep, honey? Won't it be too crowded?'

'Mom, they are used to cramped spaces. They live in one bedroom apartments. It's totally different. They can't expect what *Americans* might.' It seemed to slip my mind that I was, in fact, quite American. One kitchen and two bathrooms would *not* be enough.

From the fridge, stocked with four times our typical amount of food, Dima helped me pull shrimp cocktail with lemon and crackers and cheddar cheese arranged on a china dish. Heavy smells of body odour sifted through the essence of our small home, overpowering the lemony scent of Murphy's Oil Soap.

Tatyana emerged in her tiger-print bathrobe, and Dima's father whistled. Grandma shuffled into the kitchen, short grey hair brushed back in an owl-like puff. Viktor opened the pantry and then a closet, seemingly interested in what lay beneath our lives in this quiet town. He sighed and sat down at the table, silver cross on his bare chest. Dima mumbled behind us at the sink.

'What's wrong?' I asked.

'Champagne's flat.'

'Neechevo.' Grandma insisted on drinking it flat, but we filled our wine goblets with boxed Cabernet Sauvignon. I was still expecting a Russian-style celebration: robust toasting, eating, joking. Silence hung in the room like the heat, even though it had been years since Dima, Grandma, and his parents had all been together. My family talked excessively about everything from bowel movements to how we imagined heaven, and after years of separation, there'd be surging conversation.

I left the loud silence to wake eight-month-old Viktor. Thoughts mounted with each step. Maybe I'm keeping them from speaking Russian. Viktor's arms hung limply on my chest, his soft breath on my neck. 'Hey, little guy. Are you ready to meet the family,' I whispered. He stirred and opened wide eyes his face was slowly growing into.

Stealing him into the kitchen, Dima's mother jumped out of her skin. 'Leea, nyet,' she shook her head and frowned.

'Lea, why'd you do that? Put him back to bed. Why would you wake him?' Dima said.

'I just thought it was a special – '

'Noooo. Leea, Veektor tired. He sleeping,' Dima's father explained, head cocked.

I buckled him into the high chair with shaking hands. Our baby laughed and reached out to his grandfather over the tray. I warmed a bottle as Grandma smiled, touched a warm palm to his tender cheek, 'Oui.'

Tatyana called, 'Vitka?' scrunching her nose, puckering her lips, as big blue eyes roamed over the party.

Within days, the family had our eight-month-old rolling around the crumb-laden floor, sipping tea from unwashed spoons, and sucking lemons from their tea.

Dima's father stood beside our bed, a big smile stretching his face. 'Dima, hey, baby? It's time to get up,' I whispered, looking up at his father.

I'd leave – go running, go writing, go crazy one minute longer under their foreign gaze. 'You sure your mother's okay watching Viktor until three?' I was leaving for the University of Akron, whittling afternoon hours away in quiet work.

'She'll be fine,' he threw a butter and cheese sandwich on the passenger side seat and folded himself into our Camry.

'Listen, be home as soon as possible. I don't know what to do with your parents.'

'They don't expect to be entertained.' His keys rattled in the ignition.

'Sorry you have to go to work.'

He had planned on staying home the whole month, but our bank account faced unexpected demands. He had recently begun to work for Jerry Holmes at Gotech Electronics, drifting through the small office making copies and sales calls or filling boxes in the warehouse with small electronics. He didn't complain, though such a job seemed beyond boring to me. He worked to prove himself to Jerry, to earn a position in the company. I hoped but feared, unsure of Jerry's intentions with Dima and desperate for security. Though the job had given us more flexibility than we'd have had if he were still bouncing from odd job to the next, we weren't given unearned breaks from the Holmeses this time.

'What do you mean they couldn't borrow enough money for Grandma's plane ticket?' He didn't answer but continued subtracting from the $1,000 we had saved for their visit. Half had gone to a car repair, the other half was Grandma's. The mortgage was due, and there was nothing in the bank. When his pay cheque came, it was $180. He had used up all his paid time off.

'I don't know what he was thinking!' I raged on the phone to the accountant at Gotech. 'He'll be in on Monday.'

The book bag twisted around my wrist as I grabbed bottled water, peanut butter and bread, and my sunglasses, glancing at Grandma's enormous underwear sprawled over the kitchen chairs. Somewhere between laughter and disgust, I pressed hard on the gas pedal.

Tatyana and Grandma took to sipping Labatt Blue beer while chopping fish, chicken, and cabbage. It wasn't said until his mother had had a few beers: 'What does Lea cook? You look thin, Dimka.'

After a quiet dinner, red dishcloth in hand, I'd face a kitchen bombed with grease and shavings of carrots and potatoes.

'So much for Thanksgiving dinner, huh?' I said. Dima's eyes were glossed. Maybe it was the shot of vodka, sneaked from the freezer; the physical closeness of his family; the tension between our life and theirs. He was theirs. He was mine. I stared into his grey eyes.

'Look at the kitchen. There's no way I can get in here and put together a turkey and stuffing and all that crap.' Besides, I didn't know how to stuff a turkey, and it didn't seem important to learn any more. I leaned against the dark countertop before launching into scrubbing the refrigerator handle, stovetop, sink; before putting the clean dishes away from the dishwasher, scraping the crust from the newly dirtied ones, and reloading. I shot a dirty look over at Dima as he yawned.

'Russians know hospitality better than Americans,' he said to me on more than one occasion as the family lived with us. I came up short this time.

'What's that supposed to mean?' My voice was steel. Locked in a cage. He didn't explain, but he didn't have to. By the side door, a minimum of twelve shoes and slippers cluttered a quarter of the kitchen. Fish stained the counters, even after scrubbing at six in the morning before the family awoke to catch my 'quirky' cleanliness. Used tea cups and tea bags, chunks of cheese, salami, and dark bread littered the kitchen table. The bathroom became unusable, indescribably foreign. At one point, yellow liquid pooled in the once Comet-scrubbed bathtub.

I might have been more malleable had I not been raised to dust the stair rail and put the milk away the second after pouring it over Raisin Bran. I couldn't live in a pigsty. And they couldn't live in a pharmacy.

The vacuum roared under the kitchen table and chairs. It was ten at night. The parents and Grandma shuffled new bags into their bedrooms filled with 'deals' from another bout of shopping – a winter coat from the Salvation Army, extra wide shoes for Grandma's swelling feet, a fake spider on clearance from last year's Halloween. 'I love spiders!' Tatyana had said, days earlier, crawling through the park looking for them. I stopped the vacuum, nudging the cat away from my leg.

'Does your mother think I'm crazy?' He leaned over the kitchen table, arranging tea cups.

'She said everyone has his or her quirks.' I stared at his back. 'She's asking you to please not clean until they arrive back home once they leave.'

'Why? What do you mean?'

'In Russia it's bad omen to clean before guests arrive home. I know you won't believe this, but it's for real.' The flight itself was twelve hours long. She was asking me to wait days! My knuckles were a white cord on the vacuum's metal handle.

I would clean the minute they stepped over the threshold. Why didn't she think about this *not* being Russia?

It had been only three days since they arrived when the first drama occurred. Each time something was started, like making our son breakfast, looking for the keys, or gathering the laundry, it was soon interrupted. Viktor Junior is cold. The 'ventilator' is on his neck – it had been ninety plus degrees in our home. Or, Viktor is hiccuping. He's coming down with a cold.

I was collapsed at the table one evening when Dima's father asked, 'Leea, why drink sooo much water?' His face wrinkled with the question.

'It's good to drink eight glasses a day,' I swallowed from the tall cup, later wondering if I averaged twelve.

'No. Bad for body when drink so much. Very difficult for organs.' Dima explained his father's concern over my kidneys processing all that fluid, as he and his father sipped tea, cup six of the day.

Instead of rubbing his back, I wanted to pinch him, and hard enough to bruise his creamy flesh. Instead of relaxing beside the bonfire with his family, I wrote in my journal, worrying about my American inhospitality. Instead of accepting my status as mute, agreeable wife, I constantly harangued him for translations and sulked when these weren't complete.

'What did your family say about Susan's party?'

'Nothing. My mom absolutely thinks you should go to class instead of the party.'

'It's your citizenship party, though. I mean, Susan even said it was in yours *and my* honour, but that's stupid. It's your party, your parents' even. It's not mine, not really. Besides, it's the first class of the semester.'

'I'm telling you, my mother agrees. You should go to school.'

'What exactly did she say, Dima?' He was gathering a tray with tea and crackers for his father and Grandma at the picnic table.

'I don't know. Just go to class.'

'You piss me off, I swear. You're my only way to know them, and you never tell me everything. How am I going to really know what they think?' He was silent. Tired eyes swept over me. He pushed the side door open with his elbow and left the kitchen. The sun was setting through the sagging dusk. Sighing deeply like a wounded animal, I grabbed my running shoes.

I darted around Silver Lake, freeing blood, fire, passion in a five-mile frenzy of movement. Dream homes lined the lake, open and airy, clean and silver knobbed. My body grew weightless, numb. There were moments I just wanted to be comfortable – for days at a time.

I cracked at my niece's baptism. We arrived at Advent Lutheran Church at five. The air was sick with screaming humidity, and the church was without air conditioning. The young priest greeted us in a traditional black clergy shirt stuffed into khaki shorts and a multicoloured scarf draping his neck. He shook our hands. I looked down at his sandals.

'Pastor Kovlash, Previet!' he said. The family was silent, unsmiling, as though they hadn't understood his Russian greeting, which had been mispronounced. It grew unbearably hot. Contemporary Christian music played in the sanctuary.

'Make yourselves at home. You can take Communion. We have "open" Communion here,' Pastor Kovlash ushered us through the doors to the wide sanctuary of plain blonde wood. Nobody crossed themselves, bowed, or lit a candle before worship – as was the custom in Orthodox churches. Blood boiled in my cheeks, neck, chest. I imagined how offensive all of this would seem to Orthodox believers.

The pastor turned to me. 'This might be weird if they're Orthodox.'

'Yeah,' my voice was flat.

'Saturday night is our contemporary service. It's all very different Sunday morning.' The pastor's voice softened.

At the front of the sanctuary, a handful of men and women were dressed in jeans and singing off key. Two worship leaders slapped tambourines in front of a black statue frozen in a dance. There were no icons, no communal chalice, no incense. Instead, it might have appeared an audience and a band; a man, far too comfortable, leading a congregation, much too at ease. I pulled my eyes from the plain windows to the people slouching in the shiny pews. The family pressed together in the pew and passed the small plastic cups of grape juice down the row.

'The statue's a demon,' Grandma whispered, vigilantly eyeing the thin black wave of metal she referred to. Tatyana and Viktor were perfectly quiet. Unbreakable.

I laughed inside. The Orthodox Church had many 'statues': icons, candles, a 'showcase' of the church's patron saint. How could they mind one lone symbol of celebration? What made their symbols anything more?

We filed into the church and the ceremony proceeded. Dima and I were sponsoring our niece. At the front of the shellacked sanctuary, my sister stood in a bright dress that ended above the knees, holding her child, asleep like a limp doll. Pastor Kovlash placed an open prayer book in my hands. Dima was mute as I vowed to teach our niece of God.

Suddenly, Viktor shrieked in the middle of the ceremony. Tatyana rummaged through the diaper bag looking in vain for a bottle of water. Pastor Kovlash dipped his small hand into the baptismal font and sprinkled my niece's delicate head. Water trickled down her forehead onto the dress with a small pink bow. She didn't stir.

Tatyana muffled our son's cries against her bosom, rustling the diaper bag and taking Grandma's elbow as they left the sanctuary. Viktor and my mother followed them to the lobby. After our vows, Dima and I slipped from the sanctuary.

'Dima, where's the water bottle?' his mother asked.

I said, 'I didn't bring it. The doctor specifically told me to feed Viktor formula if he was thirsty or hungry. These sensations are the same for a baby, and he needs the vitamins in the formula.'

Grandma pushed her bottom lip even further out from the top and looked crippled with worry. Dima's father drifted to the windows at the side of the lobby.

'The child is thirsty. He needs water.' Tatyana said.

'I won't be told how to raise my son. I know what he needs. He's thriving. I've handled it fine this far! Dima, just tell them, tell them what the doctor said.'

'Look at him. He's sweating. Aren't you thirsty? Come on!' Dima said. Dagger-eyes pierced me from all angles, pinning me to the wall – the neglectful American wife. Nothing could convince them. I walked away from the bench, Grandma and Tatyana crumpled mounds of concern. Dima's father followed me. He put his arm around my shoulders, and I started to cry.

'I am Momma,' I sobbed. *Do you understand?* He chuckled. My mother and Dima followed us outside. Clouds were swollen and grey.

'Viktor is thirsty. Think about it. Are you thirsty? I don't know why you're acting like this.'

'It is not about the bottle, Dima. Are you listening to me? It's about being told what to do – '

'No one's telling you what to do. They don't understand why the doctor would say that. It doesn't make any sense.'

'It doesn't matter if they understand. It only matters that they don't interfere like this when I decide something with our son!'

My mother said, 'I understand how you both are looking at things, but listen to me. Your marriage has to be priority. You have to put each other first and work together. Lea, you need to calm down. Dima, your mother needs to back off a little bit.' But the conversation ran on and on with no resolution, despite my mother's best efforts. Straight-faced, Dima stared at the cement as I studied him as though he were the reason we were falling apart.

Viktor held our son and slowly paced. Us – door – us – door – us. He began to speak.

'Dad said that they are still trying to figure out why Viktor is always in Pampers. He shouldn't have plastic around his genitals so often or he might become infertile,' Dima nodded with his father. I was doomed. His family was impossible.

We drifted back into church as it began to rain. Grandma said, 'I can tell with the way Lea is acting that when we leave America, we will consider each other enemies.' I was aghast. Growing up, my family had been loud. We reacted in our anger: mother's pink slipper spankings when Melanie and I bickered in the bathtub. My father slamming on the brakes at the end of our street so Mom could exit the minivan and walk to McDonald's instead of coming to church with us after an argument over something as meaningless as feeding the dog. We reacted in our forgiveness: breakfast at Bob Evans after church, laughing and talking easy. Conversations as we sat on the front steps, Mom pausing from the ground meat sizzling in the kitchen to talk through a disagreement, to make my father and me hug before I left the house. Weren't family fights the first steps toward resolutions? This experience grew the seed of my greatest fear. The family would be inflexible, proudly Russian grown.

Back in the minivan for the short ride to my sister's, Viktor asked, 'How old are you?' He craned his thick neck around the passenger seat. His eyes were kind, loving; he had no idea that he'd offended me again. To him, I was just a young girl, foolish and naïve. He could forgive a child. But maybe to Tatyana I was a threat, a woman with a mind and body wedged between her and her son and grandson.

Night was falling and clouds were moving in. The breezy dark sluiced the bright echo of day. Family clustered inside the home according to kind. There were my sister's Jewish in-laws talking around the kitchen table, small women with greying hair in neat piles on their heads. My sister, Mom, and dark-lipped Aunt Vicki gathered in the kitchen munching from the veggie tray.

'You doing okay, honey?' my aunt asked. I met her blue-green stare and rolled my eyes. 'Well, darling, this time too shall pass.' She laughed a deep-throat chuckle and pushed dark hair behind her ears, leaning a tall body over the tray for a carrot. Viktor Junior and my sister's little girl squealed in the living room as they circled the coffee table on familiar laps. Dima's family was outside sitting by the pool under an old maple. Tatyana and Grandma were drinking Labatts, and Viktor sipped a glass of red wine. Dima and I flitted around the party, free.

Every face looked so appealing. Jerry Holmes had just returned from a trip to Asia. He appeared on the patio wearing a baseball cap and Dockers, a belt just bellow his healthy belly.

'Mr. Holmes is here, Dima,' I called across the kitchen.

'Hey, Mr. Holmes. How are you?' He kissed my cheek and shook Dima's hand, looking beyond him.

'Not bad, not bad. Quite a night. Man, we're in for a storm.' He spoke to me.

'Yup. It's needed, though. I can't take this heat much longer.'

'How was the trip, Mr. Holmes?' Dima peered into Jerry's small eyes.

'Ah, pretty good. There's a few aspects with purchasing I plan to change in the office ... '

With the nagging need for resolution, I swigged the water, dropped the broccoli drenched in ranch. I had to make a move. I wasn't angry any longer but numb instead and wanted to hurry up and act before anger reminded me what to feel.

I walked, unsure what to do with my eyes, and reached the family. Arms about Tatyana's full shoulders, I asked her pardon, 'Ezveneetya.' And I *was* sorry for allowing myself to break. I had no intention of letting this disagreement ruin the rest of the month we would share. She hugged me back with strong arms – crushing arms.

Again, we loaded into the minivan, finally on our way home for the night. Though I was emotionally exhausted, a part of me liked the craziness of it all. Peace settled, like a good dose of endorphins after a long, hard run. I would run for the family, as long as everyone was working to blend Russia and America. And if not, I'd fly like a bat out of hell through the sultriest summer imaginable.

On the way home, Viktor began to wail as he often did his first year when exhausted. 'Dima, stop the car. Deeeem! He's crying,' his father pressed. They were not used to Viktor's red-faced shrieks, his little body writhing in the car seat.

'I have to pull over, Lea.'

'We just need to get home. There's no point in stopping. He'll cry again when we start.'

We stopped.

'Whatever,' I mumbled, unbuckling our infant and jerking us from the minivan. Tall grass tickled my sandaled feet at the side of the highway. Viktor fell asleep against the pounding of my heart.

'He's sleeping,' I whispered gingerly strapping him into his car seat. Tatyana wouldn't meet my eyes.

We spilled out of the minivan onto the broken driveway. 'I'm putting him to sleep,' Dima mouthed, shuffling into the house. His family and I stood in the fresh night air, quiet until Dima rejoined us to translate stories of healing.

'You should walk on the morning dew because it heals blisters. Dad was in the army and had to wear boots for entire days and nights. When his feet became so raw with blisters he could barely walk, someone told him about the cool morning dew. When he began doing this each morning, his feet healed.' Maybe it was just the time spent out of the boots? But I was quiet.

Grandma shared a story about her father, who had been an officer in the navy. I had heard of him before, how he was brave and strong. Dima had been afraid of him after dreaming his ghost was chasing him. When he told his mother and Grandma, they took him to his great-grandfather's grave and said he was haunted because he hadn't said goodbye. After the graveside visit, the spirit didn't return.

Grandma told of her father when he was alive. He was a communist (so an atheist), but he had been sick when a doctor told him to visit an Old Believer, an aged Russian woman said to have healing powers because of her faith in God. Because he was so ill, he was willing to try anything. So he went to an Old Believer, who prayed over a dish of holy water and blessed him. She told him to place his arm in the water as she said another blessing. With this, a long skinny 'hair-fish' emerged from his arm. He watched as the creature wiggled in the water. As she spoke, she drifted into the distance, slight tremors of emotion rippling her flesh.

'Orthodoxy will connect the dots, I really believe this,' Dima told me late one night, rustling into bed, his father still downstairs slurping tea. I didn't believe him. His parents hadn't gone to church until recently. They didn't talk about God, or pray, or *seem* devout.

I flipped through the strange prayer books they brought and stared into the forlorn faces of icons in our 'guest' room, which had begun to feel stained by Dima's parents. I stashed the three silver crosses they had given us for 'after our baptism' in a velvet-lined box with my hair pins. How in the world would this work? I curled into a fetal position, desperate for nothing but sleep.

Living with the family would pass at the end of the summer when they returned to Russia. Yet our home would continue changing, growing, as we became family all over again.

Dima found a hummingbird's nest shortly after Grandma and his parents had left. It had been safe, tucked in the hollow of a tree stump. He held the bits of powder blue shell in his palm. 'Look. The beast next door got her.' I followed him out the flimsy side door of our kitchen. Airy tufts of nest sprinkled the earth behind our grey bungalow in late afternoon sun. A deep summer breeze swept through my hair.

I looked at the gnarled cherry tree couched in our shallow backyard. 'She'll just have to re-make the nest.'

3 'Neither the End of the World nor the Beginning': Transnational Identity Politics in Lisa Suhair Majaj's Self-Writing

SILVIA SCHULTERMANDL

Before I delve into the main questions this chapter seeks to evoke, let me start by introducing Lisa Suhair Majaj as a Palestinian American woman while admitting that this term is both too narrow and too broad. Majaj was born in the United States to an American mother with a German background and a Palestinian immigrant father. She spent most of her childhood and young adulthood in Lebanon, moved back to the United States for graduate school, has held several teaching posts in the United States, as well as in Bahrain and in Lebanon, and now lives as an independent scholar in the Greek part of Cyprus with her husband and two children. I mention these biographical details in order to illustrate that 'Palestinian American' fails to represent the complexity and, by her own definition, the contradictions, of her identity. This is an important issue not only in particular relation to Majaj as an author but also in relation to Arab American culture in general. Although I object to the notion of casting a single author as an authentic representative of his or her ethnic community in the United States, the difficult endeavour of defining Majaj's personal identity is emblematic of more general questions about Arab American culture. Does the term sufficiently convey the racial, ethnic, gender, national, religious, sexual, and class parameters that Arab Americans experience or write about? And how does one define Arab American literature as a vehicle for these experiences and as an artistic product?

These are the questions that emerge out of Majaj's work as critic, poet, and educator both within the context of Arab American scholarship and as a groundbreaking figure in transnational feminist theory. My analysis draws on her work as a literary and cultural critic, such as her introductory essays to the edited collections *Going Global: The*

Transnational Reception of Third World Women Writers (2000, with Amal Amireh), *Etel Adnan: Critical Essays on the Arab-American Writer and Artist* (2002, with Amal Amireh), and *Intersections: Gender, Nation and Community in Arab Women's Novels* (2002, with Paula Sunderman and Therese Saliba), and on her critical essays in the collections *Memory and Cultural Politics: New Approaches to Ethnic American Literatures* (1996) and *Postcolonial Theory and the United States* (2000). I also look at her poem 'Claims' (1994b) and her personal essay 'Boundaries: Arab/American' (1994a). Finally, I consider her critical essay 'Female Voices, Feminist Negotiation: An Experience Teaching Arab Women's Literature' (1992), in which Majaj raises issues about her pedagogical endeavour to introduce American students to Arab feminism and Arab women's writing. This large and diverse body of work, I believe, lends itself well to a discussion of ongoing trends in Arab American literature and culture studies, a field that still remains rather marginal in the study of multi-ethnic American studies. Reading her fiction, non-fiction, and scholarly work side by side allows me to embed it within the critical conversations she participates in and to trace the development of the various issues she raises.

Invisibility on Multiple Accounts

Looking at contemporary criticism of Arab American literature, one notices the recurrence of the word *invisibility* to define Arab Americans and their literary productions in the United States. Although many ethnic American writers have commented on the invisibility of people of ethnic background in the American social fabric, even referring to the phenomenon in the titles of their works – Ralph Ellison's novel *Invisible Man* (1952) and Mitsuye Yamada's personal essay 'Invisibility as Unnatural Disaster: Reflections of an Asian American Woman' (2003) come to mind here – Arab American critics and writers emphasize that theirs is an especially invisible status. Joanna Kadi, editor of the anthology *Food for Our Grandmothers: Writings by Arab-American and Arab-Canadian Feminists* (1994), for instance, argues that Arab Americans are 'the most Invisible of the Invisibles' (xix). Whereas many authors and critics espouse invisibility in its metaphorical sense to connote the political and social discrimination Arab Americans have experienced over the years, the social and political parameters that lead to this invisibility are unique. When Arab American authors and scholars of Arab American culture speak of invisibility, they imply three distinctly different aspects.

The first factor that renders Arab Americans invisible in the American national imagination is their racial categorization. According to the U.S. Census Bureau, they are 'white.' This categorization conflicts with the experience of many Arab Americans since the beginning of Arab immigration to the United States in the late 1880s, and is especially jarring with respect not just to the Islamophobia but to the 'Arabophobia' emerging in American nationalist discourses of citizenship in the wake of 9/11. As Lisa Majaj has observed astutely, the categorization of Arab Americans is closer in meaning and scope to the ambivalent status of 'honorary whiteness' than to enfranchised citizenship because it can be and has been 'readily stripped away at moments of crisis' (1996, 321). Not only does subsuming Arab Americans under the racial category 'white' fail to address the legal and social disenfranchisement they often face but it also excludes them from a categorization as people of colour and denies their contributions to the cultural productions of that group. In response to this ambiguous status as honorary whites, Arab Americans, so Majaj notes, have turned to pan-ethnic forms of ethnic and racial categorization that project a notion of cultural homogeneity and locate Arab Americans alongside other ethnic American communities in an oppositional space to whiteness (2000, 327). This pan-ethnic consciousness 'helps them confront the increasing politicalization of their racial categorization' (Fadda-Conrey 2006, 190).

The second factor to blur the visibility of Arab American communities is the use of 'Arab' and 'Middle Eastern' as labels. Categorizing Arab Americans as white is a legal matter, whereas foregrounding their origins as Arab or Middle Eastern at the expense of recognizing their citizenship as Americans is xenophobic and projects an image of Arab Americans as cultural aliens. For instance, although many Arab Americans do indeed participate in the political and cultural promotion of the Middle East, their active engagement in Middle Eastern affairs does not justify the negation of the American context from which their activism occurs. This contention that Arab Americans can be grouped under the same category as Arabs is problematic precisely because it precludes their participation in American citizenship at the expense of foregrounding their Arab heritage or origins. Moreover, as many Arab American critics, including Majaj, have pointed out, to assume that Arab American identities are best defined by a person's Arab or Middle Eastern origin glosses over the heterogeneity within the Arab American community and effaces the complexity that Arab American culture inherently contains. And this assumed heterogeneity results in the insensitive lumping together of Arab and Arab American identities, ultimately characterizing Arab Americans as eternal foreigners within the American social fabric, a status that many immigrant American communities have experienced over time.[1]

Furthermore, the lumping together of Arab and Arab American identities, specifies Majaj in a book review of Jack Shaheen's anthology *Reel Bad Arabs: How Hollywood Vilifies a People* (2001), exposes Arab Americans to the same cultural stereotypes that American movies have produced of Arabs in the past century, in portrayals that Majaj summarizes as 'rang[ing] from problematic to downright racist' (2003, 38). Such racism, Majaj asserts in 'Female Voices, Feminist Negotiations' (1992), includes reading Arab American texts as 'exotic, different, totally "other," and as such unknowable and uninterpretable.' Majaj's teaching goal, as defined in this personal essay, makes explicit the critical concerns related to Arab American identities that circulate in the United States based on prevalent stereotypes of Arabs.

The third problem with Arab American representation is rooted in the lack of academic status given to Arab American studies. Many critics have long bemoaned the lack of Arab American literature in the American canon, including the sub-canon of ethnic American literature that other ethnic American communities entered long ago. In their introduction to the *MELUS* special issue on Arab American literature, Salah D. Hassan and Marcy Jane Knopf-Newman contend that 'Arab American studies does not possess the status of an academic field' (2006, 5). Although Arab American studies may not have been recognized as an academic field, there has been, especially in connection with the first and second Gulf Wars and since 9/11, a growing interest in them. In this light, scholars have increasingly uncovered a genealogy of Arab American presence in American culture. The earliest awareness of the presence of an Arab American community manifests itself in the 1988 anthology *Grape Leaves: A Century of Arab-American Poetry*, co-edited by Gregory Orfalea and Sharif Elmusa. This anthology unearthed a tradition of Arab American poetry that many contemporary writers had been seeking and thus, as Majaj argues, was a catalyst for the strengthening of an Arab American literary community. In 1994, the Radius of Arab-American Writers, Incorporated (RAWI) came into existence under its first president, Ethel Adnan. Having grown out of the 1992 Arab-American Anti-Discrimination Committee (ADC), RAWI addresses issues such as the invisibility of and discrimination against Arab Americans. Not coincidentally, RAWI, which is Arabic for 'storyteller,' has inspired Arab Americans to produce literature and nurtured young talents, becoming a backbone of the Arab American literary tradition. As does RAWI, the literary journal *Mizna: Prose, Poetry and Art Exploring Arab America*, founded in 1999, also contributes to the emergence of a striving Arab American literary culture. These organizations and venues, however, as well established as they are today, are testimony to the belated onset of a literary tradition in the Arab American community. It began to come into existence at a time when other ethnic American literary communities were already flourishing.

Although the three issues just identified at the root of Arab American invisibility are distinct, it is important to point out that they often occur simultaneously. Lisa Majaj notes that Arab Americans are 'doubly invisible' (1999) because of the complex enmeshment of their various forms of misrepresentation in American culture, both in the so-called white mainstream and as people of colour. She asserts that Arab American literary tradition, for instance, is doubly invisible 'partly ... [because] there is not a great deal of it, and partly because of the lack of recognized categories to make it visible.' Although Majaj is certainly not the first American women to speak of a 'double marginality,' her contestation that 'Arab American' as racial or ethnic identity (that is, even without going into the complex entanglement of gender, sexuality, class, religion, and age) is doubly marginalized is an interesting claim. She does not comment on the particular status of women writers within this tradition or foreground the question of how gender complicates a formulation of ethnic identity, as many African American, Asian American, Native American, Latina, and Chicana writers have done before her, but grounds her assertion in the national and racial categorization of Arab Americans and the fact that the absence of a strong literary and social tradition can be traced back to the miscategorization that American society has issued and that many Arab Americans have adopted.

Questions of Gender

Arab American literature also maintains a special position within American literature because of the unique questions of gender that it confronts. Like many other ethnic American literary traditions, it seems to be carried to a great extent by female authors, a circumstance that Hassan and Knopf-Newman call the 'gendering of ethnic literature in the US' (2006, 11). Many Arab American women writers suggest that they do not see themselves confined to the margin of the literary movement, as early African American and Asian American women writers did. On the contrary, as Majaj notes in her essay 'Of Stories and Storytellers' (2005), becoming a writer seems to be a more accessible goal for Arab American women than for men precisely because 'there is more pressure upon men to be breadwinners and go into more stable fields.' More important, Arab American women writers seem to be more attractive to an American reading audience because 'Arab men are still unsettling figures to the American sensibility.' In fact, as Nada Elia contends, in 'the present climate of virulent Islamophobia, mainstream American culture seems to favour Muslim [and Arab American] women who, unlike their brothers, husbands, fathers, or sons, are not seen as a menace to American society, but rather as powerless victims of their own religion' (2006, 155). Many Arab American writers and activists, argues Elia, are aware of this racist privileging by mainstream American society, whose practice of what Gayatri Chakravorty Spivak has labelled (in the context of subaltern studies) the Western grand gesture of 'saving brown women from brown men' (1988, 296) essentializes Arab American men and women. The resulting gendering of Arab American literature within the American imagination, therefore, is not a democratic movement within the Arab American writers' community but a reflection of the xenophobic and racist stereotyping of Arab American men within American society. Many women writers, continues Elia, have produced novels that do not primarily address gender oppression within the Arab American community but articulate a 'reactionary' agenda, thereby 'foregrounding Arab and Arab American men's oppression, their deportation, their detention, the increasing harassment these men face' (159).

This complexity, along with the various discourses of power and privilege that it is exposed to, locates Arab American literature at a very different entry point into American studies from other multi-ethnic American literatures. (It is also important to note that Arab American literature emerged in the United States at a time when numerous Arab novels were also available in translation and when media coverage of the Middle East has reached a point of saturation. Because of that, 'common knowledge' of the Arab world was much more widespread in the United States than knowledge of Chinese culture had been when Chinese American literature became largely accessible to an American reading audience.) In recent scholarship on Arab American literature, critics project a keen awareness of the dangers of adopting nationalist definitions of Arab American literature on the one hand and Western feminist notions on the other. In the introduction to the groundbreaking collection *Going Global: The Transnational Reception of Third World Women Writers*, Amal Amireh and Lisa Majaj articulate their frustration with the feminist spaces being ascribed to them in Western academia:

> Discursive, institutional, and ideological structures preempted our discourse and determined both what we could say and whether we would be heard when we spoke. If we critiqued our home cultures or spoke of issues confronting Arab women, our words seemed merely to confirm what our audiences already 'knew,' – that is, the patriarchal, oppressive nature of Third World societies. If we challenged this ready-made knowledge, we were accused of defensiveness, and our feminism was questioned and second-guessed. (2000, 1)

Amireh and Majaj suggest that Arab American women scholars, in their attempt to counter the invisibility and silence that they confront, and by formulating the specific politics of location from which to speak as women, are conscious of the discrepancy between what they seek to articulate and what Western feminism wants them to say. One of the fallacies that Amireh and Majaj address is the practice within Western feminism of regarding Third World women, including Arab American women, as culturally authentic 'windows' into the Third World (2000, 2). The contested position of Arab American women within feminism, as Marnia Lazreg (2000, 35) has pointed out, puts to the test the parameters of inclusion and the definition of global feminism and its objective of projecting a sense of global equality and sisterhood among all women. Instead, Arab American women scholars actively address the politics of reception of their texts, i.e., the ideological underpinnings that result in the containment of their voices in predefined spaces within the feminist community.

Arab American Literature

Arab American literature is to an overriding extent characterized by a transnational sensibility, one that opposes essentialist categorizations even when confronting the issue of invisibility. I locate Majaj's writing at the centre of contemporary transnational feminist theory, in particular her attempt to redefine the parameters that constitute identity.[2] Although many Arab American writers admit that they seek to deconstruct prevalent stereotypes of Arabs and Arab Americans and to 'set the record straight' by correcting in their works prevalent misconceptions – an endeavour comparable to the 'claiming America' tradition within Asian American studies in the 1970s and '80s – Arab American writers counter stereotypical images of the Arab American community not by coming up with new definitions of essential and so-called authentic Arab American identity but by pointing out the limitations of the present categorizations of identity. This endeavour becomes apparent in many scholars' critical engagement with the question of what Arab American identity actually is, and, by extension, what Arab American literature is. In the *MELUS* special issue that pursues this very question, Gregory Orfalea illustrates, by looking at a host of contemporary writers, that it is insufficient to claim that Arab American literature is 'written by an Arab American with an Arab American protagonist' (2006, 119). Similarly, Majaj urges that it is premature to label Arab American literature as an account of immigrant experiences and the tensions that arise from being of Middle Eastern origin and living in the United States, for two major reasons. First, this excludes authors who write about other, non-ethnic topics. Second, this assumption is based on an understanding of ethnic American literature as merely sociological and ideological, at the expense of its artistic and creative features.

In her autobiographical essay 'Boundaries: Arab/American,' Majaj calls into question the categorizations that Arab Americans are subject to by offering the following anecdote about a workshop on racism in which she participated:

> Workshop participants were asked to group ourselves in the center of the room. As the facilitator called out a series of categories, we crossed to one side of the room or the other, according to our self-identification: white or person of color, heterosexual or lesbian/bisexual, middle/upper class or working-class, born in the United States or in another country, at least one college-educated parent or parents with no higher education, English as a native language or as a second language. Although I am used to thinking of myself in terms of marginality and difference, I found myself, time after time, on the mainstream side of the room. White (as I called myself for lack of a more appropriate category), heterosexual, middle-class, born in the United States to a college-educated parent, a native speaker of English, I seemed to be part of America's presumed majority. (1994a, 65)

This experience leads Majaj to question the social categories that the experiment replicated, speculating that 'these categories are insufficient, or insufficiently nuanced.' Majaj concludes that Arab American identity is an 'ongoing negotiation of difference.' By characterizing its status as ongoing instead of fixed, Majaj refutes essentialist notions while still achieving agency for herself as a writer and activist.

Despite the title of her essay, 'The Hyphenated Author' (1999), Majaj underscores that the notion of hyphenated identities cannot encompass the complexity of Arab American identities. The negotiation of Arab American literature also becomes apparent from the different kinds of spelling: Arab-American with a hyphen, Arab/American with a dash, and Arab American no marker, signifying neither conjunction nor division. The absence of a discernible location or identity, as Majaj resigns herself to in 'Boundaries,' pushes Arab Americans into a cultural no man's land: 'American and Palestinian, not merely half of one thing and half of the other, but both at once – and in that inexplicable melding that occurs when two cultures come together, not quite either, so that neither American nor Arab find themselves fully reflected in me' (1994a, 68).

Statements like these are reminiscent of Gloria Anzaldúa's definition of 'the new mestiza' and characterize Arab American literature, as Carol Fadda-Conrey argues, as located in 'the ethnic borderland: a constructive space in which interethnic ties between and within different communities of colour could be established and maintained' (2006, 187). Moreover, claiming the cultural borderlands between two cultures, as Majaj does in 'Boundaries,' also positions her identity politics in a critical light vis-à-vis the concept of hyphenation. Majaj echoes here Arjun Appadurai's discussion of ethnic American identity beyond the concept of hyphenation:

> The formula of hyphenation (as in Italian-Americans, Asian-Americans, and African-Americans) is reaching the point of saturation, and the right-hand side of the hyphen can barely contain the unruliness of the left-hand side ... The politics of ethnic identity in the United States is inseparably linked to the global spread of originally local national identities. For every nation-state that has exported significant numbers of its population to the United States as refugees, tourists, or students, there is now a decolonized transnation, which retains a special ideological link to a putative place or origin but is otherwise a thoroughly diasporic collectivity. No existing conception of Americanness can contain this large variety of transnations. (Appadurai 1993, 424)

Such awareness of the limited possibilities that hyphenation offers for a negotiation of Arab American identity also pertains to negotiations of Arab American literature.

Many critics have strongly urged that Arab American literature needs to find a strategy, one that 'alleviate[s] invisibility' (Fadda-Conrey 2006, 192) yet creates a sense of 'communality that is anti-essentialist' (203). And precisely because Arab American identity has yet to be defined in an inclusive and non-biased way, so, too, does Arab American literature resist easy classifications. Therefore, as Majaj concludes, 'Like Arab-Americans themselves, Arab-American texts are part of Arab culture, past of American culture, and part of something still in the process of being created' (1999).

Claims

Such politics of location becomes evident in 'Claims' (1994b), one of Majaj's best-known and earliest poems. The identity politics she exhibits in this work is an example of what Kandice Chuh (2003) defines as 'subjectless discourse.' Chuh argues in her discussion of Asian American criticism that identity can only be conceived of as 'situational' (10) and through the creation of a 'conceptual space to prioritize difference by foregrounding the discursive constructedness of subjectivity' (9). Despite a person's need to gain subjectivity, which in the case of Asian Americans equals the notion of citizenship and on this level, I would argue, offers a basis of comparison to Arab Americans, Chuh holds that subjectlessness is a much-needed intervention for the political practice of 'strategic *anti*-essentialism' (10). 'Claims' epitomizes how Majaj, with her double majority status within Arab American literature as female and a poet (poetry being the dominant genre, according to Orfalea 2006, 115), seeks to counter invisibility by correcting misconceptions without replacing them with essentialist re-definitions of herself. Although the poem articulates her close rootedness in an engagement with Middle Eastern causes, it resists classification as mere expression of a teleological quest of an Arab American woman in the diaspora in search for her true origin. And although critical of gender stereotypes, the poem also does not offer an explicit critique of gender oppression directed at an American or an Arab or an Arab American community. Instead, it projects a transnational sensibility in its subversion of prevalent categorizations, which makes it difficult to assign to its lyrical *I* an unequivocal nationality or gender.

The poem is characterized by a strong affirmative voice, established through the explicit subjectivity of the lyrical *I*. Each of the seven stanzas starts with the words 'I am,' words that also appear in primary positions in several lines within the stanzas. The continuous appearance of these words in anaphoric position creates a well-structured rhyming pattern that is missing from the line endings of this free verse. Thematically, the poem is divided into three sections, each referring to specific claims that the lyrical *I* makes by positioning herself in relation to established notions of Arab American identity.

The first three stanzas counter prevalent stereotypes of Arab women. Each starts with the assertion 'I am not,' as if responding to prescribed or assumed notions of identity. For instance, in the first stanza, the lyrical *I* distances herself from images of the exotic seductress in line with the infamous Scheherazade of *Arabian Nights*: 'I am not soft, hennaed hands / a seduction of coral lips.' Here Majaj refers mostly to an eroticized representation of Arab women, using images ranging from 'a swirl of sequined hips' and 'a glint of eyes unveiled' to 'harem's promise' and 'desire's fulfillment.' The images are explicitly ethnicized and gendered, describing without great figurative complexity a sexualized female body yet in doing so offering an extended metaphor of the ultra-feminization of Middle Eastern culture by employing the eroticism of Arab women as synecdoche for the Middle East.

The second stanza moves to stereotypes of Middle Eastern women in terms of their roles as mothers, wives, and domestic labourers. In contrast to the erotic overtones of the first stanza, the second evokes images that are unappealing, even unpleasant: 'shapeless peasant / trailing children like flies,' 'house slave,' 'foul-smelling, moth-eaten, primitive.' The lyrical *I* then refutes these stereotypes, proclaiming in response to the list of female roles, 'I am neither a victim / nor an anachronism.' Majaj is referring here to the commonplace Western habit of regarding Middle Eastern women as victims of sexist cultural practices that place them in opposition to Western modern women.

The two stanzas share the lyrical *I*'s resistance to predominant notions of Arab women's femininity and, by extension, to their victimization on the basis of gender. Instead, as Majaj argues in the introduction to *Going Global*, 'Whereas First World feminists have tended to focus on sexual oppression and on the cultural dimensions of "patriarchy," Third World feminists often seek to address political and economic oppression' (2000, 33).[3] By refusing to adopt these prevalent images, the lyrical *I* distances herself from ready-made assumptions about Middle Eastern women and thus critiques such categorization.

In contrast to the first two stanzas, the third does not use any obviously gendered images but instead rehearses a catalogue of derogatory words that denote Middle Easterners: 'I am not a camel jockey, sand nigger, terrorist, / oil-rich, blood thirsty, fiendish.' The stereotypes are so sexually ambiguous that the gender of the lyrical *I* is not clear; only in relation to the first two stanzas can we locate it as a female voice. This leaves room for interpretation, particularly because the previous two stanzas operate with such clearly marked images. Therefore, I suggest that Majaj refers to xenophobic assumptions about Arabs, and perhaps by extension Arab Americans, in order to foreground the national, rather than gender, identity that these stereotypes comment on.

The three stanzas together illustrate how Western knowledge of Middle Eastern politics and women is produced from ready-made assumptions and biases precisely because the misconceptions Majaj lists in her poem are prevalent in Western discourses about the Middle East, such as in media portrayals, or, as transnational feminist scholars have pointed out, within Western feminist theory and practice. Thus, the last two lines of the third stanza serve as a summary of the challenge the lyrical *I* issues to her spectator. By claiming 'My hands are open and empty: / the weapon you place in them is your own,' the narrator of the poem underscores the ideological constructedness of Western images of the Middle East and the construction of an antagonistic 'other.' The poem also foregrounds the construction of knowledge about the Middle East by ascribing it to an imaginary addressee. Whereas in the first two stanzas the addressee is implied through the use of stereotypes that the reader might recognize as Western biases, the third stanza speaks directly to the imaginary addressee who potentially employs these stereotypes: 'I am neither the mirror of *your* hatred and fear, / nor the reflection of *your* pity and scorn' (emphasis added). This fictional response to an addressee constitutes the climax of the poem because in no other stanzas are the images that the lyrical *I* responds to so aggressive, and in no other stanza does she talk back so emphatically.

The first three stanzas establish the context for the following three in which the lyrical *I* renegotiates aspects of the images she has just refuted. For instance, whereas she claims in the first stanza that she is 'not the enticement of jasmine musk,' she starts the fourth stanza with the claim 'I am the woman remembering jasmine,' thus emphasizing both her agency and her own process of imagination and negotiation of her identity. This creates a pattern in which she evokes images that recall the stereotypes she confronts in the first three stanzas and reappropriates them for her own definition of her identity. Yet although the images she seeks to counter are all very established criteria on the basis of both gender and national identity, the images she claims in stanzas four through six are highly ambivalent, even contradictory. In the fourth, for instance she says, 'I am the lost one who flees and the lost one returning,' an image that illustrates the cultural contradictions of the lyrical *I*'s borderland identity. This image echoes Majaj's statement in 'The Hyphenated Author,' where she speaks of the contradictions of her location as a Palestinian American woman who can claim neither America nor Palestine as her home. In this pattern of contradictory categories or elements in the fourth stanza, the lyrical *I* renegotiates her identity as a woman and as a writer.

In *Culture and Imperialism*, Edward Said offers a definition that can also be applied to Majaj's politics of location in the first three stanzas. Said speaks of a 'contrapuntal criticism,' drawing a comparison to 'the counterpoint in Western classical music, [in which] various themes play off against one another, with only a provisional privilege being given to any particular one; yet in the resulting polyphony there is concert and order, and organized interplay' (1993, 51). Unlike Said's earlier definition of an 'oppositional criticism,' in *The World, the Text, and the Critic* (1983), this definition is characterized by the aim 'not to separate but to connect' and to do justice to the fact that 'cultural forms are hybrid, mixed, impure' (1993, 14).[4]

A similar emphasis on counterpoint emerges in the fifth stanza, in which the lyrical *I* negotiates her identity in reference to her physical location through the use of images connected to the land. In metaphors such as 'I am the ancient earth struggling / to bear history's fruit,' she evokes the natural biosphere. In stanza six, she politicizes these references to the land through images that evoke the geopolitical landscape of the Middle East: 'I am opposite banks of a river, and I am the bridge.' At this point, the lyrical *I* has moved away from identity politics that define her female subjectivity and embraced a discourse that subverts the categorization she critiques in the earlier stanzas. By the end of the sixth stanza, the images the lyrical *I* brings forth speak of a different location, one that is not bound by national and geographical structures: 'I am light shimmering / off water at night.' Here the lyrical *I* places herself within the natural elements of light and water; later, she places herself within the universe at large, as a cosmological reference to the moon suggests: 'and I am the dark sheen / that swallows the moon whole.' This movement from geographical space to universal space also mirrors the poem's movement from particular to universal aspects of identity.

This idea of a universal self emerges in the last stanza of the poem, in which the lyrical *I* proclaims, 'I am neither the end of the world / nor the beginning.' It is in these last lines that Majaj suggests a strong subjective discourse, but one that refutes essentialism, that even resists the notion of classification altogether. In a larger context, Majaj's appropriation of an anti-essentialist subjective discourse – one that espouses the personal as political but does so with a keen awareness of the specific politics of location and the multiple intersections from which this discourse emerges – suggests an alternative categorization that can do justice to the large degree of heterogeneity within the Arab American community and thus also in Arab American literature.

Conclusion

Majaj's work demonstrates that the situational contexts of identity demand that her readers consider her writing both as an indication of the limits of nationalist frameworks and as an invitation to transgress these limits. For Majaj, the rhetoric of the nation-state fails in the context of the identity performances she describes, and so do clear-cut categorizations of gender. Majaj's work thus urges its readers to consider the constructedness of the categories of nation and women.

As Norma Alarcón, Caren Kaplan, and Minoo Moallem argue, 'Between woman and nation is, perhaps, the space or zone where we can deconstruct these monoliths and render them more historically nuanced and accountable to politics' (1999, 12). In Majaj's work, this space between woman and nation resists binary oppositions and refutes essentialist discourses of identity. Instead, it is a place where the personal and the political can be discovered anew in all their implied nuances and inherent contradictions.

4 Identity and Belonging among Second-Generation Greek and Italian Canadian Women

NOULA PAPAYIANNIS

Within the last two decades, research on European immigrants to Canada has provided important insights into the labour experiences, housing conditions, and efforts at community building by immigrants; the attitudes of members of the host society toward immigrants; and the immigration policies and practices of the Canadian government. Although researchers recognize that immigrants do not constitute a unitary category, not all have paid sufficient attention to the fact that the immigrant family itself is not a homogenous group. Intergenerational differences matter, and as researchers interested in transnational families we must explore the particular experiences of Canadian-born children of immigrant parents. Although members of this second generation did not undergo the journey from immigrant to Canadian, their lived experiences in Canada are nonetheless mediated by their ethnicity and complicated by gender hierarchies. Second-generation women might belong in Canada by virtue of their citizenship, but their sense of belonging to the Canadian collective is not so clearly marked. In this chapter, I focus on the narratives of second-generation Greek and Italian Canadian women and explore how the intersection of gender and ethnicity shapes their lives. More specifically, I examine how these women negotiate their ethnic identities in relation to the gendered cultural markers of family and food in order to better understand how second-generation Canadians move within and between conflicting terrains of inclusion and exclusion.

The boundary dividing sameness and difference is not rooted in biology but is socially constructed and, as such, is constituted differently in time and place. Belonging within any given group is always relational and dependent on the flexibility and mutability of the boundaries separating 'insiders' from 'outsiders.' To make sense of the shifting and complicated nature of belonging, I will begin by exploring the narrative of twenty-two-year-old Anita, a daughter of Greek Cypriot parents who immigrated to Canada in the mid-1970s. She explained to me how she perceives her ethnic identity:

> I would say I'm Greek Cypriot Canadian. Even though I was born here, I still feel more Greek. It's in my blood. My brothers and I have these conversations with my boyfriend and he says you are where you're born. But we say it doesn't matter the location, it depends on your family and where your roots are. We are from Cyprus, so I'm Cypriot first, and I say Greek because no one understands when I say Cyprus.

Anita emphatically rejects the assumption that her belonging is determined by the locale of her birth. She refuses the unhyphenated identity of 'Canadian' and instead insists that her identity is rooted in the homeland of her parents. Later in the interview, Anita told me that she wants 'to keep her culture alive' and even expressed her desire to one day 'go back' to Cyprus and live there permanently. Although Anita articulated a nostalgic longing to return, as she explicitly put it, 'back home,' at the same time she expressed disdain for the traditional gender roles that she specifically identified as part of her Greek culture. She explained how rigid gender roles dictated the roles and responsibilities of each member of the household and limited the power she could exercise as a young woman: 'I hate that rule: girls have to be in the kitchen and clean and stay in the house.' She also felt that as a young woman in a Cypriot immigrant family, she was regulated and controlled in ways that her 'Canadian' friends were not. Indeed, most of Anita's narrative focused on her relationship with her Portuguese Canadian boyfriend and her parents' unwillingness to accept a non-Greek into the family. She spoke of the ways her parents badger her to find a Greek boyfriend, arguing that marrying outside the Greek culture is improper and will make it impossible to raise her future children in the 'Greek way.'

Although Anita locates her Cypriot culture as her place of belonging, she also perceives her parents' cultural baggage as an obstacle she must overcome as a Canadian-born woman. In other words, Anita's nostalgia for her Cypriot homeland is tempered by the gendered hierarchies rooted within the immigrant family. This tension is not unique to Anita's narrative; indeed, in my interviews with second-generation Greek and Italian Canadian women, I found that all of the young women struggled, albeit in different ways and to various degrees, against their parents' and their larger ethnic community's gender expectations as they also grappled with the question of belonging. In this chapter I attempt to shed light on the gendered struggles second-generation Canadian women encounter in negotiating ethnic identities, as well as the processes by which they attempt to resolve these various conflicts and ambiguities. I focus specifically on second-generation Greek and Italian Canadian women and, based on Patricia Hill Collins' (1998) notion of intersectionality, I explore how the interplay of gender constructs and naturalized hierarchies of ethnicity shape these women's lives. As daughters of immigrants, these women negotiate their personal and collective identities within and between borders and borderlands. Viewing second-generation Canadian women through the lens of a 'transnational sensibility' not only recognizes the fluidity of their identities but also provides a useful vantage point from which to question and explore the meaning and construction of these very borders.

My understanding of second-generation women also reflects the insights of multicultural and transnational feminist writers who, like Ella Shohat, posit the notion of a 'multiply hyphenated identity,' the idea that individuals can occupy multiple spaces and positions (1998, 10). The second-generation women I interviewed for this study have all encountered discrimination as daughters of immigrant parents, but at the same time they occupy privileged positions as middle-class white women. As a feminist researcher, I recognize that gender inequality is intertwined with other systems of oppression, as Shohat explains: 'Instead of a simple oppressor/oppressed dichotomy we find a wide spectrum of power relations among and within communities' (4). Just as gender differences are socially constructed and must be critically examined as such, so too must 'whiteness' be problematized (McIntosh 1998). Race/ethnicity and gender are relational concepts structured within dichotomies that polarize 'white' and 'black,' 'immigrant' and 'Canadian.' Part of our job as researchers involves destabilizing these categories, which have historically defined immigrants as 'raced' and men as 'genderless' (Glenn 1999, 10).

Using this notion of a 'multiply hyphenated identity,' I explore the narratives of four second-generation Greek Canadian women (Maria, Helen, Sophia, and Anita) and four second-generation Italian Canadian women (Francesca, Dina, Tina, and Rose), ranging in age from twenty-two to twenty-eight, and all unmarried with no children at the time of the interviews.[1] As a feminist researcher, I strive to create space for the women to articulate their thoughts and for that reason I have chosen to place their narratives front and centre in this research (Reinharz 1992). I recognize that women's words are legitimate sources of knowledge and use narrative enquiry to examine the personal trajectories of these women.

Belonging

The second-generation women I interviewed for this study asserted multiple, and sometimes conflicting, spaces of belonging. Some identified themselves as 'Canadian,' others as simply 'Greek' or 'Italian,' although others adopted hyphenated titles of identification. While second-generation women may position themselves within a specific category, beyond the surface of these labels women's identities are shifting. Twenty-eight-year-old Tina explained that she did not feel that she belonged exclusively in either Canadian society or within her Italian culture:

> I see myself belonging to both but at the same time not exclusively to either. I can relate to both cultures well, but I don't feel like I'm 100 percent devoted. I don't feel I'm strictly Italian because I feel I have Canadian ties, but then again I don't feel I'm 100 percent Canadian because I have this culture that I grew up with which isn't in synch with all Canadian values ... [I] feel in the middle, I can relate to both, I can move between both worlds.

Tina identified herself as Canadian, but she also recognized how her Italian heritage marks her as different from other Canadians. Her narrative reveals a densely layered identity and offers a challenge to the 'cultural conflict' argument posited by some researchers. Clifford Jansen (1988) makes the point that the problem faced by Italian youth in Canada is that they are unable to identify with the hometown of their parents and at the same time they are not fully accepted by their Canadian peers. Second-generation youth feel marginalized, according to Jansen, because although they have ties to two cultures, they do not identify fully with either group and are therefore 'caught between two cultures' (1988, 178). But this simplistic paradigm not only views culture as a fixed category but also dismisses the second generation as unable to negotiate an identity and places of belonging that speak to their particular lived experiences (Handa 2003). Perhaps a more useful question to ask is how second-generation Canadians negotiate between sameness and difference, exclusion and belonging.

Numerous North American studies demonstrate how the interplay of race, class, and gender has marginalized the second generation. Mary C. Waters's (1999) research on West Indian immigrants and their children in New York City underscores how racism has severely marginalized this particular group, effectively closing off opportunities for upward mobility. In the Canadian context, researchers working on second-generation identity have convincingly demonstrated how the intersection of race and gender has operated to stigmatize women of colour. In her work on South Asian Canadian girls, Mythili Rajiva makes the point that for the second generation, 'belonging is no longer primarily about citizenship or economics ... Instead, it is the awareness of difference as a second skin that has shaped your entire life story' (2006, 170). She asserts that although immigrants themselves are discriminated against in Canadian society, there was a time before they immigrated when they did, at least racially and culturally, belong. Yet as Rajiva puts it, 'for young "ethnics," there was never "a time before" (before the loneliness of non-belonging)' (170). Rajiva's insights are well taken, yet my own research findings suggest that although European second-generation women do experience feelings of non-belonging, at the same time they also engage in processes of imaginatively reconstructing not only 'the homeland' but other spaces of belonging. These women do not represent a homogenous group but are all continually reinventing and redefining themselves as they negotiate their diasporic culture and Canadian society, and attempting to construct spaces of belonging that recognize and value the complexity of their hybrid identities.

Family

All of the second-generation women I interviewed for this study discussed the significance of cultural markers in their struggles to negotiate an ethnic identity that made sense for them. The most prevalent theme that emerged from their narratives was the role of family in the formulation of ethnic and gendered identities. Twenty-two-year-old Rose explained that her strong attachment to family was the major reason she identified more closely with her Italian heritage than her Canadian identity:

I consider myself more traditionally Italian than Canadian because of family ... Even though I'm Canadian I don't consider myself Canadian. I

see myself more with the Italian heritage because I am very family orien-
tated and there are strong bonds toward the family.

For Rose, family togetherness is the basis of her reimagining of Italian culture and identity. The importance of family was particularly prevalent in
the narratives of women who do not speak their parents' native language.

Twenty-four-year-old Dina identified herself as 'Canadianized' primarily because of her difficulty in speaking Italian, as she explained:

> In some ways I do feel more Canadianized and less Italian only because
> we don't speak it at home ... I feel that not knowing the language makes
> me feel less Italian ... When I visit family and they're all speaking Italian, I
> feel like an outsider because I can't really communicate ... so a part of me
> feels less Italian.

Not being able to converse with others in Italian, Dina feels ashamed, excluded, and less authentically Italian. However, during the course of our
interview Dina also described her experiences as a child spending sum-
mers with her grandparents, when she learned how to make Italian cookies and pasta and spent time listening to her grandmother's stories of
'back home.' Although Dina's limited language skills in some way ex-
clude her from an Italian identity, she also reimagines ethnic identity in
terms of family and food and in this way is able to blur the boundaries
between Italian and Canadian worlds and to locate her own sense of identity within a hybrid space that speaks to her particular lived experiences.

Sexuality and Control

Family was consistently identified as an important element of ethnic
identity, yet all the women in my study articulated some degree of frustration over the traditional gender roles placed on them by their families, especially their immigrant parents. A common complaint was
their lack of freedom. Unlike their brothers and other male relatives, as
teens these women were prohibited from going out with friends, forbidden to date, and generally closely guarded by their parents, particularly their mothers. As a teenager, Dina felt that her freedom was limited
by the gendered expectations placed on her by her Italian family:

> Being a daughter, as opposed to a son in an Italian family, I find that being
> a son you have a lot more freedom. I know growing up ... I just didn't

have as much freedom as my brother tended to have. At a lot younger age he was able to go out longer. My parents didn't keep as close an eye on him as they did on me, like where I was going, what I was doing, who I was with.

Twenty-six-year-old Maria also compared her experiences growing up to those of her brother, who was free to come and go as he pleased. She explained how her parents tried to control her social life by keeping her at home, discouraging her from going out, and issuing a strict and early curfew:

> To see my brother, who is three years younger than me but who has done a thousand times more than me ... just the fact that they're worried that they don't want anything to happen to me ... thinking that I'm going to get pregnant even though it was the first week going out with a guy.

Maria's narrative illustrates how her parents viewed the family home as a source of refuge from the dangers of the outside world, especially the 'threat' of premarital sex. By keeping Maria home, her parents could exercise control over Maria's movements and, most important, guard her sexual purity.

Twenty-five-year-old Sophia also described how her mother, as well as the larger Greek community, attempted to restrict her freedom:

> Greek parents are strict, especially with girls. So, if I wanted to go somewhere I would get the third degree, and if my friends wanted to go somewhere their parents would say, 'No problem, go.' When I asked my mom why I couldn't go, she'd say, 'Someone will see you and people will talk.' ... I wished my mom was more like my friends' moms ... When I started going out when I was sixteen and I wanted to stay out late, my parents would start freaking out. My friends would ask, 'What's wrong with your mom?' And I would say, 'Well, my mom is Greek and your mom is Canadian.'

Sophia's narrative underscores the role of community gossip in circumventing second-generation women's freedom. Like Maria, Sophia makes the point that it was her mother who played the key role in reinforcing familial gendered hierarchies. Within the patriarchal family, the sexual purity of daughters is considered an important commodity that must be protected through either parental controls or community gossip.

Despite the myriad restrictions placed on these women, several of my participants disclosed that they resorted to lying to their parents about their relationships in order to manoeuvre around their surveillance and still preserve the 'good girl' image. Dina explained:

It's just how females are treated in the culture ... When I was in grade 9 and I had my first boyfriend it was done in secret ... Even my cousin won't tell her father that she's dating someone right now and she's twenty-two years old ... A lot of things were done in secret.

As teenagers, the women in my study were expected by their parents to conform to a culturally constructed model of the good Greek/Italian girl. Their narratives clearly reveal that the restrictions imposed on them were closely connected to regulating their sexuality and ensuring their virginity. Tina noted the irony that although Italian daughters are forbidden from going out and having boyfriends, as adults in their twenties, their parents wonder why they are not yet married:

With my parents, there was no dating while at school ... So, it's kind of weird that they don't want you to date when you're in high school or university but after they expect you to get married right away. They ask, what's wrong with you? Why don't you get married?

These women struggle with culturally specific restrictions on their sexuality as teenagers, but as adults they are strongly encouraged to marry, have children, and conform to traditional gender roles prescribed by the family (Dion and Dion 2004; Panagakos 2003). As women, they are expected to play an active role in passing on the traditions of their culture to their own children (Tsolidis 2001). This duty may partly explain why women's premarital sexuality is so closely guarded: in order to be good mothers, they must first fit within pre-existing gendered notions of good women.

Gender Roles

From a young age, these women were taught by their parents and grandparents that men and women perform different roles, and that within Greek and Italian culture femininity is defined in terms of service to the home and heterosexual family, as well as good housekeeping. Maria recounted one of the many arguments she had with her Greek parents:

My parents were very headstrong: girls do certain roles and boys do certain roles. I remember we would have a family dinner and everyone would come over and I would have to clean the dishes with my sister and my mom, while my brother was sitting down with the men talking and I absolutely hated it ... My parents are fairly modern parents, but they still stuck to the traditional gender roles.

Like many of the other women in my study, Maria identifies the family as a patriarchal system and the prime location of women's subordination. According to tradition, although women are now highly educated and working in a professional capacity in the public sphere, they are still responsible for the home. Anita expressed particularly strong disdain for the gendered family rules:

I hate that rule: girls have to be in the kitchen and clean and stay in the house. Once I shovelled the snow and my dad yelled at me for doing 'men's work.' My brother once got in trouble for doing the laundry and I got in trouble for him doing it! Just because he's a guy, my parents think he isn't supposed to do that kind of work.

Within the walls of the family home, these women learned from their mothers and grandmothers about their expected roles and responsibilities within the family. However, their narratives illustrate that they do not passively accept these roles and instead challenge the patriarchal dictates of their cultures. By questioning and criticizing traditional gender roles imposed upon them by their parents, these women unsettle prevailing interpretations of femininity and women's work.

In addition to restrictions over dating and the emphasis on women's labour in the home, the women identified a common familial expectation that they fulfil the roles of wife and mother. Although most of them were expected to go to university and establish themselves professionally, they were also expected to marry, have children, and devote themselves to their families. Tina explained how her focus on education and career made it difficult to relate to her Italian family members:

The philosophies of Italians are not in synch with mine. For example, starting a family when you're young and the idea that everything is really devoted to family and sacrificing everything for your family ... I have more of an interest in education and career and not so much in family ... It's not that I don't want a family; it's just my focus on family isn't as concentrated as my parents' and grandparents.'

As a professional in a medical field, Tina has devoted much of her time to her study and resents her parents' insistence that she should find a good husband and have children. Rose made a similar comment when she explained why she felt excluded from her extended family: 'I don't relate to their lifestyle ... Even at weddings people will ask me, 'Where's your date, where's your husband?' In that way, I don't fit the role of the Italian woman who focuses on getting married and having children and not necessarily career.' Twenty-four-year-old Francesca articulated similar sentiments: 'With my cousins there's a difference. I value education more and they don't; they're more into going out and getting married early... I can't relate to that.'

For these women, the emphasis on family is much more a hindrance than a celebration of cultural values. However, this intergenerational conflict should not be understood simply as immigrant parents clinging to an 'old world' mentality while their Canadian-born children struggle to live as Canadians (Tyyskä 2003). Women's narratives reveal a strong desire not to simply detach themselves from their cultural heritage but to strike a balance, as Tina explains: '[My mother] was trying to preserve a cultural thing that I didn't agree with ... I try to juggle between the two, to keep them happy but keep my own identity here.'

At the time of the interview, Maria was preparing for her upcoming wedding and made a point of telling me that her fiancé is a 'modern Greek,' as opposed to the men in Greece whom she identifies as closed minded and old fashioned. Indeed, a common theme in all of the interviews was the assumption that patriarchy and gender inequality are much more prevalent 'back home' and in Greek/Italian culture than they are in Canada. Helen explained that although she wants to continue to learn about Greek culture, 'the food, the dancing, the religion, the language,' she was happy to be a Canadian citizen: 'I enjoy that part of being Canadian because you can be treated as an equal. And you can have your own rights, your own jobs. I have my independence and I can speak my mind.' Helen's narrative illustrates both her romanticized nostalgia for a symbolic homeland and her view of Greece as a static and, at least in terms of traditional gender roles, a backward place.

In her study on Greek diasporic cultural reproduction in Canada and Australia, Georgina Tsolidis makes the point that 'there is no immutable cultural checklist against which their Greekness can be judged and compared ... Instead, what we have to contend with are real and imagined feelings of origin' (2001, 206). Certainly, culture is not a fixed entity but continually reimagined and redefined in relation to other cultural narratives and practices, but why do these second-generation women identify the 'homeland' in such a static way? Anastasia Panagakos's (2003) research on transnational Greek identity may offer some clues. She explored the experiences of second-generation women who identified more closely with Greek culture than with Canadian society and therefore decided to move to Greece in order to capture a sense of 'Greekness.' Interestingly, many were shocked to realize that the Greeks in Greece do not coincide with the images of 'Greekness' these women inherited from their parents and the larger Greek diasporic community. Some of these women felt alienated by the way homeland Greeks expressed and practised religion and traditional festivals, as they did not resemble the Greek customs that had been transplanted in Canada and seemed to resemble tradition only loosely.

Although the second-generation women in my study encountered restrictions as daughters of European immigrant parents, they nonetheless felt privileged to have the freedoms they did enjoy in Canada. Anita expressed frustration over the rigid gender roles that structured her relationship with her family members, but she also explained that she felt relatively lucky compared to some of her peers: 'Sometimes I think back and I'm proud to be Greek ... My Muslim friends ... can't do anything ... I know compared to them I get a lot of freedom.' Anita's comment speaks to my earlier discussion on the 'multiply hyphenated identity.' As a young woman Anita encounters gendered restrictions, yet at the same time as a white ethnic, her social and racial position allows her to distance herself from 'other' women, notably her 'Muslim friends.' Her comment might also be related to the tendency among ethnic women to defend their own communities. Indeed, studies on violence against women show that immigrant women are often reluctant to speak out against their abuse because they worry that the negative press might hurt their community (Jiwani 2001). In a similar way, Anita may want to protect her Greek immigrant community from being labelled 'backward' and excessively patriarchal.

Gender Roles and Food

Although all the women recalled vivid memories of conflicts with their parents over such issues as curfews, boyfriends, and household labour, another source of intergenerational conflict was related to the reproduction of cultural traditions. The women discussed the various ways in which they felt pressured by their families, particularly their mothers, to maintain cultural traditions and to pass on to their own future children the markers of Greek or Italian culture. Immigrant mothers expected their second-generation Canadian daughters not only to speak the family's native language and to teach their future children about various religious and cultural values but also to reproduce the gendered roles of cooking and baking passed on from mother to daughter. Three of the women in my study were engaged to be married at the time of the interviews, and they all noted that they felt pressured by their mothers and future mothers-in-law, as well as their fiancés, to learn to cook traditional Greek or Italian dishes.

One of the women I interviewed simply rejected the efforts of her mother to teach her how to cook traditional Italian dishes. In my interview with Tina, she recalled the embarrassment and cultural shame she experienced as a child in elementary school when her Italian lunches brought intrusive stares from her Canadian classmates:

> When I went to school, the kids whose parents and grandparents are from here ... I felt that I didn't have the same connection as they did ... and that I was different than them ... I remember in elementary school ... seeing the other kids with their peanut butter sandwiches and their drinking boxes and I had my Italian bread and my salami sandwiches.

Growing up in a rural area dominated by white middle-class families, Tina felt that her Italian heritage marked her as different, as an anomaly in the fabric of her mostly white, non-immigrant community. Although she recognizes that Italian food is now in vogue, she told me that she would not force it on her own future children.

Although Tina rejected Italian food as a marker of difference, some of the women in my study expressly embraced food as a celebration of culture. For Dina, food is both a symbolic and a tangible reminder of love and family togetherness: 'Food is, to my grandmother, just to feed us, it would just mean love, food would equal love ... I think it's just that in Italian culture, I always feel that even if you didn't have anything else, if you have food then you're ok.' Helen spoke to me about the importance of food and recounted some of the vivid memories she had as a child, watching her mother and grandmother lovingly preparing large traditional Greek feasts:

> It's nice to know how they used to make the food and how they used to live ... As a little girl I would always be around my mother in the kitchen

and watch her as she baked or made a meal. And it was nice to be a part of that, to be a part of how my mom grew up. One time it was nice because we were making a sweet and my grandmother was helping; it was nice to have three generations of women together making a sweet.

Throughout the interview Helen stressed the importance of keeping her Greek culture alive by reproducing the gendered roles of cooking and baking passed on to her by her mother and grandmother. Helen identifies herself as a deeply religious woman and spoke of how certain foods are closely tied to the Greek Orthodox faith and hold important religious and symbolic significance. In learning to cook traditional Greek meals, Helen is not only maintaining a cultural and religious tradition but is also recreating what it means for her to be a Greek Canadian woman within the context of family. In this way, Greek food for Helen is both a source of cultural pride and a part of her redefining of ethnic identity.

Reimagining Ethnic Identity through Family Stories

Just as the cultural markers of food and family were identified as significant elements of ethnic identity, the women in my study also discussed the ways in which they used family stories of 'back home' told to them by their parents and grandparents to help them construct their own place of belonging in Canada. These family memories provided helpful roadmaps for women in their own journeys toward a symbolic homeland. Dina recalled parts of her grandfather's war stories and explained at length the impact they have had in her own life:

> Those stories about World War II, it brings two worlds together. By understanding where he came from, I feel like I can relate to him ... I like to hear his stories, I feel they're important to me. I don't want to lose that heritage, that culture. I feel like if I can continue to hear stories about what it was like in Italy that I feel like [I am] a part of it.

These family stories are significant for second-generation Canadian women because they provide them with a way to connect to the place from which they came and with insights into the struggles and sacrifices of their parents, especially their mothers and grandmothers. Considering that second-generation women feel constrained by traditional gender designations that relegate them to subordinate roles within the family, it is interesting to note that many of the family stories they remembered about their mothers, grandmothers, and great-grand-mothers emphasize courage, perseverance, and, above all, strength. Dina's narrative underscores this point particularly well:

> The way my dad describes his grandmother and how strong she was and what a strong woman she was ... it gives me a sense of who I want to be when I hear those stories ... Those stories help me to understand where I came from and who the people were who basically made us who we are.

Sophia also recalled her mother's stories of her early years in Canada working minimum wage jobs as she tried to learn to speak English:

> My mom has been working every day of her life ... She's not working for herself, she's working for her kids. That's something you have to respect because a lot of mothers these days will leave their kids alone to go dancing. That's not a mother. A mother is someone who will provide for her children, who will work her ass off so they can have anything they want.

Using her mother's stories of hard work and sacrifice, Sophia reinterprets womanhood and motherhood in positive ways and contests the dominant assumptions of Greek women as simply passive wives and mothers in the home. Interestingly, she offers a celebratory vision of womanhood by replicating the gendered narratives imposed upon her by her parents and the larger Greek community. Her accusations against women who 'leave their kids alone to go dancing' partly reflects the same patriarchal attitudes that negatively affect the lives of second-generation women, the idea that in order to be a good Greek/Italian woman and mother, one must conform to gendered notions of woman's place in the home. Nonetheless, remembering and reinterpreting family stories of female strength enable second-generation Canadian women to engage in a process of creating a gendered intergenerational culture and, as Vappu Tyyskä has asserted, a 'transnational intergenerational feminine narrative.'[2]

Conclusion

In listening to second-generation Greek and Italian Canadian women's stories, I found that these women are continually negotiating the meaning of a Greek or Italian Canadian identity and that they base their shifting identities not merely on the culture passed onto them by their parents but on their own reinterpretation and reinvention of the diasporic culture. Family and food emerged throughout women's narratives, both as markers of a reimagined culture and as sources of inclusion and exclusion. The tensions in these women's narratives are rooted in conflicting generational interpretations of gender roles. As daughters of immigrant parents, they struggle against prescribed gender roles but also actively create new spaces of belonging that speak to their particular lived experiences. As women, they are controlled in ways that their brothers and other male relatives are not, yet as white ethnics they are themselves relatively privileged. Using their parents' stories of sacrifice and survival, women reimagine their own journeys in positive, self-affirming ways.

5 Time and Space in the Life of Pierre S. Weiss: Autoethnographic Engagements with Memory and Trans/Dis/Location

Fantasies: Numbers: Body Inscriptions: Dislocations

It is my sixth session with Dr. Gonçalvez-Smith and, like the past five times, I press '11' on the plastic display of floor numbers in the elevator and am reminded that exactly the same model of elevator led to my shrink's office when I still lived in Washington and that it was also situated on the eleventh floor. Like the past five times, I am also reminded with more than a hint of disgust that I used to believe in, or more precisely, be scared by, all this numerology crap. How could I have been so naïve, so egocentric, ethnocentric, and anthropocentric as to believe that the universe contained a perfectly orchestrated plan for me, a plan that could very occasionally be discerned through the recurrence of certain numerical sequences which indicated patterns to follow? How could I have believed for one second that the universe, 'thinking' in human and positivist terms, 'knew' that 'I' existed, and was trying to let me know numerically? What a sad, sad, joke. Like that time I almost didn't board that flight from Johannesburg to New York but spent two hours going around the departure hall stepping over cracks and shadows to counter the negative energies of the universe, which had assigned me to seat number 13 and would no doubt have caused the plane to crash if I had not done something about it. Isn't it beautiful that I, as the sole recipient of seat number 13, was the only person aboard the Boeing 747 who mattered to the universe and had been entrusted with a mission to save all 300 passengers? At least in those days, there was no doubt in my mind that I existed, that I mattered, and that it all mattered very much. Now I know. I know that the universe, whatever it is, does not think like me, does not compute itself in positivist term, and does not know that I exist.

I know that I do not exist coherently, that different apparatuses have assigned different sequences of numbers to me, and that those numbers grant me different ranges of possibilities (spatial and existential) in different layers of imagined space and time. I know that the sequences that define me are all incompatible but that they rely on one another to tell me that I am not complete. In the end, the numbers in the databases and those I once imagined were sent to me by the universe do not mean anything. They mean absolutely nothing, and neither do I.

My name is Pierre S. Weiss, and I am a collectively mediated fiction. I am a co-construction of fantasies inscribed onto me by the family institution, various institutions of culture, the delusional memories of others, state apparatuses, corporate apparatuses, biomedical apparatuses, ideological apparatuses, religious apparatuses, legal apparatuses, schooling apparatuses, media production and diffusion apparatuses, and aleatory encounters within a mostly close-ended range of constraints. I am a series of disjointed constructs engineered by mutually unintelligible and dispersed hegemonies. I grew up in diasporas. I am dispersed, decentralized, and multiple. I do not form a coherent whole. I am constructed by incompatible sequences of digits on different pieces of plastic, paper, and laminated forms. I am determined by the fantasies behind the numbers on my Canadian Social Insurance Card (SIN), my Quebec Medicare Card, my American Social Security Number (SSN) (not valid if laminated), my Irish Personal Public Service Number (PPSN), my British National Insurance Number (NIN), my French *numéro de sécurité sociale* (NSS), my Brazilian *Cadastro de Pessoas Físicas* (CPF), my student ID number, my French passport number, my credit card(s) number(s), my employee payroll number, my bank account(s) number(s), my bank branch number(s), my Swift code number(s), my personal identification number(s) (PIN), my phone number(s) and area code(s), my *Diagnostic and Statistical Manual of Mental Disorders* (DSM-IV) diagnostic code, my Quebec Permanent Code, my genetic code, my date of birth, my grade point average, my gross annual income, the income per capita and gross domestic product (GDP) of my countries, the numerical value of my height, weight, girth, and intelligence, the comparative numerical value of the currencies with which I operate my daily transactions and those that have an impact on my daily transactions, the paper numbers I pick from dispensers when I wait for service in square, concrete buildings. 'Can I help the next number in line, please?' 'What is your number please?' 'May I ask for the last four digits of your credit card, please?' 'In order to identify you, I will need the three numbers in your postal code and your personal security code.' I am asked to describe myself by ticking a square in a close-ended range of boxes that will identify my physical health, mental health, criminal record, ethnic group, income range, education level, consuming habits, sexual preference and habits, the degree to which I agree with a statement, or the degree to which a statement describes me.

I am the rhizome that connects these numbers, the body on which they are inscribed, and the projection of all the fantasies they document. I am a diseased rhizome with severed connections, ruptured links, pathways that lead to more pathways that lead to walls, and no continuities between my many ends. I am disembodied, disembowelled, dislocated, dislodged, dispersed, disjointed, disjunctured.

I fill out many forms: paper, electronic, online, and editable Adobe PDFs. I am those forms. Credit card application forms, provincial and federal immigration forms, I-95 visa waiver forms, tax forms, grant application forms, fellowship application forms, graduate student research objectives forms, and medical insurance forms; FBI, Scotland Yard, Polícia Federal, Gendarmerie nationale, and An Garda Síochána police criminal record check forms; passport application forms; videostore, health club and American Anthropological Association membership forms; magazine subscription forms, daycare (government and private) application forms, discount coupons application forms, document translation and certification forms.

I receive bills in the mail. I receive phone bills, gas bills, electricity bills, water bills, parking tickets, speeding tickets, property tax, credit card bills, overdue rent fees, bounced cheque fees, account maintenance fees, overdraft fees, shipping and handling fees, processing fees, import tax fees, ATM service charge fees, books and video late fees, immigration overstay fees, lost or stolen or both document replacement fees.

Beginnings

I begin. A house on the edge of a small village in the Algerian province of Kabylie. A steep path (*un raidillon*, as my parents call it) through the dunes separates our house from the beach.

We came here from northern France before my memories began. Mother teaches French and biology at a public high school in a mountain town, farther south. At first, father stays at home with me, but he soon finds a position as a math teacher in a local school.

Sometimes, mother brings me with her, up the dry and windy mountain roads. There are days when the shepherds lead their sheep down the mountain. Then, mother stops the car and we let the long river of sheep submerge us.

At night, jackals roam around our house in search of food. They grunt and howl. I am terrified of them. One November there is an earthquake, and then, unexpectedly, snow. A bush fire, on both sides of the road. A trip to the desert, to Tamanrasset. I hide in the shade, in the van. I am given water. I have a fever. Outside, everything is white: the sand and the heat, the sky.

The house is white, too. Inside and outside. Outside, there is another white house. Neighbours. The mother wears dark clothes, loose. She is always moving, talking. A dark mass in motion with an indefinite shape. She calls out to her children. Her words are hurried, loud.

The children move faster. Sometimes, I play with them.

At night, my mother finds me in my room, in bed, muttering sequences of words to myself. In the Kabyle dialect.

On occasion, a wild boar ventures into the fields from the mountains, ravaging the crops. At night, the farmers get together and hunt the beast down. Later, in the morning, we find the swine, massive and inert, lying before our front door. A present. A gift from the village people, whose religion forbids the consumption of such meat, of the pig's untamed cousin.

My father manoeuvres the beast away from the door and ties a rope to its legs. He throws the rope over a beam and hauls, until the dead mass is left dangling in the air. With a diving knife, he sections the boar's stomach and releases a thick, bubbling stream of entrails and dark blood. Then, the bloodless, gutless animal is skinned, and its head and feet are severed and discarded. The red meat is quartered, salted, and left to dry. At night, sitting in my highchair, I am fed a soft, greyish slice of fibrous meat.

An uncle from France, one of my father's younger brothers, is called upon to look after me. He arrives. There are no more trips to the mountains. I spend time with my uncle and the other young expatriates he befriends. One of them is another French teacher, with long hair and a Viking moustache.

I am taken to a beach where a dead dolphin dries in the sun.

Often, I ask to be taken there, to see the dead dolphin.

Dead Dolphin Beach becomes my first solid point of reference beyond my immediate surroundings. My awareness of that beach is purely mental and spatial

A trip to France. Snow. My father and I are driving to the hospital, to see my mother and my new sister. A sister. Laure.

In the hospital, Laure is smaller and uglier than I expected. Her eyes are closed and puffy. She does not look like a girl.

Another plane journey, with a stopover in Rome. We are back at home, in the white house, above the *raidillon*. I want to play with my sister, but I am told she is too little; she cannot play yet. When will she know how to play? I ask. When she is big. *Quand elle sera grande*, I am told. But that does not answer my question. All this answer produces is more questions. When does one become big? How does one become big? How does one know when one is big?

Relentlessly, I ask, Is Laure big today? Is Big-Laure here yet?

Mother responds. It takes time, bigness happens gradually, But I cannot understand.

One morning, my sister is dressed with a green skirt and black stockings; her skirt a funny bulge above her diaper. She looks like a girl. I am overjoyed. Big-Laure is here, I cry out.

The reply comes. Not yet. She is getting bigger, but she is not big enough to play, not old enough.

I am puzzled. What is big enough? What is old enough? By comparison, I am big, old enough to play. But what is bigger? What will I be like, look like, when I am bigger? What will Laure look like?

My father makes a drawing. With a pencil, he begins with my sister. He draws a woman, naked, with protuberant breasts and a triangle of hair where the inside of her legs meet. On the right, he draws a man, taller, angular. Above his penis, there is another triangle of hair. This is what you and Laure will look like when you are big, he explains. *Quand vous serez grands*.

The threshold of my concept of bigness has been pushed farther, but I still do not grasp the idea, the process. One does not wake up big; bigness happens slowly. But how can one get so tall, so hairy, without noticing? How will someone who is immobile in one's crib, unable to speak or sit up, learn to laugh, run, and play without there being visible change one morning? And what happens after the drawing? Does one still get bigger?

Our belongings are packed and shipped, the house is closed, and the sea is crossed. Of the crossing, there are no recollections.

All there is left is a colour picture of my father with his white cotton shirt tied around his shoulders, sitting on the metal floor of the boat. *El Djezair*. Below the picture, the handwritten caption says, *Retour d'Algérie*. *Retour* – return – signifies that we are coming *back* to something. But back where? I have just left my home. What are we coming *back* to?

Another house by the coast. Another steep path to a beach. The path is steeper and overgrown with ferns and thorns. The beach is littered with pebbles. This is Brittany, my father's house.

I live farther south, also on the coast, with my mother, sister, and the French expatriate teacher with the Viking moustache, who is now a civil engineer. I am visiting my father. His house is big, old, dark, and damp. There is no real village, just a small number of scattered houses and fields, fallow land, grass, grey granite rocks with yellow lichen, cliffs, and the sea. This part of Brittany is the westernmost department of France, it is called *finistère*. *Fini* – ended, end – and *terre* – soil, land, earth. *La fin de la terre*, the end of the land, the end of the earth.

From this indefinite cluster of adobes before the end of the land, my father's house seems detached, farther. A muddy path with a streak of grass in the middle leads to the house. Along the path: an untidy hedge of white and blue hydrangeas. In the summer heat and humidity, the hydrangeas emit an overpowering odour of urine. The house is white; it has a black slate roof and yellow shutters, like the lichen. The paint on the shutters is cracked and flaking.

We park behind the house. The front door is at the back. One has to walk around the house, past the wooden cabin that houses the toilet and the metal jug for flushing, and along the edge of a corn field.

Already, images of Algeria are beginning to fade. My points of reference are shifting. Dead Dolphin Beach is still here, but it is no longer central. Or rather, it retains its centrality in my cosmology, but it is I who drifted away.

In my mental geography, there are now two solid points of reference.

There is my mother's house, where I seem to reside permanently. A grey house, with orange tiles on the roof. The sea is still present, but it is out of sight, out of immediate reach.

And there is my father's, at the end of the land.

In between, an indefinite lapse. Yellow and red car lights, a dizzying slideshow of white bands and stretches on the black asphalt, and a wet and grimy frame with wavy contours on the parts of the windshield where the wipers do not reach. A nauseating smell of gasoline.

There is a third landmark, a third substantial area in my geography. It is somewhere in the middle, between the two houses, between two lapses. There is an immense suspended bridge, with metallic cables. After the bridge – before the bridge the other way – we stop at a crêperie. When I am transferred from one world to the other, stopping at the crêperie becomes customary, becomes a ritual. Images, noises, and tastes from around the metallic bridge become engraved in my memory.

There are more beaches.

By my mother's, the sky is high and blue, and the coast extends as far as one can see. Miles of sand. High dunes, wind swept. And pines. Long and deep forests of tall stone pines, some of them inclined, deformed by the wind. We gather pine cones, many as big as my head. At home, in the fireplace, they make crackling sounds and release a sweet, comforting smell.

By my father's, the sky is lower, greyer, foggier. The shore is rockier and the sea colder. When the tide is low, the sea retracts beyond my view, leaving an endless stretch of grey sand, with small, scattered pockets of salt water, speckled with bright green algae. With a pair of Wellingtons and a bucket in hand, I follow my father into the grey area. In the small ponds, under black rocks, inside the sand, we find yellow winkles and limpets, purple razor clams, green and dark-red bits of polished.glass, orange crabs, maroon urchins, silver clams, blue mussels. All vibrant with colour. When we get home, the treasures dry and the colours grow fainter.

Staring at the World Map

I grasp the idea rapidly. A little above the middle of the map, at the tip of the green stem that ends with finger-like protuberances, is my father's house, the fog, and the yellow lichen on the rocks. Below, past the point where the stem merges with the mainland, just above the notch where the Gironde River merges with the sea, is my mother's house, in which I stand, looking at the map. Lower, across the oval-shaped Mediterranean sea, is Algeria, the village in Kabylie, and the Dead

Dolphin Beach. An unmarked dot in a thin strip of light green at the very top of Africa. Beneath, the green turns into a reddish brown that becomes yellow, then burgundy, and light green again, and dark green. The Atlas Mountains, the Sahara, the Sahel, the savannahs, and the jungles of the Congo.

On both upper corners of the map, the antennae of Siberia and the Aleutian Islands are duplicated. I enquire. I know the earth is round and the repetition is a mere reminder of that fact. On the real earth, however, there cannot be two Siberias and two Aleutian archipelagos. On the map, therefore, one of the two representations must be false, and the other must depict the real places. Which side of the map is the true one?

Mother replies that both sides are true. There are two depictions that represent the same place; the purpose of the repetition is to highlight the proximity, the connection between the two ends of the map. But I still cannot comprehend. If there is one place in reality, and if that place is shown twice on a map, one of the depictions is necessarily superfluous, fabricated, untrue. But which one? This question causes me great anxiety.

Years pass, we shift.

We now live in southern France, a small village in the Languedoc.

There are concentric circles everywhere. Around me, people's identities are organized in concentric circles of geographic allegiance. To the people of southern France, geography is identity. They belong to their village, to their department, to their region, and then to France, and perhaps to Europe. There are newspapers and rugby teams for every circle of their concentric identity. Language, dialects, accents betray geography. There is little diversity and little racism. There is regionalism, parochialism, villagism.

The circles of my identity are fragmented, disjointed, blur. In the village, I am an outsider. I am a Parisien, but I have never lived in Paris.

I am nine years old.

In the village, there are other outcasts: sons and daughters of Moroccan immigrants, who carry with them the spatial disjuncture of their parents' exodus. They, too, seem condemned to define themselves around a skewed focal point they have never known or cannot remember. They are sentenced to walk around surrounded by bubble of exclusion that comes with the price of dislodged allegiances. They are sentenced to live 'à l'interieur de l'exterieur, et inversement' (Foucault 1972), Inside the outside, and vice versa.

How can that be? How can we all be sharing this space and reality, and yet not be?[1]

My own private Algeria, around which I had defined myself, has almost ceased to exist. I know I can no longer claim allegiance to a land that is still bleeding from the pillage of its resources and the rape of its people inflicted by my ancestors. I know I can no longer define myself around a land whose tongue, sounds, and smells I have forgotten.

As for memories, I no longer know how to trust them. My own private Algeria exists as a fuzzy image in the back of my mind when I ask my parents about it and listen to their stories or when I look at the photo albums.

The photo albums are organized sequentially; they document a chronology of frozen moments in my parents' and my life, and are silent about so much more.

Flipping through the thick folders at my mother's, I can retrace the outline of our story. The beach, the house, and the man with the Viking moustache. He appears as a peripheral character at first, on the far side of an image, displaced from the central focal point, working his way toward the centre as the pages unfold.

There are two pictures, in separate albums, that defy the laws of my cosmology and that I can view only in absolute privacy. The second one, chronologically, is set in an Algerian landscape, with acacia leaves in the background. My father and the man with the Viking moustache, playing chess. How symbolic is this game? How much of a real battleground is captured here?

The first one precedes my birth. In the background, brown rocks on a Scottish beach. A close-up of mother and father, kissing. Their touching lips slightly open. My mother's eyes are closed, and father looks skyward. This picture joins two realities that cannot exist simultaneously, two universes that can only collide. Two separate and incompatible cosmologies of which I, incomprehensibly, am the product, the outgrowth.

The distress.

At my father's, there are no photo albums. When I enquire, father replies that he does not trust photography. He tells me about Thamus, the

Egyptian king who rejected the invention of writing presented to him by Theuth, the inventor god, because he said writing would impair humanity's ability to remember, an idea he gleaned from Plato's *Phaedrus*. One should not rely on cold, lifeless external signs to remember; one can only lose memory if one relies on such signs, and photographs are such signs. One should cultivate one's inner memory. Thus, when there are no lifeless signs to suggest a story, I rely on my father's memory. But memories conflict. Mother's memories tell different stories. 'No, no, it was I who gutted and skinned the boars. Your father didn't have the stomach for this.'

Which story is true then? Whose story is true? Whose memory is true? If all I have left is lifeless signs and conflicting memories, how can I know where and when my own story begins?

Escaping the Grid: Movement, Indeterminacy

After a restrained adieu to Ana, overcome by a profound sense of warmth and sadness as I catch a glance of sleeping Carl Phillip Emmanuel's back and the sweet scent of urine from his gorged diaper, I get off at Bonaventure Station and board the 9:50 train to New York.

Watching the Montreal cityscape and its little Mohawk of high-rise from behind the grimy train window, I cast aside the feeling of nausea that is in the back of my throat and scrutinize city and the cold white sky with an attempted temporal distance. As in the attempted epistemological distance with which I approach letters, signs, sounds, and objects, as though they were utterly alien to my cosmology, in a effort to strip them of their culturally constructed meaning and be faced with the unknowable nature of the thing itself, I am contemplating this picture from an imagined return to the past, recovering the gaze I first lay on this city when it appeared in my northbound horizon some eight years ago. I find, almost eerily, that I am quite adept at alternating my gaze and feelings between a routine outlook on a marked space that has now been inscribed with my own sense of place and a new area that has yet to be mapped out and displays strangely exotic lights and forms. In fact, it is as though I were in possession of a lens on which I can manually set the focus to familiar look/new look.

The inner and outer Amtrak trainscapes are by now permanently set to familiar mode, and I am too tired to try a fresh outlook. Even the impossibly absurd act of border crossing and its impossibly absurd rituals, through which hegemonically engineered arbitrary hierarchies of relationships between place, space, identity, identification, value, and access (somehow, incomprehensibly, taken to be true and normal) are enacted in a most violent manner, fail to evoke in me more than the customary sneer, and it is only by force of habit that I ask myself, 'How can they go along with this? How can they all play in this farce and accept its violent, violent rules?'

Later, I am almost moved by the beauty a few scrawny pines, bare birch, black waters. But not quite, not fully.

By force of habit, I proceed to reflect on the collective spatial practice of train travelling, but fail to find any real collectivity to it. Unlike previous journeys, when I had sat in dining cars, marvelling at the snapshot episodes of camaraderie that would spring up between various passing protagonists, my sulky mood forces me to notice the scattered schizophrenias of awkward travellers engaging with various electronic devices and decentrally connected to distant schizophrenias via cell phone networks, trying at all costs to fill the void of their thoughts and feelings and the fear of impromptu conversation or proxemic invasion. Trains might be designed as moving spaces where human trajectories momentarily converge, but I fail to notice any real convergence today. During extended trips – that is, practices of spatial mobility – I usually despair/marvel at the strangely dialectical relationship between institutionalized distrust and xenophobia (literally, the fear of the stranger, the other) present in all of us and what often seems like the proof that we are, in the end, all part of the same species and have an inherent, some would say biological, interest in getting along. Sure, the xenophobia is omnipresent and has in fact permeated the deepest layers of social reality, to the point at which we are not even bothered by the constant reminders that the other is not to be trusted. We are not moved to tears of despair when we are bombarded by visual and auditory reminders not to leave our luggage unattended, when we are invited to report anything suspicious at a given number, or when we see the many padlocks on suitcase zippers. We do not weep in desolation when we meet the fleeting gaze of passengers, or when we ourselves flee other people's eyes and devise complex stratagems to prevent newly embarked travellers from taking the empty seat next to ours. What usually fascinates me, then, is that in spite of this, there almost systematically develop silent rules of trust between proximal passengers, so that, after only a few wordless hours spent in another's immediacy, they feel confident to take a stroll and leave their belonging under one another's protection. Despite so many cultural-institutional legitimations of distrust, paranoia, and fragmentation, then, is it possible to venture that there subsists an urge to mark travelling space with a temporary sense of place and community?

Later. Somewhere above the ice shelf on top of Siberia. The white iced earth is quite an impressive sight. Even more impressive are the long fissures, the sharp, zigzagging dark holes that fracture the shelf. According to the flight locator, we are right at the juncture of Siberia with the ice shelf, though where a hypothetical coastline would lie under all that white, I do not know. It is a little eerie to think that I will be in the so-called 'tropics' in a matter of hours, and that I have had to fly over polar regions to reach the tropics from a 'temperate' point of departure: temperate, tempered, well tempered / tropical, feverish. What awful, awful binary constructions. It is eerie and disturbing because, now more than ever, I am faced with the limitations and utter falsehood of the two-dimensionality inscribed onto bodies and space by projection maps and the colonizing cosmologies of Empire. What is more, I am faced with the absurdity of two-dimensional directionality and the arbitrariness of cardinal points.

I take off from New York, on what appears to be a south-westward journey to reach the southeast: a point that lies almost equidistantly east and west of New York, albeit several degrees to the south. Yet we are flying north; we are flying straight up until north becomes south, and west becomes east, and today tomorrow. So after passing the pole, which as far as I am concerned may or may not be real – meaning, in realist tradition, that the thing itself, the pole itself, and its properties exist in and of themselves outside a fuzzy consensus of collective imagination – our straight trajectory can no longer be considered northbound. A lapse later, after crossing the international date line – which I *know* is not real – all notions of temporality are shattered as we enter the future. So flying across time zones and space zones is completely absurd, at least if one is to interpret this spatial and temporal practice from within the laws and language of the inhuman Grid inscribed with fantasies, numbers, straight lines, and more fantasies.

In fact – leaving other trivial mechanical matters aside – I can safely assert that I *do not understand* the spatial and temporal implications of flying through multiple 'time zones' because this very act exists outside the possibility of knowing delineated by the Grid, and because I am a prisoner of the Grid. I am an unruly prisoner, often condemned to corporal punishment and solitary confinement, and prone to the occasional illusion that I have found cracks that reveal spaces for subversion. But in the end, I remain a prisoner. Yet today, in this unknowable moment of flying, of flight, and fleeing, I feel good, precisely because this is a rare moment when I seem to have escaped the Grid, and I want the illusion to last.

After two sunsets in one seventeen-hour lapse of flight, at a local time designated as 10:00 p.m., I land in Hong Kong, of which, from the descending aircraft, I can distinguish only a zigzagging ridge of vertical cubic light on Lantau Island. Descent into my first journey to the 'East.' As I have done for most of my life, I enter the immigration line for Non-National/Alien/Foreign Passports, and scan the Permanent Resident line for evidence of diasporic or ex-pat people, but fail to see any. I am momentarily amazed by a sparsely frequented separate line labelled 'Frequent Visitors' and wonder with a tinge of jealousy about the type of ID card one must possess to qualify. Another absurd moment passes, and I am officially stamped and led into quasi-Chinese space (One Country Two Systems) by a silent immigration officer. After collecting my rolling suitcase, I hit an inward identity switch and immediately enter a new social-acting mode, playing the role of a confident academic traveller familiar with his surroundings. The role requires little effort because the arrival hall through which I pretend to know my way is littered with the usual sanitized corporate logos (Tie Rack, McDonald's, Starbucks, KFC, The Body Shop) and is constructed according to the aggressively legible and universalized principles of the Grid. After realizing that I have lost my Hong Kong guidebook but that I have actually memorized the Grid airport map and instructions to get into town, I purchase a Mass Transit Railway (MTR) ticket to Kowloon station with my World Bank Fund Staff Federal Credit Union Visa card, and pull out HK$2,000 from an HSBC, (formerly Hong Kong and Shanghai Banking Corporation) automated teller machine (ATM), which spits out my cash with a receipt that includes my account balance, bumped up to six digits in the local currency.

On the MTR, I watch through several layers of glass and yellow light the surreal sight of São Paulo–style vertical, closed condominiums with little figures playing tennis next to empty swimming pools. After patches of tunnel dark and city lights, I get off at Kowloon station, and meander through deserted underground parking lots until I reach a congregation of collective transport minivans that I would call *kombis* in southern Africa, and *combis* in hispanophone South America. I almost accidentally find my way to a combi going in the direction of the Jordan

MTR station, which I have decided will be my temporary destination because I remember the guidebook's description of guesthouses along Nathan Road. The 'East' hits me in the face at full speed when the combi emerges from the subterranean lot, and I keep my composed look while my throat tightens as I suck in the clutter of neon lights on dirty white buildings and the multidirectional bustle on and through the intricate network of sidewalks and overpasses.

I get off in front of the MTR sign for Jordan station and, catching sight of the Nathan Road intersection, drag my rolling suitcase and laptop briefcase in a well-performed confident manner in one of two possible directions that I imagine to be north and toward Mong Kok, on the opposite side of the harbour. Mong Kok, as I remember, is described in my lost guidebook as the most densely populated urbanscape in the world but, more interestingly, as home to a Triad-infested area west of Nathan Road where the lone traveller is advised not to wander at night: precisely the kind of area sought by me, Pierre S. Weiss, in his desperate, temporary attempt to elude the Grid of Empire and find those spaces of indeterminacy where he can become the *flâneur* anew: Baudelaire and Walter Benjamin's Idle Man About Town (Benjamin 1986), indulging in non-directional, experience-driven ambulating, perambulating, and, above all, the precious act of getting lost, of escaping control, one's control, anybody else's control.

As I brush past and collide with new fleeting gazes and shoulders along Nathan Road, following my imaginary north, I reminisce internally with a smile over my adolescent and deliberately disorganized – alas, an oxymoron – bouts of *flâneur*-ing in the French countryside with David V and Greg C, impulsively getting on and off random trains, sleeping in fields and forests, and wandering off mountain paths in what seemed like the wildest, remotest, and surest way to get lost and enjoy an illusion of freedom from the highly regulated spatial regimes of parent-controlled dwelling and state-controlled schooling.

I hook a left, any left, into one those over-cinematized Hong Kong dim alleys and get a pleasant flashback of early encounters with urban indeterminacy, in that prison southern French village, where, as a lone walking child of nine, I would seek to escape the growing solidity of my mental geography by meandering through geometrically incoherent and olfactorily charged narrow lanes, alleys, dead ends, and abandoned houses and yards.

I settle into a pleasantly grimy, starless hotel in the vicinity of Yau Ma Tei MTR, and jump right back Out after a cold shower and a change of socks. Memories of not-so-distant claustrophobias come back to haunt me as I fidget in the urine-scented hallway while the elevator cables squeak, and I suddenly plunge down the stairway with different kinds of mouldy carpet adorning its different floors, rationalizing that the limited mobility of the shoebox lift would have been decidedly anti-*flâneur* in its spatial logic. I am, of course, on the verge of panic at the thought of suffocating in the narrow-narrow box in the event of a blackout.

It is 12:30 in the morning, and I have no idea what that means. I walk back toward Jordan MTR in the direction of the harbour, making detours in littered and steamy side streets frequented by an odd combination of strolling families, sitting shopkeepers, stumbling drunks, and stoned-looking whores who divert their eyes when I walk by. This is the kind of street where I expect to encounter rowdy American seamen, but it is not until I get to Tsim Sha Tsui half an hour later, that I see the first gringos, locally known as *gwai los*. As we near the harbour, the *gwai los*, diasporic subcontinent workers, and djellabah-clad Nigerians outnumber the Chinese; the dirty-white concrete buildings have turned into glass and steel, the jumbles of wire and Cantonese neon signs have disappeared, and if the left-side driving and double-decker buses reveal that this urbanscape cannot be American, there are no solid clues that could differentiate it from any other Commonwealth megacity, like London or Melbourne. Some would find this depressing but not I, not today, because I like being in global, or rather glocal, diasporic spaces. The architecture of this end-of-the-city zone, however, fails to impress me, and the modernist urban design, with its chequered, geometrical logic, constantly ushers the wannabe *flâneur* back to the coherent and familiar, threatening to depress me until I cast a glance back toward the delightfully PoMo sight of the crumbling Chungking Mansions at 36–44 Nathan Road.

I am even more delighted when I fail to see any backpackers around that *futur anterieur* vision of a tower block, and the congregation of Indian, Nepalese, Sri Lankan, and African subaltern ex-pats loitering on the sidewalk fills me with hope and excitement. The absence of backpackers makes me momentarily wish that I had stayed at one of Chunking Mansion's many guesthouses among the vertical labyrinth of Indian shops, working-class restaurants and residences, and god knows what else in a surreal building that is said to house 4,000 people. I enter it from the flank and frown at the unpleasantly sweaty odour of a white-haired, fat *gwai lo* in a Hawaiian shirt who is discussing the possibility of going up to his room with a chubby, sari-clad sex worker.

I am a little self-conscious about making awkward conversation after having been silent for more than twenty hours and brush off the Indian guys who try to sell me counterfeit Rolexes and Gucci handbags, wondering if those who were born here can speak Cantonese, have Chinese passports, and perhaps a local sense of place.

Along the harbour walkway, I suck in the tackiness of the Hong Kong Central skylights across the bay, and try to determine whether I am impressed by this sight. I decide that I am after noticing that I am breathing very deeply, and I start walking again to cast off the dizziness, enticed by the hyperreal, sitcomesque vision of Cantonese yuppie couples snuggling on concrete benches with tall glasses of red wine.

PART TWO

Redefining Nation

6 Contemporary Croatian Film and the New Social Economy

JELENA ŠESNIĆ

Iva: 'How do I know what I will shoot?'
(What Iva Recorded on October 21, 2003)

Recently, Croatian critics and cultural pundits have applauded the return of domestic audiences to Croatian film. Whether this trend is because of improved artistic standards, a revival of cinema coming out of the postwar stupor and financial restrictions, or a changed horizon of expectations is still being debated (Polimac 2006; Škrabalo 2008; Turković and Majcen 2001). Be that as it may, this chapter addresses the capacity of the new Croatian cinema – here represented by three recent and noteworthy feature films: *Oprosti za kung fu* (*Sorry about Kung Fu*, 2004), *Što je Iva snimila 21. listopada 2003* (*What Iva Recorded on October 21, 2003*, 2005), and *Što je muškarac bez brkova* (*What Is a Man without a Moustache?* 2005) – to engage new types of social arrangements emerging in post-communist, transitional society. It does so most often in a mix of mild irony, comedy, or melodrama. (In terms of genre, *Sorry about Kung Fu* is a comedy/drama, *What Is a Man* is a comedy/melodrama, and *What Iva Recorded* is a drama.)

Two of the fault lines for my observations are sex/gender roles, here refracted through the notion of the (representative) family and broadly defined family values, and regional setting as a strong indicator of changing social values. In very broad terms, setting often signals the emergence of new cultural economies in which, somewhat unexpectedly, there is an interaction between traditional and intransigently local cultural practices (for which read also nationalist, pure, and unadulterated) and the global, transnational forces intruding upon them. It is at this intersection that we observe the emergence of a transnational sensibility – which we can identify as an alternative code, inflecting both social and cultural practices and engaging women as its principal agents or carriers. I find it intriguing that these films insist that women are simultaneously more vulnerable because they are more exposed to overwhelming transformations, and better attuned to deal with, respond to, and disseminate the effects of those transformations. Such a disposition seems to stem from their relative invisibility (as in *What Iva Recorded*) and their socio-economic marginality (as in *Sorry about Kung Fu* and *What Is a Man*).

To understand the cultural economy within which these films circulate, a few observations are in order. A recent survey of the principal markers of post-communist Croatian identity puts Catholicism, or more broadly speaking religion, and vaguely defined 'family values' indisputably close to the top of national priorities (Aračić et al. 2005). In post-communist society, religious sentiments can be publicly acknowledged for what they in considerable part were during the communist regime, a vehicle for sustaining national(ist) feeling and salvaging national consciousness. There is no denying that the communist project of fashioning a new pan-ethnic, Yugoslav identity failed to perceive the importance and entrenched nature of religion as a component of various ethnic or national identities. This omission, among a few others, seriously undermined the project's viability, as proven by its lamentable outcome. To go back to contemporary Croats, however, when one looks more closely at this resurgence of, or more precisely, this acknowledgment of an abiding concern for, religious affiliations, it can be seen to derive from a close interrelation, indeed a causal link, between a specific, home-grown variant of Catholicism and national identity. I have in mind the traditional, popular, folk aspect of religion that in some cases (which I will discuss presently) does not quite see eye to eye with Catholic orthodoxy or with the official teachings of the Church. For instance, with respect to ethical values, sociologists note a discrepancy between the teachings of the Church and more pragmatic aspects of Catholicism lived daily (Aračić et al. 2005, 55–6), and put it down to differences in 'personal,' 'social,' and 'civic' morality' (236).

Thus, religious affiliation serves as a stand-in and almost doubles for a more overarching form of affiliation, namely, national. The bonds created and sustained by reliance on, and activation of, the ideological power of Catholicism are more or less co-extensive with the boundaries demarcating ethnic/national community. In other words, religion reinforces a specific concept of Croatian national identity, which is in no small degree based on the idea of nuclear family, implicitly supportive of traditional gender roles and sustaining a generally recognizable division into the public sphere for men and largely private sphere for women. This presumed division looms especially large in some geographical areas of Croatia, specifically in the hinterland, rural zones that form a distinctive setting for two of the films discussed here (*What Is a Man* and *Sorry about Kung Fu*). The third film, *What Iva Recorded*, takes place in an urban milieu but implicitly engages this cultural reading of regions. Sociological research indisputably reveals Croatian society as largely traditional with respect to women's roles. These embedded values are rooted in the regional economy and in *What Iva Recorded* are hinted at through the likely rural background of Iva's father and some elements of popular folk culture.

Such predictable gendering of national identity is more often than not buttressed by religion in the course of identity-building processes (Čičak-Chand and Kumpes 1998, 113–67). The films question the sociological truism that situates the making of the national subject in the alliance of patriarchy and religion, which the female characters disrupt. Religion, while providing 'a symbolic identity frame for the majority of the population,' is not the most important factor in understanding new female roles. Among other significant factors are social forces such as the 'economic system and the media, which create woman's new image' (Aračić et al. 2005, 79, 230). The films use and enhance the field of the popular visual culture and media-generated models in order to display the new sex/gender arrangements in modern-day Croatia.[1]

Family and Nation: A Tenuous Partnership

Ties of fictive or imagined kinship bind potential members of a national community. A nation is very often figured on the model of the family (Freedman 2002; Hill Collins 1998; Yuval-Davis 2003). Because the discourse of the Catholic Church has been heavily invested in promoting the heterosexual nuclear family unit, we should observe a certain convergence between the family model as interpreted by nationalist proponents and as promoted by the Church. Inherently, both nationalists and Church proponents centre on the family as an appropriate analogy for an apposite social order. The family's capacity to mediate between the public and the private, religious and secular, nationalist and catholic (here in the sense of all-inclusive) prerogatives makes it understandably a focus of interest for these positions. As cogently expressed by Patricia Hill Collins, 'The power of [the] traditional family ideal lies in its dual function as an ideological construction and as a fundamental principle of social organization' (63). She further looks at family as a locus where race, gender, and 'constructions of ... national identity intersect' (63). As such, the family performs an important ideological task, that of naturalizing various constructed arrangements: 'Individuals typically learn their assigned place in hierarchies of race, gender, ethnicity, sexuality, nation, and social class in their families of origin. At the same time, they learn to view such hierarchies as natural social arrangements, as compared to socially constructed ones' (64).

Without intending to overemphasize the role of the traditional family in the changing circumstances to which even entrenched family structures must defer, and narrowing the focus of my investigation to a few of Hill Collins's hierarchies, most notably, those of gender, ethnicity, and nation, I concur with her interpretation of the family's supreme ideological performance as the agent of the individual's earliest socialization.

Given this latent potential of the family to function as a paradigmatic form of cognitive and ideological mapping of our social reality, it is perhaps not surprising – but still well worth considering – that several younger and middle-generation Croatian filmmakers focus on family in a more or less traditional context, but then strive to show how variegated forces (from war to emigration and from post-communist to proto-capitalist economy) transform these traditional, commonsense, and received notions of what a representative Croatian family in postwar transitional society should look like and how it responds to and in turn initiates significant transformations.

Both the Church and the state have claimed a woman's body as a procreative source to produce future nationals/citizens. The urgency and frequency with which appeals are made to women to fulfil that role, however, testifies to a possible lack of responsiveness on their part to assume the reproductive role. Even though it is hard to generalize, the decline in birth rates in Croatia suggests at the least that fewer women decide on having children and that, as frequently as in the rest of Europe, they postpone that decision (Aračić et al. 2005). So the insistent calls on women to have children (even if, or especially when, that expectation is at odds with hard reality) produce a complex picture of a family structure in a state of constant redefinition, in which those principally affected by and mediating the transformation are women, although they are neither the agents nor the initiators of it.

My preliminary thesis is that gender has the potential to be disrupt-ive and transformative with respect to traditional family structure, but that this potential has to contend with other forces that significantly qualify its impact (e.g., religion, traditionalism, region, cultural expect-ations, popular consumer culture, and so forth). Therefore, although the three films in question come to espouse a new family structure, it is far from certain how this arrangement is to come about and, signifi-cantly for my focus here, whether it really signals a newfound sense of agency on the part of women or is simply a by-product, an unexpected, unintended side effect of larger shifts and transformations in society.

My reading of the way new Croatian cinema conceptualizes one of the structures salient for the new national, post-communist, postwar identity thus complicates the by-now well-articulated critique in Croatian film of patriarchy as one of the principal obstacles to not only female but also male self-realization (Kovačević 2001).[2] The patriarchy is clear-ly and forcefully cited and mocked as an underlying reason for the stunted and stifled emotional lives of characters, both women and men, even if the next step in the narrative logic of the films fails to produce a viable or straightforward response. (For instance, one could argue that despite all the rebelliousness of the young woman's character in *Sorry about Kung Fu*, played by Daria Lorenci, the final bond, which she does not want to sever or invalidate, is affirmed as a strong emotional attach-ment to her father. That bond presumably overpowers even the one she has with the father of her child, who is absent.) Patriarchy is no longer uniformly positioned or universally operational as a way to foil women's agency. Also, men increasingly come to understand the ways these patriarchal strictures bind them too, even if no significant action materializes from this realization. While *Sorry about Kung Fu* is poised between the woman's self-realization and her deep bond with her re-lentlessly patriarchal family, in line with its generic template, *What Is a Man* presents greater crossing between the two spheres, showing women gaining the upper hand and a consequent softening of the male principle. In the last film, *Iva*, we see how an alternative perspective, also informed by gender, enables a serious examination of the depth of social crisis in contemporary Croatia.

Regionalism/Localism: New Cultural Geography Arises

The traditional, local setting in *What Is a Man* and *Sorry about Kung Fu* – a barren, economically depressed, heavily patriarchal, folk Catholic, ethnically homogeneous, and war-wrecked Dalmatian hinterland – is at first projected as a place that still contains undiluted, unadulterated (national and moral) values, apparently under threat in all other locations. But these films also show to what extent this is just a comforting fantasy in the face of the forces of cultural levelling and unification. *Sorry about Kung Fu* opens with the long shot of a plane landing, and then a coach stopping in the middle of nowhere; similarly, *What Is a Man* features a long shot of the motorway cutting through the region. The shots are metaphors of uncontainable and intrusive forces intervening in these localities. The advertising material for Sviličić's *Sorry about Kung Fu* focuses on the fascinating and somewhat depressing barrenness of the monotonous landscape that engulfs the characters. This setting, however, has already been criss-crossed by the all-pervasive, widely syndicated *telenovelas* (which through their embeddedness in Latin folk Catholicism have some definite appeal for Croatian audiences in addition to their sentimental plots, stereotypical characters, archetypal moral situations, and so forth) and other TV-introduced entertainment culture. And far-ranging economic change has been brought in by the construction of the motorway. As well, the workings of the international European labour market impinge on the characters. In *What Is a Man* the restitution money for a work accident suffered by the husband as a *Gastarbeiter* in Germany is partly what that sets the events in motion. Similarly, in *Sorry about Kung Fu*, the space of Germany, where the protagonist finds work as a refugee from the war, figures as a threatening outside where dangerous transgressions take place, materialized in a mixed-race baby.

Recently, literary and cultural studies have demonstrated a resurgence of interest in regionalism, not simply as a thematic concern but as an abiding and viable critical perspective somewhat on the margins of the canonical, dominant cultural forms.[3] This has been articulated, for instance, in the densely argued *Writing out of Place*, in which Judith Fetterley and Marjorie Pryse (2003, 257) claim that regionalism – especially though not exclusively as exercised by women writers – is a critical practice that also uses gender as a point of view to launch a redefinition or critique of the normative. They add that, in fact, regionalism's geographical metaphors co-exist with the feminist epistemology articulated from the 1970s: 'Regionalism is both a discursive construction and a cultural location grounded in the everyday lives of women and other non-dominant regional persons' (258). Unlike the more standard label 'local colour writing,' regionalism in American turn-of-the-century literature, according to Fetterley and Pryse, explicitly seeks to ground itself as 'the rhetorical awareness of difference as critique' (258). This contention is especially interesting for the ways in which these processes partly correspond to those that operate in the production of Croatian regional cultures and partly depart from these conclusions, here meant as a convenient and relevant point of departure with a sense of the intervening cultural and temporal distance.

It is interesting how regionalism/localism has lately begun to figure prominently in this new – and ever more globalizing – constellation and is not simply a retrograde force stalling change and transformation and clinging to the old standards. As suggested by Arjun Appadurai (1996), the production of locality is a serious cultural enterprise that entails a careful balancing between the global and the traditional. I have said before that regionalism is not simply a straight opposite to globalization (here also encoded as transnationalism), but neither is it merely an extension of nationalism. It manoeuvres between adopting certain modes of global economic and cultural behaviour and retaining the contours of the old order. The characters who on the surface struggle most assiduously to maintain the status quo in the arrangement of family and gender roles (the economic emigrant in *What Is a Man*, played by Ivo Gregurević, for example) are in fact the carriers of a new, culturally hybrid (not to say multicultural) orientation who have, by getting away from local cultural geography, initiated the process of cultural exchange and social transformation.

As suggested by Hsuan L. Hsu, 'For readers, tourists, and politicians alike the region often serves as a focus of nostalgia and a privileged site of geographical feeling,' while 'progressive cultural critics represent the local as the scale of familiarity, loyalty, and authentic experience, in contrast with the merely imagined community of the nation and the passionless economic space of globalization' (2005, 36). Simultaneously, however, Hsu demonstrates how the global and the national overlap understanding of the local and its (self)representation.

Let me turn briefly to a text by Croatian journalist and film critic Jurica Pavičić (2006). We may begin to see how readings of Hribar's film *What Is a Man* differ and get inflected by individual point of view and political orientation; in fact, they even split along the lines of politically 'correct' or 'misguided' readings. So whether one sees characters as worthy of our sympathy or mired in their patriarchal and redneck sensibility beyond recuperation, in the end is a function of wider sociopolitical concerns and crystallizes the ideological positions found in

Croatian culture nowadays. (The same could be said in connection with Radić's film *What Iva Recorded*.) Pavičić criticizes *What Is a Man* for failures in dramaturgy, for leaving protagonists somewhat out of focus, and for favouring a witty scene over larger narrative structures. Still, when Pavičić comes to the film's quite unprecedented popularity in a day and age when the Croatian film audience is shrinking or is disproportionately exposed to Hollywood production, he no longer holds back his political aces. Pavičić's text, it becomes clear, debates with and refers to an earlier column by a compatriot who is a political opponent from another regional newspaper.

Where I pointedly disagree with Pavičić's analysis is in his contention that the film mediates for traumatized national audiences a painful but inevitable soul searching, culminating in the cathartic recognition of our mutual implications in all our recent sociopolitical deviations. I think a simpler, and perhaps less flattering, explanation is that the backward regional space of the Dalmatian hinterland still retains its symbolic role as an abject zone, where the most undesirable elements of national culture reside. The audience can laugh sympathetically at the characters not because, as Pavičić contends, they identify with them but because they still believe them to fall short of their own high, tolerant, and multicultural standards. This reaction, of course, differs regionally, but the overall feeling is that of a smug relief that provincialism and staunch patriarchalism reside somewhere else. Also, my guess is that the closer to Dalmatia the film-going public resides, the more closely its response will approximate the panicky feeling of being exposed and thus the more the film will provoke a need for disavowal through comedy and laughter. Although the possibility of unambiguously positive identification is still possible, I deem it less likely, owing to the defamiliarizing signals inherent in comedy.

If comedy is to some extent an acceptable mechanism for grasping this particular sociocultural milieu, the elements of melodrama, especially in *What Is a Man*, raise other concerns. Melodramatic conventions work in two directions: centring on the inescapability of familial structures supposedly solidly grounded in emotions, and thus reconfirming the overdetermined status of traditional family; and opening 'space prohibited by the so-called classical realist film text, which is restricted to oppressive patriarchal norms' (Kaplan 2000, 52). This means, to paraphrase Kaplan, that melodrama in its apparatus of representation and spectatorship inscribes a place for a female-identified gaze. (Interestingly, the third film discussed here, *What Iva Recorded*, a family drama and black comedy, goes one step further by reaching a point at which it effectively grants to the unstable, marginal, and unsituated protagonist an active position of looking, turning her into a central spectator and thus making the whole film the effect and content of her gaze.)

What Is a Man brings together some salient features of the new Croatian social landscape: the Church representative and the new *homo politicus* (two types of masculinity that have already been paraded in cultural representations), and also an emergent type, a more sensitive (or, dare I say, feminized) new man. It does so while launching a serio-comic consideration of their respective roles by tracing cracks in traditional, by and large patriarchal, social structures. This reconsideration is reinforced in turn by the film's ambiguous agenda in representing new types of female characters, who function within the patriarchal context that forms their 'natural' surroundings even while they seriously undermine its logic (the assertive widow, the entrepreneurial sister, the emigrant's daughter, the female defence minister).[4]

The other unexpected outcome of the way the regional is implemented in the new Croatian cinema is the way it is turning into a cultural critique. This in itself certainly does not depart from age-old generic models that successfully exploit the differences and imbalances between various locales, especially the rural (encoded also heavily as regional) and the metropolitan (representative of the national cultural and, by extension, also political capital). However, what is relevant for the war and postwar Croatian contexts is that this critique proceeds from a space that is unlikely in several respects. To remind ourselves of Fetterley and Pryse's arguments, they wish to make an explicit link between regionalism and feminist critique, and this is also one of the running themes in *Sorry about Kung Fu* and *What Is a Man*. The reader should be reminded here of the popular perception, deriving from centuries-old practices, that it is precisely these regions that are most unlikely to indicate, let alone sustain, this kind of connection, and yet this is what has happened, and this trend has been taken up in all three films as a sub-plot.

Where this view of the regional gets complicated, but also enhances its potential to generate new cultural modes not simply against the national norm but as a corrective to it, is in the region's disproportionately large share of prominent politicians, especially during and in the immediate aftermath of the war. (Hinterland Dalmatia extends here for the purposes of my cultural reading across the border into the neighbouring Herzegovina.) In this respect, the region can be perceived as a container of solid, vaunted, and healthy national values. So this re-reading of re-gion is a very significant, sometimes sensitive and sometimes less so, recording of the changing fortunes of its manifold functions.

Now let me go back to the conjunction of the Church, the family, and the nation, so appositely figured and metonymically recreated in *What Is a Man*, a rural, local drama, advertised in the media as a 'comic pas-toral' (HRT trailer) or a mix of comedy and melodrama (*Večernji list*).[5] On the face of it, there is something subversive in the romantic attach-ments of a character who is a Catholic priest; however, as suggested by another critic, this does not contradict but is in fact 'in concordance with the setting up of a crucial family principle,' in this case the bonds of feeling that override all other concerns in melodrama (Čegir 2006; see also Nenadić 2006).

It may seem as if I have stretched my arguments unduly by inserting the element of nation, especially as it intersects with the image of the exemplary family. However, one of the plot lines in *What Is a Man* con-firms this reading. Consider the splitting of a protagonist into an inhib-ited, sensitive priest (representing perhaps a changing image of the Church in post-communist times) and his hypermasculine, overbearing identical twin, a general (both roles are played by Leon Lučev). As I men-tioned at the beginning of my discussion, religion is perceived as an es-sential and essentially indisputable component of ethnic identity. In this respect, the priest is not only represents the institution to which he be-longs but also signals one of the forms of dominant national masculinity. The same logic, from a different point of view, applies to the general.

Thus, when a young widow in mourning (played by Zrinka Cvitešić) after her husband's untimely demise shifts her attention to another li-bidinal object, namely the priest, she does not necessarily opt for a new kind of man. Because of the logic of melodramatic plot, her desire will not be deterred but rather enflamed by very strong taboos surrounding the ambiguous (because suppressed) masculinity of Catholic priests. Significantly, she refashions herself as an active, desiring subject: it is always she who initiates their meetings and in other ways takes control over the evolving relationship. Once she has pronounced her desire – ironically through the sacrament of confession (somehow rendering her impulses more dignified) – she proceeds to assert herself. She does not even flinch from conceiving and having a baby out of wedlock (the same holds true of a self-reliant young woman in *Sorry about Kung Fu*), even though nothing would be more 'natural' and expected but to re-sign herself to a union with the general, whose baby she is carrying.

That she foregoes this intensely phallic impersonation of the new 'national' man, however, underscores the transformation that she, and tangentially her sister, have undergone since the moment of her husband's death and the onset of their economic self-sufficiency. Thus the outlines of a new national family, as one among several viable models, begin to emerge, hatched in a barren and intransigent region that has so far taken a backseat to more dynamic (because more hybridized and more urban) littoral and northwestern parts of the country. The film thus charts a new cultural geography even when it is clear that the characters are subject to more overwhelming forces.

In Ognjen Sviličić's authorial project *Sorry about Kung Fu* (he figures as a director, screenwriter, and composer), one of the principal concerns is stated in the opening motto, an ordinance from the late medieval *Poljički statut* (Statute of Poljica, 1440), a document regulating for centuries the political and social life in the Dalmatian hinterland, where the action of the film takes place: 'If a daughter or a granddaughter who is not yet twenty-five years of age and is fit to be married chooses instead a dishonourable life or to her own shame finds herself with child, it is her father's prerogative to banish her from the house' (translation mine).

Scenes ushering us into the film – an air-craft landing and shots of the motorway and a coach arriving in a desolate country – point to another frame of reference, alerting us to the existence of an outside world that impinges on a way of life seemingly immutable for generations. Literally, the (forced) mobility of the population induced by economic and political forces initiates a cycle of events that disrupts traditional expectations. Germany, traditionally a place of refuge for Croatian political and economic exiles, is in the film a force of disruption that has 'corrupted' Mirjana (Daria Lorenci), a wayward daughter who finds herself bound by the statute, which is even more deeply engrained in the oral than in the written tradition. The other place that metaphorically spells an alternative, with freedom from parental and community strictures, is imagined by Mirjana's younger brother, Marko (Luka Petrušić). For him, the United States as a country of rock and heavy metal bands, with its attendant counter-cultural thrust, offers that space.

Importantly for my focus here, not only does Mirjana come from the outside world but she is obviously pregnant with no husband in sight. Literally, something foreign, in the form of a baby, is implanted in her, as a physical sign of her dissociation from her family and social environment. After the war, Mirjana returns to her village from Germany, where she had emigrated. Because she is pregnant and un-married, her parents desperately try to find her any match, soliciting the help of a local marriage broker. Despite all odds, Mirjana evades the unwanted suitors and gives birth to a Eurasian baby boy. As pressure on her mounts, she has to leave once again. It is only on his deathbed, in the final sequence, that her father acknowledges his grandson and 'forgives' Mirjana. Needless to say, once it becomes obvious that this difference is also foreignness on a very literal level, because the baby is part Asian, Mirjana's family and the community brace themselves for this double challenge. The rebellious daughter has overstepped the rules twice in a very disrespectful manner, and she will be made to feel the enormity of her transgression. The drama is even more poignant for Mirjana because she is decidedly not a feminist, and she has not come to upturn the traditional order; she obviously has respect for and an ingrained sense of duty and obedience toward her parents, especially her father, despite their elliptical communication. It makes it all the more difficult for her to reconcile the two sides of her life.

Hence, it is almost a truism that certain regional constellations histor-ically support and reflect a specific dispensation of gender/family roles, here notably the Dalmatian hinterland and other inland, rural areas. However, these two films make clear the extent to which varying social processes disturb traditional roles and cause them slowly to adapt to new circumstances. Let me just note here that traditionalism has persisted as a structure of feeling, despite the communist/socialist professed commitment to gender equality. Even though officially en-dorsed and implemented in some areas (access to jobs, equal pay, labour rights, regulation and protection of women's reproductive rights) this new ideology cannot infiltrate these geographic sites.

Thus it is indicative to see how in a transitional society, in its tortuous passage to capitalism, new structures of feeling emerge. Encroachments promulgated by capitalism, its economic logic, and its promotion of consumption of popular images bring about changes that socialist slo-gans and more earnest commitments could hardly accomplish. What incipient capitalism – through economic emigration, later tourism, and finally through unlimited consumption of popular artefacts and global capitalist products inundating the region – finally brings is an overhaul of sex and gender dispensations. At the same time, while the audience witnesses the regional being morphed into the ideal of an idyllic com-munity in *telenovelas* or long-gone pastoral, German-produced Westerns (such as the Winnetou series and its referencing in *What Is a Man*), the urban space in the third film points, it seems, in a different direction.[6]

Meanwhile in the Metropolis ...

Perhaps not surprisingly, Sviličić is a screenwriter for Tomislav Radić's film *What Iva Recorded*, which succinctly combines all the major moral and ethical concerns plaguing contemporary Croatian society. This is a view from the metropolis but one that cleverly and by implication invests in the critical potential unleashed by regionalism and localism, and is sceptical of bland globalism. By a very simple narrative device, a home party at which various guests arrive and interact with Iva's family, the film skilfully uses the ironic procedure of a semi-innocent narrator. (The question is, of course, to what extent an urban, grungy, fifteen-year-old is inexperienced, innocent of the world around her.)

The whole film is presumably shot by Iva (Masha Mati Prodan), who gets a camera for her fifteenth birthday, on 21 October 2003. The handheld camera, carried by Iva around the house, turned on and off at her own convenience and unobtrusively planted in places and at times when only she knows that it is on, thematizes on one level the process of watching and making films as proceeding from an intense impulse of scopophilia, spying on others and, ultimately, debunking them. The whole film is in fact shot as a sequence of subjective shots determined by Iva's decision about what to shoot. Consequently, the audience can only speculate on what she has decided to leave out (occasionally, though, parental strictures also apply).

Let us consider for a moment what Iva's position as a girl with a camera means in the context of her family's troubled dynamics. On one hand, it clearly empowers her, putting her in a position of a privileged observer who manipulates her prerogative: she stalks her parents (especially her mother) through the house despite their remonstrance; she leaves the camera on without the knowledge or consent of others and violates her family's hallowed privacy. Despite her initially vulnerable, weak status, denied either a vantage point or a voice, her acquisition and use of a camera turn her effectively into a critical, observing, watchful, censorious consciousness, perhaps even some kind of the superego.

For the moment, it is important to understand the paradox of Iva's situation: that she can from her position of utter marginality (a teenager, a stepdaughter, a minor still dismissed as an uncomprehending child) advance to the position of a controlling element in the household.

Unexpectedly, she turns the tables, and by choosing what and whom to shoot assembles her own version of her family and the larger society in which she does not yet figure as a competent participant. This underdog position, depicted through Iva's eyes, is a vantage point from which the audience can see moral bankruptcy of the society and certain inevitable fault lines in its institutions.

Of course, Iva's subjective shots are subjected to a secondary revision by the implied author, which places a possibly ironic layer between Iva's and the implied author's manipulations.[7] The point, however, is that both manipulations operate with the camera, and that once the camera begins to mediate between an individual observer (in this case an alert, intelligent, sensitive, but also shrewd girl) and the observed, and then, later on, between the content of the film and the audience, we are caught in a very intricate system of meaning production.

The question for me here is why Radić chooses to present Iva with a camera when he could easily have simply made her into a critical, wry, and ironic observer and commentator through a hypodiegetic narrative situation. Instead, he creates a slightly disturbing situation in which an insistent and sharp observation enabled by a portable camera, easily moved and concealed, and with admirable technical features (zoom, sound system), renders the characters as both helpless objects of our pity because of encroachments of the insistent eye of the camera and as butt of our contempt for what they turn out to be in this intense and emotionally strong disclosure of certain pathologies of social life in present-day Croatia. It is definitely worth considering how Iva's marginal position can by a rather simple trick be transposed into a position of covert authority, even if only while she is holding a camera. Iva does not simply comment; she actively participates in the production of meaning in the scenes before us. She is the director. But that also means that she to some extent manipulates, censors, cuts out, or leaves in what she finds appropriate for her film. (Why film her mother repeatedly helping herself to a bottle of vodka? Why film Božo, her stepfather, walking around all riled up and shouting? Why record the sexually titillating behaviour of a multi-accomplished escort girl, played by Barbara Prpić, who makes more money at her substitute job than she does with her diploma?)

In a telling reversal of the weak subject position into an active vehicle of meaning production and guide to interpretation, Iva actively invites us to see the world from her perspective, not simply as a helpless bystander but as an active producer of images and meanings. This alerts us to the simultaneously liberating and empowering but also insidious potential of technologies of visual reproduction. In addition, it uncovers a basic premise of the film: not to take the visible for granted but to allow for perspective that is askew, and not to give in to preconditioned, stereotypical cultural expectations.

Stereotypes are paraded in the film from the beginning, as the camera sweeps across the Zagreb cityscape and zooms in on Novi Zagreb, the socialist, high-rise working-class buildings from the days of centralized city planning and enforced industrialization and heavy urbanization, stretching across the River Sava. Iva's family, most probably *nouveau riche*, resides on the river's northern bank in one of the newly erected 'urban villas' sprouting uncontrollably in fashionable neighbourhoods on the slopes of Medvednica Mountain, above Zagreb. This provides an appropriate setting for the display of snobbery and hypocrisy abiding within the four falls of the family mansion. Božo (Ivo Gregurević), the head of the family as described by his hysterical and slightly vodka-doused wife, Željka (Anja Šovagović Despot), is 'primitive, immoral, and calculated.' Darko (Boris Svrtan), Željka's bohemian brother, an artist and struggling painter, is denigrated by practical and money-grubbing Božo. According to Darko, Božo is also a fascist, and judging by his heavy accent is not from the metropolis but from the rural regions, a self-made businessman sprouted by the post-communist transformation of Croatian economy. Božo is also desperately trying to buy into genteel respectability, but it falls mostly to his unstable wife to assert the family's high-class aspirations through her snobbishness. The camera unfailingly records all the characters' faults and foibles.

Iva's position as a camera operator is highlighted repeatedly as she is condescendingly humoured by other characters, especially by Herr Hoffer (Karl Menrad), a hypercorrect German businessman. But at the same time the characters continuously evoke the feeling that they are at the camera's (Iva's) mercy. The line between life and art is blurred. What is Iva's gaze like? From a few shots when she turns camera toward herself or is being filmed by somebody else, she seems to be a young adolescent, pretty much in line with her urban counterparts elsewhere in Europe, confused and with a sense of irony and self-irony (as when she pulls faces at the camera). At the same time, she is committed to representing her protagonists from different perspectives (hence the prevailing medium shot accompanied by skewed shots). The medium shot alienates the characters and shows them to be rather pathetic and unlikeable puppets embroiled in very suspect pursuits.

(Božo's agenda apparently is to broker a deal with Hoffer even if he has to use an escort or to prostitute his own wife. Darko is happy to squeeze money out of Božo and then belittle him as an intolerant right-wing pig. Željka is sensitive to the status of the escort but fails to recognize herself as stuck in a house where she toils and satisfies her husband's whims in turn for the comforts he is providing.) The skewed angles and close-ups either humanize the characters or show them to be sympathetic caricatures. However, given that Iva is prone to caricaturing even herself, a hint of truth behind these grotesque, overblown, yet revealing presentations opens up.

A dinner at home and subsequent orgy of eating and drinking at a restaurant is a carnivalesque episode, in which anything becomes possible. The camera mercilessly records the absurdity of the characters' roleplay and unmasks them in their blatantly obvious pursuits: the Bakhtinian sphere of gross carnality and the belly. Still, even here, the high and the low, the represented and the implied, the surface and the deep meaning are intertwined. The reversal of roles, although short of the encompassing effect of carnivalesque regeneration through subversion, still achieves a cathartic effect, and what is more overturns the viewer's expectations concerning most of the characters.

That is, in *What Iva Recorded*, the space that beforehand figured as a framework for sustaining relative female independence, in transitional Croatia becomes a place carrying another set of traditional values, now imported from the script of Western middle-class domestic ideology: a comfortable home, a family provided for exclusively by the husband as a competent and high-powered bread winner, with a stay-at-home, incipiently hysterical wife.[8] In effect, the changes that capitalism brings into transitional economy paradoxically contain the already won positions of empowerment for women in the urban milieu while causing upheaval in the backyard. Whether it is a step back or a step forward, and from whose point of view the audience should gauge it, are just some of the questions enigmatically flashing at us from the screen in recent Croatian films.

7 Identity, Bodies, and Second-Generation Returnees in West Africa

ERIN KENNY

I was precariously balanced underneath a new laptop and a nursing baby heavy with sleep, 'Hey, Mom,' I blurted, 'I got Googled!' The idea made me laugh.

'Wow! Who Googled you?'

'Some big New York attorney.'

She stopped chopping onions and looked at me strangely. 'Oh?'

'He's looking for an expert witness who can testify about female genital cutting in Guinea.'

She winced visibly. 'Sweet Jesus,' she swore on the inhale, the way she always does when she's embodying motherly responsibility. 'Do you know about that? What could you say about that?'

Until that moment, I'd not even considered testifying. I was just tickled that I'd been Googled. I didn't really consider myself to be an authority on FGC, despite attending twelve or so ceremonies in Mali and Guinea. I don't 'do' FGC.[1] I study return migrants and their families. I was back in the United States. I had a new baby. A new tenure-track job. Syllabi to write. No time to jet off and testify. No inclination to talk about this topic with Americans.

'Well ...' I waffled.

'Erin,' she cut me off. 'Do you know something about this woman's situation? Do you know about this?'

In fact, after more than three years in West Africa, I knew more than I was really comfortable knowing, and definitely more than I was comfortable with my mother knowing I knew. 'Sure. But it's not really something I like to talk about.'

She looked at me in that same curious way she did when I told her I was pregnant. To my Irish-born immigrant mother, being a woman is always heavy with responsibility, rich with joy, replete with sacrifice.

She said, 'If you can help this woman, you have to. You don't really have the choice of talking about it or not.'

There are a number of places in this opening vignette where I want to stop and explain, to do analysis. I love that my mother, who never had access to a university education, leapt immediately from the abstraction of a foreign practice to the life of an individual woman. No one 'trained' her to do that. She does it, and she's done it all her life. My mother believes that women have obligations to each other, no matter where they live or what they believe. My mother – one of eleven children – sees women as sisters, full stop. The other thing I want to point out is by way of foreshadowing. My daughter, the sleepy baby, is Malinké: according to the principles of identity construction in her father's culture, she is and always will be Malinké, despite having an American mother and unquestioned access to a blue passport with a proud, golden eagle on the front. Her name, Kiera Belle Kaba, was carefully chosen to reflect her Irish and Guinean heritage, and the beauty in linking the two.

My mother continued, 'What about Kiera?'

What she meant was, what about Kiera's future? Could she go to Guinea? Would she be subjected to FGC? Would Kiera's father expect her to undergo this rite of passage? Was her only granddaughter 'safe' from such a violent coming of age?

One of the things I always regret now that I teach at a small liberal arts college in Springfield, Missouri, is how quickly students seize upon the practice of FGC to reaffirm their beliefs in the 'backwardness' or 'barbarism' of the non-West, by which they really mean People Who Grow Up Outside Driving Distance to an Abercrombie and Fitch Store. Lately, in an effort to be provocative and outrageous, I've been challenging students by labelling their knowledge of FGC as analogous to pornography. I ask them why they think it's okay to know more about the genitalia of a woman in another part of the world than they know about what (and if) that woman eats, or what she believes, or what she thinks about the music of Céline Dion (which is inexplicably omnipresent in Guinea). Too many discussions about FGC on television or in the mainstream media take the genitalia of a woman out of context. In other words, like pornography, these representations separate labia and vagina from a real person. Students say this is an unfair comparison. 'I really care about that woman's pain,' they say. 'I know it's wrong.'

To which I say, maybe you should also know something about that woman's joy, because we are always more than our bodies and perhaps you're failing to see a bigger picture about what a woman is (and is not) – and what a body is (and is not) – in another cultural context.

But, these aren't exactly things I can say to my mother. The idea of telling my mother that her notion of her 'sisters' in Africa is somehow tinged with pornographic representations of ripped and sewn labia hurts me, as I admittedly fall into old-world-style restrictions about intergenerational manners in conversation.

Besides, my mother raised an important point: What about my daughter? Since my first moment as a shiny, idealistic Peace Corps volunteer in Mali in 1995, I have heard many cases of African professionals who return home to the village from the city with their children in tow for a wedding or a holiday, only to have their parents or in-laws sweep the children away to have an excision performed by the village blacksmith without their knowledge or their blessing.

A very cold awareness – totally visceral – pervaded me in that moment, fingers poised above an expensive laptop and the rest of me nursing my heavy baby. Ultimately, in this particular transnational context, my own notions of gendered identity for my daughter – and myself, as her mother – were definitely out of my hands. In Guinea, rights to my daughter's body are not owned by me, or her father, or even herself. Those rights continue to be collectively determined. And since I was not able in that moment to admit that totally intellectualized, stinging cultural paradox to my mother, I agreed to answer the email to the New York attorney.

Through stories, this chapter introduces a few women I met during my dissertation year of ethnographic research in Guinea in order to merge two themes that stand out in literature of the past decade: transnational mobility and cultural constructions of the body. Just as contemporary emphases on transnationalism reflect a theoretical move away from bounded units to reflect new conceptualizations of space and place, our understanding of the way the body is culturally constructed yields insight into the human experience (Csordas 1999). Studies abound on the ways that culture marks bodies (Van Wolputte 2004), simultaneously constructing both the individual body and groups of bodies. Inspired by Merleau-Ponty's notion of 'the embodied self' (1964), many feminist analyses of the transnational experience challenge universalist attitudes about the body in Western thought and offer alternative perceptions of identity, cultural values, and gendered moralities.

Because the body houses a nexus of cultural tensions that emerge in the context of transnational childhoods, in this essay, I refer to particular bodies and experiences (as described to me during fieldwork)[2] in order to locate constructions of 'ideal' gendered morality (which I identify as 'personhood'), and to further examine rites of passage in West Africa, and, more specifically, the significance of 'missing' these rituals for foreign-born children. Most significantly, this chapter outlines areas of potential tension in the experience of 'second-generation return migrants,' children born to returnees while they have been living abroad, who return 'home' to a place they have never been. For many second-generation returnees, tensions revolve around ambiguity governing passage through stages of a prescribed life course and the construction of Malinké personhood, specifically female genital cutting.

The 'Homeland': Transnational Households of Return Migrants

Within the past decade, global forces have yielded unprecedented numbers of returnees worldwide (Brettell 2000), yet little systematic ethnographic work examines the identity processes of children of return migrants. Transnational studies emphasize the interconnectivity of people as national boundaries continue to loosen and everyday experiences of people around the world place them within a simultaneous field of the local and the global. Transnational studies of human mobility, however, present distinct methodological challenges. They deep time exposure to account for life course changes in individuals and relationships and to trace the influences of multiple localities and attention to the situated locality of various household members (Miles 2004). The transnational lives of migrants are often rife with contradictions as the process of identity construction tends to be fused to specific, nostalgic localities of 'home' (Gupta and Ferguson 1992). In Africa, migrant identities reflect fluid sets of relationships that evolve as migrants move through lived social worlds. Awareness of transnational forces may produce profound ambivalence, as ethnographic studies in Africa reveal the many 'malcontents of modernity' (Masquelier 2000, 84) across the continent. Continual negotiations between accommodation and resistance necessary to maintain the 'self' relative to others take place within a widened range of possibilities, creating the alternating rhythms of sameness and difference, self and other (McKenzie 1999; Taussig 1993, 246) common to the transnational experience. These patterns are further complicated when a migrant returns 'home,' usually at the time of retirement. In this particular study, for those who return to the deeply Islamic and historically rich region known Upper

Guinea, the decision to return home after living abroad constitutes the fulfilment of a cycle expected of 'successful' sons (Safran 1991) and a return to idealized Malinké notions of intergenerational obligation and personhood.

The lived experience of a transnational migrant typically involves many people in many locations. Attention to the dynamics of loss in the home community enriches mobility studies (Long and Oxfeld 2004; Rouse 1995); so, too, does attention to the host community dynamics upon the entry of the migrant (Chavez 1991). Participants in this study had lived outside of Guinea in other areas of West Africa for anywhere from five to fifty years; each had returned to their household of origin, usually with foreign-born children and/or spouses, for a variety of reasons (Kenny 2005). For them, the home community and the host community occupy the same place, which is itself replete with symbolism, expectations, and obligations. Drawing on lessons learned abroad and nostalgic notions of the 'homeland,' return migrants actively construct 'moral identities and communities in relation to the wider world ... as a means of scrutinizing one's own life, questioning the validity of the social order, and creating a space of contestation' (Masquelier 2000, 85). Return migrants often embody a 'return of conservatism' (César 1974): they enjoy relative advantages they feel are 'due them' within the constructs of an idealized nostalgia combined with the practical agency of accrued social capital from their successes abroad. Often, returnees in this study expressed anxiety about the challenges of parenting abroad and actively promoted the maintenance of a distinctly Malinké, multigenerational household to regulate and to produce 'good' children. Connections to transnational business opportunities and increased capacity for business investment often allow returnees to occupy positions of enhanced status within the natal household following their return, further enabling them to provide for foreign-born children.

Located in eastern Guinea, the region known as Upper Guinea is populated primarily by Malinké horticulturalists. The term *Malinké* refers both to the ethnic group (a sub-group of Mande) and to the language, which is spoken in Guinea, Mali, and western Côte d'Ivoire. Malinké society is self-consciously ancient: oral history stretches back to the time of the legendary ruler Sundiata Keita, around 1200 AD. The Malinké recognize polygynous marriages, patrilineal descent, and residence in the home of the groom's father, usually in three-generation extended families of averaging thirty or forty people. Authority usually rests with the oldest male relative (*dutigi*), and internal household hierarchies are organized on principles of age, gender, lineage, marital order, and birth order.

Upper Guinea, the 'homeland,' is called *fabara*: it is a physical place, but it is also a meaningful social construction that resonates with Malinké notions of history, lineage, and identity. (See also Feldman-Bianco 1992, 145, for a discussion of migrant identity comprising 'multiple layers of space and past time'.) Two key concepts in Malinké identity construction essential for understanding the context of children of returnees are that children 'belong to' the *fabara* regardless of the geography of their birth and, as outlined in the next section, that in the *fabara*, personhood 'accrues' incrementally, through relationships (Brand 1998) and prescribed stages of a distinctly gendered life course (Bledsoe 2002).

Personhood and Gendered Bodies in the *Fabara*

Incremental, earned changes in personhood[3] via progression through a prescribed life course in a gerontocratic society cannot be underestimated, and must always be considered *with* gender in determining opportunities available to individuals at different times in their lives. Life course refers not only to biological maturation and aging but also to the social system that gives meaning to relationships and grants status to individuals as they progress through these processes (Bledsoe 2002). Therefore, what I refer to as 'personhood' *includes* aspects of the body but is not *restricted* to essentialist definitions of the body. Analyses of kinship, marriage, and productive activity in Africa demonstrate how the notion of 'personhood' shapes significant aspects of daily lived experiences (Brand 2001; Grosz-Ngaté 1989, 168). In most African societies, gender and sexuality continue to be tied to reproduction. If we view this aspect of gendered embodiment as transfer points for relations of power (Foucault 1980a, 103), then we most definitely see Malinké notions of 'the body' as reinforcing cultural supremacy of male over female, age over youth. However, because gender represents only one of many indexes of personhood (Brand 1998), other personal attributes may also figure heavily into determinations of relative status within the household. Feminist research demonstrates that households display an enormous range of women's economic influence, including the ways that public performances of patriarchal ideology may be challenged by private matrifocal behaviour in the absence of male members. Transnational migration studies therefore increasingly avoid theorizing gender as a single analytical category in transnational re-locations (Brettell 2000).

For adult men and women in Upper Guinea, the life course is divid-ed into distinct stages that may be marked by membership into core Malinké age-grade organizations called *ton*. Rites of passage for men reflect certain social obligations and establish key relationships that bind the initiate to other men in a community through shared experi-ences. Until the age of eight or nine, boys are called *bilakòrò* (wearer of foreskin). After circumcision, they progress through stages of *cèmisen* (small man), *kamalen* (unmarried man), *cè* (usually thought of as a hus-band, or married man), and *cèkoroba* (an old man, a grandfather) based on their choices, actions, and behaviour. Being called a 'man' in Malinké society is very much a collective and earned title.

For women, progression through the life course stages tends to be less about their membership in a group of women and more about the ways in which rites prepare them for relationships with men (Levin 2001). A Malinké woman maintains the *jamu* (lineage name) of her fath-er throughout her life, though her children will receive the name of her husband's family through *kulusijala*, strict patrilineal principles of des-cent. It is said that 'the two ends of the belt are closer than the breasts,' symbolizing that identity, continuity, and group membership are more reliably transferred through *ji* (semen) than through *sinji* (breastmilk), symbolizing the nurturing relations constructed at the breast.

Mande Initiations: Making Bodies in the *Fabara*

Within the Malinké context, female excision marks a preliminary stage in the social construction of an appropriately gendered person: it dif-ferentiates a female from a male, a girl (child) from a woman (adult), a Malinké person from a non-Malinké person. As a Western feminist and an anthropologist, I occupy an undeniably uncomfortable space for thinking about excision.[4] I did not set out specifically to research this issue; rather, it became an unavoidable part of my research, especially as my relationship with a Malinké man deepened in a romantic way and his family began to think of me as a relation. I presented a bit of a conundrum that drew a great deal of discussion and laughter as I frequently did not have a preappointed 'typical' in-law role to occupy relative to other family members.

As I observed it, female excision is a quick procedure. Squatting, the initiate is held by adult women, and a female *numu* (caste-based specialist) kneels between the knees of the child. The *numu* 'calls' to the clitoris with a small song, and flicks it with her fingertip to achieve a partial erection. Then, in what seems like one motion but is clearly a practised skill, the *numu* pulls the clitoris with the fingers of one hand while expertly slicing down and across with a razor blade that has been sterilized in fire or alcohol. The goal, in my understanding from speaking with this group of practitioners, is only to nick the clitoris, not necessarily to remove the entire thing. This ability, of course, varies according to the skill of the practitioner and the degree to which the helpers are successful in subduing the terrified child. Specially prepared leaves and gauze are then packed between the child's legs, she is seated on a clean mat in a skirt of new cloth with her legs stretched straight out in front of her, her legs are loosely bound to prevent her from moving too much in the first day or so.

The pain experienced by the child is not inconsequential, and she is soothed and praised by all present. It is important to remember that all this takes place in the context of celebration: the child is congratulated for her courage, and she is welcomed into a community of adult women. Men were never present at these events, nor did I ever attend a boy's circumcision procedure. I typically provided non-aspirin pain medication, ranging from Tylenol to Motrin, but my own interventions were relatively minor. At the first operation I attended in Mali in 1996, I wept openly and expressed my fears for the girls' safety with enormous concern to anyone who would listen. Mostly, I was mollified by the senior women, who spent as much time comforting me as they did the children (also see Aud Talle's essay, 2007). To the best of my knowledge, all of those girls recovered without complication, and I have spent the intervening years regretting my emotionalism on that day, which must have frightened the girls terribly.[5]

According to Malinké identity processes, gendered personhood is a process, culturally enacted through ritual and marking of the body. In very important ways for the Malinké sense of identity, these categories govern the path not only to becoming a man or a woman but to being a *person* with obligations and responsibilities to others within the household. Bodily factors must be governed by cultural regulation enacted by the community. *Bilakòròw*, uncircumcised boys and girls, are seen as androgynous non-persons because they have not yet begun the cultural transition to becoming community members. I often heard it said during my year in Kankan that children 'know nothing.' They could not be trusted to tell the truth or to act with integrity, preferring instead to think only of their own pleasure by playing and behaving foolishly. Uninitiated children in Upper Guinea do not fully possess 'person-hood.' Ritualized genital cutting, circumcision and excision, dispels gender ambiguity by removing the substance of the 'other' sex and re-making a non-person into one who is fully and unambiguously male or female (Grosz-Ngaté 1989), but these ceremonies also mark the construction of a new person. Malinké families in Kankan conduct two key ceremonies, *solisee* and *kolakadi*, to celebrate the rites of passage of children into the status of 'person.'

An all-night ceremony (*solisee*) marks the genital cutting operation. In 2003, I attended several *solisee* events for male and female children. Large celebrations are increasingly common as families and neighbours collaborate to consolidate the costs of the elaborate celebrations. *Solisee* begins at sunset, usually on the night of a full moon, and usually during the summer, when children do not have school. The initiates are cut, one by one, by a *numu* in one of the huts of a family's compound, while the female members of the family and female celebrants assemble in the common space outside. Women sing and dance in a circular pattern, led by *jeliw* (praise singers). Male celebrants arrive around midnight and, except for a few drummers, do not participate in the dancing. The adults keep this vigil through the night, and as the sun comes up, a few of the key members of the ceremony begin the work of instructing the child initiates in adult matters of proper behaviour for the next ten days to three weeks. During this time, the children heal from the surgery while remaining isolated with other initiates, engaged in an intense period of learning. Parents and older siblings bring food to the new initiates daily, congratulating them on their bravery and new social status.

At the end of the period of isolation, initiates are 'reintegrated' into the community with a joyous *kolakadi* celebration. Beginning in the afternoon, the new initiates parade through the streets of the neighbourhood dressed proudly in new clothing, accompanied by drummers, cars, and motorbikes (and throngs of younger children, singing and dancing). The procession wends its way to a household of one of the initiates, where celebratory food and more guests await them. As before, women – especially the mothers of the initiates – dance enthusiastically to celebrate this important step in the life course of their children and also to celebrate their success as mothers in bringing such disciplined new adults into the community.

According to Malinké logic, removing the desire of a woman to 'play,' or behave sexually, allows an excised woman to assume a role as wife and mother. A woman who remains uncut shows too much 'sentimentality,' a Malinké euphemism for nymphomania, and lacks ability to control *jàràbi* (passion). The operation allows her to become more fully female, in that it releases *nyama*, the dangerous and fire-prone male-like part of her (Gosselin 2000). Likewise, boys must have the female-seeming part of their genitalia, the foreskin, removed in order to behave more appropriately like men. In the 'old days,' the procedure (called *soli*) was done by *numu* (members of the traditional occupational caste blacksmiths). Today, *numu* may still be used, but some people prefer medical professionals to conduct the potentially dangerous operation. Unlike the dramatic clitoral removals and infibulations of Sudan and Egypt, in Upper Guinea, many traditional practitioners may only symbolically nick the clitoris, leaving most of the organ intact.

However, those I interviewed also cited the necessity to prepare the body to remain 'clean' for Muslim ablutions. Daily prayers require all adult Muslims to purify themselves before presenting their intentions to Allah. A number of women informants confided concern for lingering 'impurity' they feared would accompany the female body following intimacy if the clitoris were fully present; specifically, they suggested that a *suma djuma* (bad smell) would prevent them from praying (e.g., Johnson 2000, 219).

To ensure a 'proper Muslim husband,' I was told, women must be *kablakoraya* (excised). Members of the older generation explained to me that bad behaviour or *la débauche* (debauchery, often attributed to exposure to Western values) lead young people astray and encourage them to engage in sexual acts too early in their lives: they go 'wild.' Most interviewees acknowledged that the Qu'ran does not call for excision per se, but they adamantly believe that the result fulfils the Prophet's proscriptions on female sexuality. They view Islam and excision as entirely compatible within the constructions of modest female sexual behaviour. They cite well-publicized HIV rates among city dwellers and refugees to strengthen arguments for the continuation of the practice and perhaps to mask anxieties about other structural economic problems. That Malinké youth are radically changing their sexual behaviour is debatable (Launay 1995; Prazak 2004), but increased global access to external debates and information strengthens local discourse about the significance of the practice and the value of maintaining a well-disciplined, gendered body.

Officially, the practice of female genital cutting is outlawed in Guinea according to Article 265 of the Penal Code; however to date, no cases have been brought to trial (US Department of State 2001). I attended approximately ten ceremonies celebrating genital cutting for boys and girls in Kankan in 2003. Some groups in Guinea, like Tostan,[6] actively promote anti-excision education campaigns and try to encourage alternative coming-of-age rituals for girls. These groups cite the high rates of complications and maternal mortality in excised women, but also face allegations by locals that they function as 'puppets' of the West by spreading misinformation, especially about rates of maternal mortality.

Typically, Western discussions about FGC include human rights discourse about forced 'amputation' and sexual violence, sometimes revolving around the notion of female sexual enjoyment. Most of the women I spoke to confirmed that sexual activity could most assuredly bring great physical pleasure despite the operation, unsettling Western assumptions about necessary correlations between excision and sexual sensitivity (Johnson 2001, 227). One woman even stated that the Qu'ran does not prohibit sexual pleasure between a woman and her husband. However, the way this pleasure should be expressed points to other underlying rationale for excision. One return migrant I interviewed told me that his mother remained very critical of his decision to marry a foreign-born woman who was not from Upper Guinea because of complications such a marriage could present between co-wives. She told her son that an excised wife would never tolerate an unexcised wife in her household because of the possibility that the uninitiated wife would 'cry out' during sex. Another man told me that unexcised women he was sexually involved with during his travels abroad 'cried out like donkeys.' Excision very dramatically disciplines the female body to respond as a person, not as an animal. Unrestrained vocalizations in Malinké ideology belong to the nonhuman realm of animals and witches, and must be avoided at all costs in persons to be mothers and wives.

Dilemmas of Foreign-Born Children: Gender and 'Reputation'

I came to know Ami, the hostess at Kankan's only 'ex-pat' restaurant, because I admired her penchant for animal prints and impractically high heeled shoes. Meeting as I did with the ten or so other Europeans and Americans living in Kankan in 2003 during our standing Saturday night dinners, Ami charmed me with her fashionably outré wardrobe, her warmth, her excellent English, and her bright sense of humour. Over time, I learned that she had been born in Liberia and brought back to Kankan only a few years earlier, as a young teenager, when her family fled the conflict there. We grew increasingly friendly, and eventually, Ami came to my home in the city centre. Until this point, I'd enjoyed friendly, easy interactions with my neighbours. Following Ami's visit with me, however, my devout Muslim neighbours shook their heads discouragingly; they tried to make me understand that 'the girl from the *boite*' was virtually the same thing as a prostitute, that she had loose and questionable morals, and that no good could come of my association with her.

Many children of Kankannais returnees, born abroad in large anglophone cities like Monrovia and Freetown, treat their new home with a combination of respect and ambivalence, well aware that they usually do not participate in the *solisee* and *kolakadi* ceremonies. Because of the ways that kinship and identity are reckoned within this region of the world, children are raised with a knowledge of the *fabara*, a place that connects them to their patrilineal relatives. Under some circumstances, they may have travelled to the *fabara* for a wedding or funeral; or they may have spent as much as a summer vacation with their father's relations. Often, though, children are raised in urban environments with little real experience of the homeland of their father, except through stories or the experience of visiting relatives. The challenges for acclimating to the *fabara* vary for male and female children returnees. Usually with other family members, they 'return' to a place they have never lived and do not know well.

A combination of circumstances (including political instability under former president Sékou Touré and the policies of structural readjustment) drove the fathers of these foreign-born children to leave Upper Guinea during the 1970s and '80s. The return of these families since the mid-1990s was also driven by regional factors, including guerrilla warfare and instability in the wake of crippled central governments. A few families in this study lived temporarily in refugee camps in Kissidougou, just south of Upper Guinea, as they attempted to make their way back to their natal Kankan.

Many children of Kankannais returnees share the experience of extensive travel within West Africa. Not infrequently, they reported feeling disappointment on 'returning' to the economically neglected region of Upper Guinea to live. For my fashionable friend Ami, aged ten at the time of return, her most vivid recollection of the newness of Kankan was the first night, when her mild mother struck her across the mouth after she asked for meat to accompany the common bowl of rice and sauce. That night, she was frightened to sleep in a house covered with a thatched roof. She wished for the bigger houses, cars on the street outside, the hum of the refrigerator, and the blue light of the television that she had known in Monrovia. In particular, Ami recalled that her gifted culinary mother did not know how to prepare the local foods after arriving in Kankan. The family ate pasta and meat in Monrovia. In Kankan, they felt 'reduced' to locally grown grains and they ate sauces made of leaves. It took Ami some time to get used to the new tastes.

Second-generation return migrants also comment on the newness of the visceral aspects of Islam when they first come to live in Kankan. As early as AD 1100, Upper Guinea was central to West African Islam as home to an Islamic university that was a sister to that of Timbuktu (Mali). Today, Kankan houses no fewer than 106 mosques, many of them built by donations from successful return migrants. During the call to prayer, one can stand in the market and hear *muezzin* from all directions. In Kankan, Islam is embodied in a daily rhythm and set of bodily procedures (Delaney 1990): the pace of the day is punctuated by the slowing down that accompanies ablutions and the collective experience of people falling to their knees on mats, always handily stored nearby. Children of returnees are often more familiar with Christianity than Islam. This was the case for my friend, Saran.

Saran's Liberian-born mother, who never married her father during the fifteen years he lived in Liberia, consciously raised the children in a Christian church and sent them to a Catholic school in Monrovia. Years later, when Saran's father decided to return with the children to the home of his first wife in Kankan, Saran's Liberian mother refused to come. Despite bitter arguments, Saran's father claimed custody of the children, and returned them all to the *fabara* as the culture considered that to be the most appropriate course of action. With the help of her younger brother, who supported the decision of Saran's father to assume full custody of his nieces and nephews, Saran's mother went to English-speaking Nigeria to begin a trading business. Now, Saran's mother visits the household in Kankan every few years, usually with a great many gifts that she affords through her successful business venture. Today, though Saran speaks with equal ease about Christmas and Ramadan, she remains aware that her household disturbs some Kankan neighbours for what is considered 'moral laxity,' due principally to children born out of wedlock to both herself and her older sister. As I came to know Saran better and better, she revealed that her Liberian mother's trading activities were actually the economic engine that drove the household. Her father, unemployed since the return to Kankan in 1997 and apparently chronically unskilled at business ventures, relied heavily on the remittances of his Liberian second wife, who was also remitting income to her own parents, still in Liberia. Additionally, like many return migrants, Saran's father went through a phase of deep Islamic piety upon his return to Kankan, and made the pilgrimage to Mecca with funds secured from Saran's mother's brother in Nigeria, a Christian who apparently hoped that the trip would generate some opportunities to expand his trading business. It appeared that the strategy had been unsuccessful, but it did allow Saran's father to spend large amounts of time at the mosque with other elite *hajji*, many of whom subscribe to fundamentalist Wahhabi principles and agreed that the illegitimate children of Saran and her sister should be most appropriately raised by the families of the fathers of those children.

Children of returnees may also initially find themselves at a linguistic disadvantage: though they usually speak English and Malinké, they do not speak the French required of them at school. The sudden loss of cultural competency on the part of a second-generation migrant produces intense alienation, and also profound reflexivity about their own unique identity (Ang 1994). Youssouf, a teenaged son of a returnee, grew up around other Mande speakers from Upper Guinea in a diamond-mining region of northern Sierra Leone. He articulated a key gendered dilemma for the children of returnees: while most of the male children *are* circumcised, most of the female children are not. Youssouf said he never reflected much on the potential differences between countries or places as a child, or the hardships he and his sisters might face in other places. Throughout his life, his father returned occasionally to Kankan to fulfil family obligations, including taking another wife who stayed in the household of his father. Youssouf himself did not see Kankan until 1998, when the family quickly fled the violence fuelled by the quest for diamonds by guerrilla factions. Youssouf said:

> Really, if my father was not Guinean, I would not come here. He obliged me to come and recognize Guinea as my home. When I first came here, I could speak Malinké, but not French. I had to learn it and people thought I was stupid! Guinea is my home country, but I did not always think it was a place with advantages. My father always gave me advice so that I could love Guinea. From the time in Sierra Leone, I had friends from other countries, and even other religions! I knew people who ate pork! But now, I am a man here, and finally I understand my father. I want to marry a woman

from here, so that she can educate my children in the right way to live. That is the most important thing for a man.

For female children, expected to be involved with household chores, the move to a more rural setting may reveal the limitations of 'foreign' training. Ami was a quick learner; she even remarked that sometimes, it was 'fun' to carry water and pound millet, but these activities were much more difficult for her mother and her older sister, Tigedanké, age twelve at the time of the move.

Female children of returnees also suffer the stigma of their foreign birth, which lingers in the imaginations of the local population. Conventional wisdom suggests that girls born abroad are more sexually promiscuous, especially because they are not excised. Even in cases when the operation has been conducted (in a hospital, for example), older Kankannais shake their heads and say that the operation alone is not sufficient; it must be coupled with the period of socialization that accompanies *solisee* and *kolakadi*. This was the case for Tigedanké, Ami's older sister, who found the relocation more challenging than her younger siblings. Three years after the family returned, Tigedanké 'fell pregnant' and was forced to marry. Her father refused to attend the marriage and reportedly recriminated himself for not insisting that his daughters undergo excision. Ami feels sorry for the life her sister leads: 'Now she has too many children and a husband who will not be faithful. It is not a good life for my sister.'

Transnational Parents, Ideal Children

My American brothers and I were raised by an Irish mother. Not infrequently, we were reminded of the relative wealth and advantage we had according to our mother's nostalgic recollections. When we first visited Dublin as teenagers, we were prepared for dour poverty and thick, heaving repression. Instead, we were mystified by the Celtic Tiger affluence that we saw: the music, the confidence, the healthful joy. Later, when I spent a year volunteering in Ireland, I met Nigerian asylum seekers who spoke openly of their concerns about raising their children in a land of such excess and impropriety. Excess and impropriety, I thought, in *Ireland*? The morally ambiguous Ireland they described for their children did not resonate with the buttoned-up-and-tidy Ireland my own mother often described to her American children. Not yet a parent myself at that stage, I began to think about this dilemma of raising children abroad, and wondered what it revealed about the nature of identity. Now the single mother of a biracial four-year-old in the American Midwest, I continue to puzzle this out, and I am beginning to suspect that this profoundly difficult dilemma of raising children strikes at the heart of what it is to be a person, what it is to be embodied, and what it is to be enculturated. We desire all the things we were taught to value for our children, we are transformed through our own experiences of transnationalism, and we are profoundly anxious about our ability to help guide our children through those choppy and unpredictable waters of 'becoming.'

I discovered that children born abroad often miss significant, communal experiences of 'Malinké-ness.' As discussed, in the *fabara*, bodily experiences stand as metaphors for transformative episodes within the life course of a Malinké person. While much recent African literature on migration deals with moral ambiguity by employing metaphors of consumption through witchcraft (Geschiere 1997; Masquelier 2001), eating and drinking (Bayart 1993; Mbembe 2001; Weiss 1996), or vampirism (White 1993), I focus on anxiety about raising 'proper' children and Malinké identity construction. The women I interviewed described acute anxiety about the identity and morality of their children while living abroad. I share the stories of two of these women here.

Aicha, a divorced returnee born in Kankan who spent decades in urban Mali, vividly remembered her concern that her three daughters would miss the excision ceremonies and thus lack the proper training that would eventually ensure their marriages to proper husbands. Aicha remained convinced that even though her daughters were well educated and could potentially marry 'modern' men in the city of Bamako, they could not make good matches with men of 'good quality' if they were not excised in the traditional way. Aicha insisted, 'Even if a man tells you that he does not care about such things, it is his mother who will insist that a daughter-in-law be properly initiated into womanhood.' According to Aicha, many old people feel that a *bilakòrò* daughter-in-law (one who is not excised) cannot be trusted to raise their grandchildren because she will lack the ability to raise them with strong moral principles. In this assertion, Aicha articulated the continued Malinké belief that marriage between two people, even modern city people, involves intergenerational obligation to the family of origin, and that parents continue to be crucial to endorsing marital appropriateness.

Because she deliberated so long about returning to Kankan for a traditionally sanctioned ceremony for her first daughter, Aicha missed the window for the hospital operation. (In Mali, doctors will perform the surgery on infants. Recent legislation has changed this, but it is likely that the procedure is still conducted regularly.) During her oldest daughter's early childhood, Aicha actively saved money for an elaborate party, anticipating an opportunity to return home to celebrate the ceremonies. With time, however, her oldest daughter began to fear the surgery and, wise to her mother's plans, refused to accompany her home to Kankan during the summer of her thirteenth year. Aicha's husband, a Malian, refused to persuade or punish the girl, believing that female excision was a woman's issue. Aicha sought an ally in her husband's mother and while her Malian mother-in-law agreed that the excision should be performed, she was reluctant to send a teenaged girl to a ceremony so late in her development. Finally, when her oldest daughter was fifteen, Aicha spent the money she had worked so long to save since she suspected that her daughter had already begun to 'play' with boys. She remains profoundly disappointed that her oldest daughter remains *bilakòrò* (unexcised).

However, for her second and third daughters, Aicha paid for the operation to be performed at the hospital. She explained:

> It made me sad for my daughters [to have the excision done in a hospital]. The *kablakoraya* [excision] was done without a *solisee*. I wanted them to have the celebration and prepare the food for them. But my mother was dead and my husband would not support me in sending them ... to have the operation.

Importantly, Aicha felt strongly that being a Malinké woman comprises more than just an act of surgery. For Aicha, gendered personhood must be culturally enhanced and communally acted. Surgery alone cannot produce a proper Malinké woman: the rituals must also be enacted by the group to contribute to the relational nature of the emerging person. From Aicha's perspective, her daughters missed this opportunity and could never become 'properly' Malinké.

Hawa, another Kankan-born woman who also lived in Mali with her Kankan-born husband, confessed to profound anxiety for her uncircumcised children while living abroad. However, instead of bringing her children (both sons and daughters) to the hospital in Mali as Aicha did, Hawa returned to Kankan to stay with her mother for a summer so that her children could be properly indoctrinated in the *solisee* and *kolakadi* ceremonies.

I came on the [boat, via the Niger River]. Oh, it took days! And when I came with Binta [oldest daughter], Madi was nursing, and he became very sick! I thought we would never get back here! But my mother arranged everything: we had the ceremony with the drummers and we danced all night. My husband's mother was present, too. She came, and she danced all night with us, even though she was very old. But wasn't it an obligation [to have the children circumcised]? It was expected by the family. It means Binta can marry a good man. She can expect a good husband.

Two circumstances mark Hawa's experience as different from Aicha's: first, Hawa's mother was still living. Her mother, still in Kankan, was able to make arrangements for the ceremonies, such as contacting drummers and making sure that the proper foods would be available for guests. She was also supported by her husband's mother, for whom age did not seem to be a deterrent for the appropriate observance of all-night dancing. Second, Hawa's husband, himself from Upper Guinea, assisted Hawa in the preparations for travelling back to the natal household to have the ceremony done at the appropriate time in the life course of each of the children. As attested to by Hawa's long and uncomfortable journey, few household resources could be spared to support such a return. However, both parents were willing to make the sacrifice for the sake of the proper initiation of their children into the roles of gendered persons.

Hawa returned with her husband to his natal household, the *fabara*, after twenty years abroad and she often claimed that all her children were grateful that their parents were able to return 'home.' The youngest of her six children also accompanied them to Kankan, a 'home' that she had never lived in for longer than a summer. Hawa pays for two of her older children to attend school in Bamako, asserting that the 'education system' is better in Mali and provides her children with significant advantages in the business world, but is clear that what she means by 'proper education' begins within the household.[7] For Hawa, as for many Malinké, the issue of 'education' must be divided between that of the mind and that of the body. A family may send a child abroad to be 'educated' to improve his or her chances at success, but the child must also have access to the 'education' of the body that comes only from observing the proper rites of passage and disciplining the body through frequent communal and cultural interventions, including excision.

Conclusion

This chapter has had a long gestation, but it began when I was jolted into thinking about my own daughter's transnational embodiment, and the implications of that for parenting in the United States with a Guinean man. Kiera's experience of 'self' is of course tied to the ways her father and I have contributed to her physicality. We note, with a great deal of pride, that her 'personhood' is a distinct hybrid that surprises us both: she switches easily between French and English (with random expressions of Malinké and some Irishisms, like 'rubbish'), she is comfortable eating rice and sauce with her hand, and when she was three and a medical technician drew a blood sample, she shouted at him indignantly, 'No! You're a bad man! That's my mommy's blood and she gave it to ME!' While I am not entirely clear on how she came to internalize this particular belief about her body, her ideas of self are clearly relational and contextualized to her early life with an African father and a Western mother.

Transnational mobility and the construction of identity, however, continue to be challenging terrain. Kiera's father, struck hard by both the abundance and the alienation of life in America, moved out of our home last fall. My greatest fears about parenting alone have become a reality. Recently, on a rainy afternoon that perforated my heart, my Guinean ex-husband launched into a lengthy and excruciatingly specific diatribe about my lack of 'education' (he repeated it in French, 'éducation'), and his perception that I was entirely unqualified to raise our daughter. He said, several times, that I lack the appropriate manners and social abilities to model proper gendered behaviour for our daughter, and he lamented the lack of role models. Given the last year or so of bitter arguments, this rare and unexpected emotional outpouring from a normally stoic man was less surprising than it was hurtful, exposing a mountain of insecurities and fears about my own competence as an adult. His judgment of my mothering, coming as it did at the end of a long, intense teaching semester on a conservative Midwestern campus, sank me into despair. My fingers went numb; I could hear my heart thumping. I longed for the supportive networks my husband and I had relied upon so joyfully during our early relationship in Africa, when the future was bright with promise. I sat on the floor heavily, broken, as he slammed away, and it was hours later when the wiggling body of my laughing, four-year-old daughter brought me back to myself. Foucault was right, I thought: the body is a dense transfer point of power.

The theorist in me asserts that in this difficult project of raising transnational children, the body must be situated as a product of specific social, cultural, and historical contexts that carry different obligations and expectations on two sides of a border (Silvey 2005), but ultimately that body must become a lived reality to be experienced by the 'person' within. Perhaps more than any other group, children born on a different side of a border from the place of their parents' birth experience a lived reality that may be fraught with tensions and ambiguities. Their bodies are simultaneously essential and social: they *have* bodies that they must discipline appropriately and they *are* bodies representative of the hopes and dreams of their parents. And crucially, those bodies must be called upon to interact with the bodies of others. Anthropologist Thomas Csordas (1999) argues that though children may establish a sense of self through embodied awareness, they do not necessarily have to achieve the classic Western mind–body split:

> On the level of perception it is not legitimate to distinguish mind and body. Starting from perception, however, it then becomes relevant (and possible) to ask how our bodies may become objectified through processes of reflection ... when both poles of the duality [mind–body] are recast in experiential terms, the dictum of psychological anthropology that all reality is psychological no longer carries a mentalistic connotation, but defines culture as embodied from the outset. (Csordas 1999, 36–7)

The experience of transnationalism is profoundly embodied, and the individual profoundly aware of that embodiment, as his or her physical body navigates and plunges through a variety of environmental circumstances, demanding that the individual process and respond appropriately to changes in climate, food, and comfort, while also posing continual emotional and intellectual challenges. A long period of the transnational experience must be devoted to learning – or relearning – appropriate responses to the environment. Suddenly, with this knowledge, I recall those afternoons spent with Hawa and Aicha, Youssouf, Ami, Saran, and Tigedanké to more fully appreciate what it was they tried to explain to me about their experiences at home and abroad, and to more fully understand their concern with properly gendered embodiment.

Happily, the young woman mentioned in the introduction to this chapter was granted asylum to remain in the United States. I spoke with her grateful Guinean mother by telephone, and we cried together. Last Saturday, Kiera competed in her first gymnastics meet, with a host of other bouncy only children, and her happy, shining face was quickly transmitted to computer screens on three continents. As the daughter of an immigrant, I wrote this article for my own daughter, and our story remains incomplete in many ways. I imagine that it is she who has the most to teach me as I continue to navigate this path of transnational parenting, and I look forward to the evolution of our lives together.

8 What Is an Autobiographical Author? Becoming the Other

JULIAN VIGO

'I know this and you don't' (Steedman 1991, 2). These words written by Carolyn Steedman regarding her 'unique' access to working-class experiences elicit anger, indignation, dialogue, or even silence from many readers of her autobiography. It seems to me that as readers of an autobiographical text, we assume a position of author-ity twice removed, subsuming a space in which the reading of the text becomes not merely an act of critical interpretation, a dialogic interaction with the author as other but a response of perpetual synthesis, an overlaying of our individual experiences, utterances, thoughts, a superimposition of our subjectivity between the lines, the pauses, the unspoken/unwritten, often obfuscating the subjectivity of the author. Yet inasmuch as autobiography is discussed in terms of a 'minority voice,' there seems to be a critical move here, if not altogether unconscious, to challenge and even negate Steedman's own minority voice, the paradigmatic basis for her autobiography, which is essentially her subjectivity, her knowledge, her experience, in order that we might interpret the text through our own empirical initiative, trying to make her individual experience our own, to know what Steedman claims we simply cannot.

I find that much of the interpretation of autobiography today tends to disseminate and disguise the individual utterance under the metanarrative of 'minority' in order that the 'majority' not only understand difference but also be able to assimilate these voices within the various master narratives of Autobiography – Working Class, Homosexual, Latino, Black, Woman, AIDS – rather than an autobiography of a woman raised in the working class, a homosexual man, a Latino youth, and so forth.[1] We contend that the experience of an other must somehow be equated to that of the masses, ourselves, or as Michelangelo

Antonioni's 1966 film *Blowup* or Don DeLillo's novel *Mao II* (demonstrate, 'This isn't a story about seeing the planet new. It's about seeing people new. We see them from space, where gender and features don't matter, where names don't matter. We've learned to see ourselves as if from space, as if from satellite cameras, all the time, as the same. As if from the moon, even. We're all Moonies, or should learn to be' (DeLillo 1991, 89).

As Jean-François Lyotard's postmodern condition confirms the breakdown of the master narratives of the world into a plurality of *petits récits* (1984, 60), Michel Foucault's panoptical structure embraces these *récits* as narratives of legitimation or of resistance, the 'antagonistic articulatory practices' (Laclau and Mouffe 1985, 128–37) whereby the utterance, including the resistant voice, is already inscribed within a certain monolith of knowledge/power. Thus, the individual narratives of experience end up legitimating their respective master narratives, orbiting the moons of the Gay, Black, or Chinese American experience. The individual voice is positioned, consumed, fetishized, and shelved in Women's Studies, for instance (because the author is a woman before an autobiographer), and her life/text becomes part of the master narrative of Minority Voice where we can confirm that we are really, after all, the same. Yet autobiography is never only about the self and instead tends to use self-narrative as a means of relating a story that is often identifiable within society at large.

In a general sense, autobiographies have also taught us that identity politics in the United States and Canada are deeply problematic discourses that do not hold any one single truth valid for a group experience at large. We may refer to Samuel Delany's 1988 autobiography of being queer and African American wherein the supposed contradictions of sexuality and race emerge. However, as we know from more recent autobiographies, there is no collusion between whiteness and homosexuality any more than between blackness and heterosexuality; hence any such perceived 'contradiction' is in itself problematic (i.e., that somehow homosexuality in the African American communities is less tolerated than in other communities). Moreover, many publications and – to a large extent – academic institutions have struggled with the notion that identity politics of the individual somehow correlate to that of the perceived group. Hence we see courses offered and texts published that deal exclusively with communities we call African American, Latino, Gay, and Woman, as if these nomenclatures really could speak to 'the group.' Even on an international level, as Hans Massaquoi's memoir, *Destined to Witness: Growing Up Black in Nazi Germany* (1999), demonstrates, notions of race or nation are simply not reducible to any monolithic formula of comprehensibility. His text chronicles his childhood in Germany during the Third Reich, but his 'minority' experience was one of assimilation rather than difference, which was sublimated in favour of the more relevant and temporal narratives of his childhood, namely his dream of joining the Hitler Youth as a 'German,' even as a second-class citizen by virtue of his colour. ('Neger, Neger, Schornsteinfeger!' ['Negro, Negro, chimney sweep!'] were the words he was taunted with as a child.) Eventually, Massaquoi's self-revelation critiques the very delicate, if not problematic, terrain of identity politics through his personal struggle of living between two worlds, the conflicting histories of nations in which he was brought up and lived (Germany, Liberia, and later the United States). Massaquoi's autobiography ultimately interrogates various discourses of race – fictions of racial purity and racial mixings – whereby identity is always postured after some ideal fiction of 'pure identity' and being.

Thus, as is true of writing autobiography, reading engenders an act of synthesizing difference negatively, so that we may see the differences, the mirror held up to our eyes in which identity, like difference, becomes the centrifugal force that separates the text within a preordained self/other, difference/resemblance context. Likewise, the experience of the 'minority' voice is exorcised and often revealed to be not so *minor*. In fact, autobiography often creates communal strength in shared experiences whereby the narratives of identity are not in the least unreal or 'minor' but instead transcend the silence of shame or invisibility while breaking barriers that are presumed to be common ground (i.e., race, gender, nationality) and creating newer spaces for identifying with an other. Because subjectivity presupposes that we can know and understand difference, we are thus empowered to use this perceived difference to sift the remnants, these fragments of resemblance. And in so doing, we name them. But does this naming make identity? Does identity have a full stop, or is it something always in progress, never fully representable? Massaquoi would certainly argue against pure identity, as his autobiography represents his life as a series of collapses between nation, race, time, and place. In fact, it is through Massaquoi's transnational life that he is able to put together the pieces of his identity; inasmuch as he is a product of the places he has spent his life, he cannot be interpreted on the level of pure identity nor through the looking glass of one particular nation or culture. Massaquoi's autobiography renders bare the fictions inherent within discourses of race and nation and like-wise attempts to corrode the possibility of seeing difference: he posits himself as that very difference, as the only black boy in his neighbour-hood who did not join Hitler's army.

So what is autobiography for the reader if not the ritual act of seek-ing both difference and similarity in the life of a person the reader does not know? Walter Benjamin writes that 'the fight of seeing resem-blances is nothing other than a rudiment of the powerful compulsion in former times to become and behave like something else' (1977, 333). Here, Benjamin suggests that representation and interpretation are the art of becoming the other. Furthering Benjamin's theory of the mimetic faculty, Michael Taussig asserts that the act of thinking is simply 'the ability to discern resemblance' (1993, 33) whereby one maintains, as Hegel contends, 'pure self-identity in otherness' (1977, 111–14). In this way, interpretation, like representation, is an act of becoming other, of utilizing difference to 'discern resemblances,' to attempt to view our-selves in the text, the text as mirror, ourselves as other. The act of read-ing autobiography embodies our desire to become the other, in part, to author, to identify, to understand, or perhaps, to resolve or better com-prehend emotionally.

This paradigm would necessarily change the act of self-representation, of autobiographical writing, and of reading an autobiographical text because implicit within the rendering of any given text is the monologic voice, the authorial intent, the subjective account of a life that the au-thor freezes, frame by frame, meticulously accounting for the past. Within the empirical foundation for analysing autobiographical dis-course we tend toward a reading of a 'life,' a narrative that mimetically, linguistically, attempts to mould some simulacrum of the past, a frag-ment of an existence, the memory of a hidden, deeper pain. We concern ourselves with the notions of 'betrayal,' narrative distance, and 'truth,' as if, living in the present, we were actually in a better, more objective position to discern the truth through the act of writing or reading auto-biography, inscribing a life onto a blank page or lifting it off the page through the steady strokes of our eyeballs sweeping the text.

In *Mimesis and Alterity*, Michael Taussig describes the act of storytell-ing that plunges the reader into a textual–temporal continuum where-by one is removed from the self and forced to become other:

> The fundamental move of the mimetic faculty taking us bodily into alterity
> is very much the task of the storyteller too. For the storyteller embodied

that situation of stasis and movement in which the far away was brought to the here-and-now (archetypically that place where the returned traveler finally rejoined those who had stayed at home). It was from this encounter that the story gathered its existence and power, just as it is in this encounter that we discern the splitting of the self, of being self and Other, as achieved by sentience taking one out of one-self – to become something else as well ... It is at this point that the freedom and foreboding bringing the traveler home insists on audience and attains voice, and it is here, in this moment of apprehension, that the listening self is plunged forward into and beyond itself. The storyteller finds and recreates this staggering of position with every tale. (1993, 40–1)

In this way, the autobiographer as storyteller is positioning herself within the metanarrative, her life, as well as within the discursive moment, the text. Through allochronic distancing, the author is both a discoursing subject and the object of her discourse. The author as self also seems to struggle with the 'truth' as a measure of her own honesty and representational authority (as if one static representation could ever be said to be truer than the next). The notion of temporality seems to be a point of disjuncture in which the subject represented maintains an ideal, historical status while the subject representing seems to imply, through the act of representing, a kind of renewed interest in the represented. The subject representing thus calls upon her transcendental powers to overcome the consciousness, the space, the time of the represented – to rise above (somehow) the faults, fears, confusions, or anger that she once embodied, once felt. The act of writing autobiographically implies, even asserts, a distance while overcoming antagonism, the feeling whose resolution is signified by the act of writing. Autobiography holds the writer captive, the simultaneous subject and object of her own desire for both a literary and extra-literary resolution.

Reading autobiography reproduces this same process allochronically, superimposing the reader's subject-ivity/object-ivity onto the text, as he/she meets the page in a different time and space, interacting with the subject/object of the autobiographer from the reader's own vantage point as object, the identified within the text, and as subject, the readerly, the scholarly, the identifier. From the title of this essay, 'What Is an Autobiographical Author?' I am taking cues from Foucault's essay 'What Is an Author?' in which he predicts the end of the author as an 'ideological figure' and a time when 'fiction and its polysemous texts will once again function according to another mode, but still with a system of constraint – one that will no longer be the author, but which will have to be determined, or perhaps, experienced' (1984, 119). I believe, then, that the function of the autobiographical author is one of transference whereby the act of experience is what ultimately authors the narrative, mediating the status of both the writer and reader in relation to the text in which they are in a sense both authors positioning their subject-ivity, the power of authorship, between their lives and the text. Just as in writing, reading autobiography is performance – we identify with the other of the author and thus 'discern the splitting of [our] self,' we 'stagger,' positioning our other within the sphere of the storyteller's other. Discarding the Hegelian purity of identity, we nonetheless realize our 'self-identity in otherness.'

The idea of authorship that I am questioning is ultimately linked to the power of mimesis. According to Taussig, when mimesis has 'sprung into being, a terrifically ambiguous power is established; there is born the power to represent the world, yet that same power is a power to falsify, mask, and pose' (1993, 42–3). We prize this power of falsification dearly in writing and reading autobiography – we are obsessed with notions of accuracy and truth that are threatened by the lapse of time between the moment experienced and the moment recounted. The idea of time, then, is to be held up as static, held up as atemporal in the sense that as narration, time is frozen, through the ontological position of the subject represented, yet synchronously fluid, temporal, through the act of storytelling, a narrative that reveals the pauses, the anger, the forgiveness. The use of time, like truth, is something that can be twisted, melted, yet consistently framed; it seems to locate the narrating subject in a more advantageous position than the subject narrated. It is the narrator who ultimately decides the 'truth,' or her 'truth,' and thus frames the route through which she overcomes the past and transcendentally marks the present as the position of author-ity, of mimetic supremacy, of her otherness.

Autobiography is the act of seeing resemblances, of becoming the other, through the mimetic faculty of language and through historical and cultural articulations. Autobiography can be viewed as the space between incongruent truths, such as Samuel Delany's two memories of his father's death: 'My father died of lung cancer in 1958 when I was seventeen. My father died of lung cancer in 1960 when I was eighteen. The first is incorrect, the second is correct.' Autobiography is the domain in which, as Delany states, the 'wrong sentence still feels ... righter than the right one' (1988, xviii). As historical or cultural criticism, autobiography is the space between 'difference and particularity,' what Carolyn Steedman calls the 'landscape' that serves as the sphere of mediation between the universal and the autobiographical 'I' (1991, 16). Autobiography is ultimately performance, a dialogical continuum cultivated within the symbiotic domain shared by the universal and the individual, the public and the private, the writer and the reader, the self and the other, the empowered and the disempowered. Autobiography is an act of terror that attempts, through allochronic positioning of the subject, to distinguish the true from the false and memory from experience, while reinscribing a new truth, a new story, a new memory. Autobiography engages both the living and the 'disquieting' souls of the deceased within the space of death (Hertz 1960, 35–7).

7 December, 1990

Dear Mother:

I just don't know where to start. You may have been told this is a priority search which means usually 'not good news.' In this case the news is not as bad as it sounds. Mother, I have 'AIDS,' yes this is in most cases deemed to be fatal. I feel with my strong mental convictions, this condition can be controlled and eventually beaten!

My desire to meet you has been strong ever since I knew I was adopted. My life is comfortable. I have a good pension. The majority of my life I have split between living in Windsor, Kitchener, Detroit, and New Orleans. My favorite city was New Orleans. I still like to return from time to time.

I am excited and scared [about meeting you]. This is something I have wanted to do for a very long time. I am listening to music to help me write this. My interests in music extend far beyond just listening. I love to play too. I am a somewhat accomplished trumpet player. My new interest is now keyboarding. I hope to hear from you soon.

Sincerely,
Mark

This is the letter that my brother Mark wrote to his biological mother after having been given a priority search by the Canadian adoption authorities. He found his mother in December 1990 and a year later, Mark died at twenty-four of complications resulting from AIDS. I have as many problems stating that he died 'of complications resulting from' AIDS as Delany has in stating his age and the year of his father's death. Whenever I say, 'My brother died of complications resulting from AIDS,' I wonder, did he die as a result of AIDS, from AIDS, or with AIDS? Then I realize that he, in fact, did not die because of AIDS. The space of death has made strange, in the true fashion of *ostranenie*, the concept of my brother's death and its relationship to AIDS, a narrative whose construction from the early 1980s as the 'gay disease' is still widely, monolithically understood within the context of sexual aberrance or (over) activity. For me, the silence, the invisibility of my brother's death, of his dying, cannot escape the underlying narratives of which AIDS was as much a symptom as were my brother's sexual practices, 'race,' family, and society. I will always understand his death in terms of AIDS as a physical metaphor (and I am not referring to Sontag)[2] for the underlying, much more terminal illnesses, diseases, rot that our current society represses in favour of more wholesome, straight projections of the nation, the community, sexuality, the family, and childhood.

For me, then, autobiography is the process of writing in which I use words, language, to grasp the past, restructuring my memories and pulling them into the present so that my childhood no longer seems so distant, so silent, so invisible. In his book *Close to the Knives*, David Wojnarowicz describes the power that language exerts upon memory and history: 'Words can strip the power from a memory or an event. Words can cut the ropes of an experience. Breaking silence about an experience can break the chains of the code of silence. Describing the once indescribable can dismantle the power of taboo. To speak about the once unspeakable can make the INVISIBLE familiar if repeated often enough in clear and loud tones' (1991, 153).

Like Wojnarowicz, I hope that my words will break a code of silence – rupture a taboo that bars access to certain experiences and memories in order that the invisible not only become familiar but also interact dialogically with the visible: that the 'once unspeakable' interrogate both the collective, homogenizing narratives of the majority and of the emergent minority voices that in their attempts to become less invisible, often become marked. They are often generalized, stereotyped, and then, easily forgotten. Autobiography is the movement between the domain of the visible and the invisible, the self and the other, in which identity does not hinge on the ability to represent but, as Peggy Phelan contends, 'Identity emerges in the failure of the body to express being fully and the failure of the signifier to convey meaning exactly.

Identity is perceptible only through a relation to an other – which is to say, it is a form of both resisting and claiming the other, declaring the boundary where the self diverges from and merges with the other' (1993, 13). Contrary to its conventional definition, autobiography is the performance of seeing and becoming the other in order to represent and reproduce ourselves to ourselves.

I was one of three children, adopted from different families and from various parts of Canada. Our parents remained married for only a short time after we were adopted. They divorced, and the next eight years were spent being pushed around from one parent or grandparent to the next until we moved in with my mother and her second husband, who then moved us all to New Orleans. I cannot really describe my child-hood, nor do I wish to. It just sounds like a cheap paperback ... (and so, too, may this). But that is the difficulty in describing one's life: once the words are committed to paper, or even to a screen, they no longer re-semble what they describe thirty years prior. The pain has slowly diminished and time has in many senses washed away the bitterness of the tortures to which I was subjected. Likewise, there are other mo-ments when I recount my childhood and I focus solely on a few surreal situations that involve Mennonites, a potato field, and Bible camps, stories our father told us of the Mogul empire, and I realize that my childhood was surreal in most every way. So I beg the reader to allow me the gaps, the non-narrative fogginess and the irreconcilable nature of descriptions here. What I can offer are blips, momentary glimpses into a life that I still cannot believe is my own.

I did not realize how terrible my childhood was until university, when I was with a group of friends watching the movie *Mommy Dearest*. Everyone started laughing when Joan Crawford pulled the 'Tina, bring me the axe' routine. I remember thinking about how my mother made us get up at 2:00 a.m. to clean the bathroom with toothbrushes, among various other acts that only an ABC Monday night movie of the week could truly depict. But is memory usually not like this? We tend to re-ject certain experiences in quick, jerking responses to some outside stimulus, some seemingly trivial moment that forces us to recognize, re-view, and restructure the past ... a past that childhood orders as nor-mal, a past that now appears unreal: the normality of syringes, cruel tasks, unthinkable punishments, fear. To see a mother smiling, the white, perfectly straight teeth shining, can be the most horrific, fore-boding vision in the world. In rewriting these moments, however, words cannot fully represent the experience: language cuts the yoke between memory and kitsch. One's life vaguely resembles another's; one's pain becomes everyone's; one's death is owned and maintained by a collective and often popularized narrative. Language becomes the commodity that lays itself bare to the masses' attempt to find the common denominator that makes it bearable, acceptable, twelve-step treatable, co-optable, saleable, and sometimes conquerable.

Growing up in Canada in the 1970s, adopted with other adopted siblings, living with a series of different parents until the age of ten, I experienced nothing but difference in our households: a blonde-haired sister, a black brother, an Indian father, a red-headed mother. Hence I gave the name 'the Benetton family' to my own family because we were just like the Benetton advertisements of the 1980s and 1990s, without the smiles. There were many moments before the age of ten when suddenly my sister, my brother, and I were sent upstairs to pack our bags to move in with a different parent (and new spouse) or a different set of grandparents. Our childhood was constantly and dangerously marginal from each of our births – from the egg producers and womb holders who gave birth to us (I dislike the term 'natural mother' as anyone can copulate and push out a child) to the Canadian government's mismanagement of our adoptions to parents who were clearly unfit, to our many composed families thereafter, most of whom did not care for us in the least. I recall mostly feeling tolerated as a child. So, our move from Canada to the United States was brought on by our father and second mother giving birth to *their* daughter. Within months we were shuttled off once again to our mother's and second father's home and we were moved to the United States shortly thereafter.

In many respects I realize that it was this transition from Canada to the United States that allowed for the final rupture of my family. Perhaps certain things became visible to my older sister and she felt suddenly able to leave home? And maybe this had an indelible effect on us all and each in our own time? Inevitably, we would all leave the home that was never really ever a home, able finally to recognize that we had never been *home*.

In 'The Politics of Location as a Transnational Feminist Critical Practice,' Caren Kaplan analyses Adrienne Rich's notion of the 'politics of location' that functions as a 'marker of Western interest in other cultures and signal[s] the formation of diasporic identities' (1994, 138). Emphasizing the dangers of Rich's theory, Kaplan goes on to warn about the aporia of historicizing and specifying difference in contemporary critical practices:

A politics of location is also problematic when it is deployed as an agent of appropriation, constructing similarity through equalizations when material histories indicate otherwise. Only when we utilize the notion of location to destabilize unexamined or stereotypical images that are vestiges of colonial discourse and other manifestations of modernity's structural inequalities can we recognize and work through the complex relationships between women in different parts of the world. A transnational feminist politics of location in the best sense of these terms refers us to the model of coalition or, to borrow a term from Edward Said, to affiliation. (1994, 139)

I find this passage relevant to the story I here present, this series of realizations with which we were faced as children in our passing through and confronting various families, not to mention our having to adjust to the quickly paced changes of our own races, sexualities, and nations. On the one hand we were assumed to be well treated coming from the home of a doctor, a wealthy family, and were perceived as having a family that 'loved us enough to adopt us.' All of New Orleans, and later Picayune, looked on at our parents in admiration of their courage for adopting three 'helpless' children, and the stereotype of the loving, selfless, wealthy family were all markers that actually kept the abuse coming. Indeed, the signs served to deflect all criticism and even blind the onlookers, who saw mostly the plasticity of a loving family, never the putrid stench of abuse rotting, simmering beneath the surface.

It was this relationship between various familial and societal abuses and transnationalism that served as the means for us to accept the conditions to which we were exposed. Changing countries simply provided another form of destabilization that went perfectly hand in hand with the bizarreness of being bumped from Mennonite country in southern Ontario to Alcoholics Anonymous and Parents without Partners meetings in New Orleans, and to sitting on school buses listening to other children either lash out at me with racial slurs, or worse, assume I was white and feel comfortable sharing their bigotry with me (thinking that I would simply nod my head in agreement). The domestic abuse seemed to fit right along with the social abuse of racism in the south, and each violence bled into the other to such a degree that everything began to feel completely normal, although I felt that something was not right, as did my brother and sister. Hence the sense of not belonging (I did not understand many of the expressions used in the deep South; when a classmate told me to 'scoot over,' I just stared), the idea of coming from a place that was not 'here' ushered in a sense

·of normality all around because both my person and my everyday life were out of place, even unevocable. Kaplan argues that stereotypes of identity are problematic because they presuppose knowledge and certain constructions of identities that can only really be known by the subject herself. Yet when this theory is translated from a feminist paradigm to the autobiographical/transnational narratives of children, there are simply no models to follow, no stereotypes to mimic, especially because children are still considered objects – not subjects – in their own lives in most parts of the world, including the United States and Canada. Acknowledging psychological abuse is still a legal hurdle that most governments have yet to confront, and children are expected to be the only interpreters of difference when they have barely the experience to recognize their own thoughts and experiences.

For instance, Mississippi's laws recognize children who run away because of abuse, but if the abuse is psychological the child will be treated as a delinquent by the system and eventually be returned to the parents because mental abuse is not grounds for labelling a 'child in need of supervision' and thus permitting the court system to intercept parental abuse.[3] In Mississippi, as in most parts of the United States and Canada, children who are mentally abused go unacknowledged, their parents do not face redress, and the abuse continues until these children grow up and eventually leave their 'homes.' When faced with youth courts, these children are often labelled as 'lacking discipline,' 'disrespecting their parents' – even 'wilful' – and they are eventually handed over to the very people who have been abusing them. So what Kaplan's critique of a 'politics of location' does for an understanding of the polemics of 'first' and 'third' world feminisms, I assert can also be applied to the judicial paradox of 'good child'/'bad child' that is often at work in child welfare cases across North America and across many geographical boundaries. Many unmarked identities are seemingly non-existent simply because nobody speaks up for the children whose voices are silenced by such facile, Manichean schemes of 'justice.'

It was moving between geographical boundaries that over time allowed my siblings and me to see the reality, the horror, of our everyday lives. In thinking of the word *transnationalism*, one can easily conjure the idea of a physical moving between two spaces. However transnationalism for us as children meant not only moving between Canada and the United States as a physical experience but also as the metaphorical and symbolic marker of a childhood in which we were forced to change everything quickly: we were expected to become adults overnight, taking on adult responsibilities, and even more swiftly we were ushered from one home to the next for fear that our presence as the 'unwanted children' would scar the biological fantasies of each passing parent as they gave birth to their newer and more 'legitimate' children. Moreover, the constant change of geographies kept us from having any constant childhood friends, and thus from interacting with parents who would have been shocked at our treatment at home, from having witnesses to decry the actions of our 'keepers.' And so transnationalism became our new 'skill' – we were able to adapt as quickly as we packed our bags and the specificity of location took on less and less importance as we became masters of adjusting to new schools every six months. Eventually this translated into the transnational affiliations that I would later have to explain when my classmates in New Orleans inevitably asked me if I knew 'how to speak Canadian.' 'Yes, I do,' I would answer. Every question had an answer and it did not necessarily have to make sense.

Adapting to our surroundings – a new family, a new country, new abuses – served in both positive and negative ways. First, we were taught to accept everything that came our way as 'pure difference,' and we never questioned the abnormality or unhealthiness of the situations into which we were put; abuse became normal to us because everything else was equally odd, and thus equally acceptable. Conversely, after years of moving around and accepting abuse as 'normal,' we were exposed to many stories of people whose childhoods (even those described as 'horrible') were far healthier than our own. Transnational passages thus obscured the strangeness of new abuses while also forcing us to see up close new situations that were markedly different from and healthier than our own.

Soon after moving to the United States, my sister Laura ran away at the age of fourteen. She kept running away every time the police brought her home for several years thereafter. I was ten the first time. Mark was nine. From the time my sister ran away, Mark and I used to plan to run away together. Being so young, we were not quite sure what was wrong with our parents – we did not have the language to name it all – but we were aware of being incredibly unhappy as children. To be totally honest, we were never really children; we were child slaves. My mother fancied herself a woman of high society despite her and my father's addiction to alcohol and various illegal and legal drugs, including Vicodin, which reigned high on their list. Because they were constantly 'indisposed,' we were left to take care of everything. It was a magically and torturously real childhood: a father who would squander his salary on drugs, alcohol, and horse racing bets while quoting us stories from Indian history, telling us about when, as a young dental student in Mumbai, he cleaned legendary film actor Raj Kapoor's teeth, recounting stories of his time in Birmingham, Alabama, when he witnessed the civil rights movement as a young immigrant to the United States, and eventually sitting us down in front of the television to watch *Roots* as he screamed in Gujarati at each scene of cruelty. (Later he assigned us a series of books to read including Martin Luther King's and Mahatma Gandhi's auto-biographies.) Those were the good moments. But most of our waking moments were spent in the service of our parents' needs: going to the store to pick up prescription drugs or six-packs of Dixie beer, or both, cleaning, cooking daily meals day, and taking care of their biological children, who were permitted to eat freely while we were given older food, less food, and only powdered milk. It was the kind of childhood that I found only in Dickens and other cruel narratives of the sort. It even seems unreal to describe it here simply because in the almost thirty years that have transpired since I left home, of all the hundreds of people whose personal horror stories I have heard, I have rarely heard a story that matched mine in terms of sheer cruelty. Was it so surprising when Laura ran away from home? Not really. I remember picking up the telephone and hearing a police officer tell my mother that my sister had been arrested for 'solicitation.' I remember thinking that she must have been selling Girl Scout cookies door to door with-out a licence, as I had seen those signs often on neighbouring homes to discourage door-to-door salespeople: 'No Soliciting Please!'

Less than a year apart in age, Mark and I usually attended the same schools. Fearing our mother, we dreaded coming home and would pro-long the school day as much as possible. I grew to love school so much that the last day of school before summer vacation I always cried hys-terically. Mark, on the other hand, hated classes but managed to escape home through band rehearsals and trumpet lessons. During the sum-mer, we had no reprieve from our chores because of the school day. Summer meant that we were full-time parents to our younger siblings and servants to our parents. This was the hardest time of all as we were routinely kicked out of the house for forgetting to unload the dishwash-er, or even more typically, given lines to write. 'Writing lines' as our mother liked to call it, went something like this: writing 20,000 times 'I will not forget to take out the garbage on Tuesday night.' Our week-ends were often spent in our rooms on such literary tasks. And if too much white space showed at the end of the line, our mother would have us add 'Mother' – always capitalized – to the sentence just to give us one more word to write.

Quite often, on the way home from school we would be harassed by neighbourhood kids who ran around yelling 'Zebra' and 'Nigger' at us. One of Mark's natural parents was black, and with my very short, curly hair, nobody ever thought we were adopted from different families. The curly hair, the darker skin, and our Indian father marked us. To everyone we were both visibly black. Soon, Mark stopped telling certain friends that he was black, which got us into even more uncomfortable situations. His white friends who thought he was white and his black friends who thought he was black collaborated one day and beat both of us up. Although being black was problematic for us, being both black and white proved even more dangerous. I was thrilled when I started middle school the next year: I would have one year of invisibility before my brother came along. Eventually I was able to get into a high school that his grades prevented him from entering. At this school I was viewed as white. Today, my memory of passing as either 'black' or 'white' is quite haunting: the visible inscriptions that society marks on the body through language necessitates the individual's choice to accept or reject a pure race – one is compelled to be either 'black' or 'white.' My brother's insistent reconstruction of his race affirms, in much the same way as Adrian Piper's video installations demonstrate, that to understand race as skin colour, the visible, is to be 'cornered' into a static, homogeneous identity.

My mother got divorced from our second father and married yet again, so we moved to Picayune, Mississippi. The family and racial troubles grew even worse. In Mississippi, our mother felt freer to discipline us publicly; she rented us out to neighbours to clean their houses in addition to the domestic chores we had to do at 'home,' a huge estate with hundreds of pine trees on it. So Mark and I were always raking pine needles, especially on Mississippi's hot summer days. Our mother would lie next to the pool and yell down to us, 'You missed a spot!' pointing as if we could see where she was indicating from fifty yards away. After about a year in Mississippi, Mark finally did run away. He was fourteen at the time. He did not have any friends to turn to; he was ostracized by the community because he was not white. And because we came from a wealthy family nobody in the town thought we were abused. Our mother worked with Nancy Reagan's 'Just Say No' program in Mississippi; our second father was a doctor; our third father a psychologist. To neighbours, we could not have been abused. Mark left one morning without saying a word to me. He returned a week later and told me that he had run away after our third father made racist comments to him about the 'nigger ducks,' referring to the American Black Ducks on the lake behind our house. When my mother found out Mark had returned, she called the police to arrest him and, as was typical in small-town Mississippi in the 1980s, the police obliged. When they released my brother the next day, my mother refused to pick Mark up, telling the police to make him walk home (a mere ten miles) because it would 'teach him a lesson.' Instead Mark hitchhiked back to New Orleans and I would not see him again until five years later.

I finished high school early because I had transferred from a college prep school in New Orleans to a pretty pathetic high school in Mississippi. I had no courses left to take after my third year except meat cutting. Owing to my mother's interference and her determination to keep me near, I went to college fifty miles from her house. And she told me a few days before I left home, 'As you know, we are perfectly capable of paying for you to go to school, but we don't want to.' I went back home that Christmas vacation so she would co-sign a student loan, but because I had received a B in a history class, she locked me in my room for three weeks. I left to finish the spring semester and never returned. College became my refuge. I took on several part-time jobs and even joined the army and became a military intelligence officer. I buried myself in my studies and my military service, and throughout college I slowly came to see the horror of my childhood.

Yet the knowledge that my mother was a despicable person never completely sank in until I found out what Laura and Mark had done in New Orleans. What they did was to escape home. I, by comparison, was somewhat comfortably gaining refuge from the past within the covers of books, in battle dress uniform, jumping out of airplanes, planning my future. I remember my mother calling me up one day at school to say that Mark was working as a busboy in a New Orleans restaurant. She added, 'But you know what he was doing before ... He's going to get AIDS, I bet.' The excitement in her voice was as if she were guessing the answer to a *Jeopardy* question, waiting to hear the winning bell.

When I returned from a stay in Central America in 1989, I found out that my mother had hired detectives to find me. I had painstakingly distanced myself from every member of my family. I did not want to be in contact with my mother, my past. I received a phone call from a friend in Mississippi telling me that my mother had called her to say that my brother had a brain tumour and to ask for my phone number. I laughed, knowing that my mother was lying. My friend called me back the next day and said, 'No, he doesn't have a brain tumour. He's sick.' The tone in her voice, the simplicity of the phrase 'He's sick' ... I knew the 'sickness' ... I had no choice but to call my mother to find out where Mark was.

She picked up the phone and with her newly cultivated southern accent said, 'Hi, how's your hair?'

'My hair?'

'Yes, your hair ... Is it short? Long?'

'It's long,' I said. I will never forget the sound of her drivelling on about her nose job, face lifts, oil wells somewhere in Texas. I got the necessary information from her and flew to Canada to see Mark. Mark with tubes, potassium, and more drugs than I care to remember, than I can remember. Mark recovered from the spinal meningitis he had in the fall of 1989 and was released from the hospital. I visited him almost every month and we spent most of our time filling in the past, playing chess and talking about our mother or, as he referred to her, Sheila. Mark had a much better sense of humour about her than did I. He laughed when he recounted the story of her hair turning green in the swimming pool and he revelled in the thought of her face lifts causing her jaw to snap open whenever she sat down.

Mark talked openly of his experiences on the streets of New Orleans describing to me in depth the bars and baths in the French Quarter, the men he would pick up, the men he would fuck and get fucked by. Crisco, towels, blow jobs, rimming, animals, old, fat, bald, uncircumcised men. At times he was able to avoid prostitution by running drugs, but usually he ended back on the streets. He returned to Canada when he was sixteen. Even though he was a prostitute, he never denied his attraction to both men and women. I always felt guilty about visiting my brother only once a month ... I guess I still do feel terribly guilty. I was in college studying biochemistry ... My brother was rolling over for money. I had no idea how he survived until I was nineteen. I had found my escape: books. I used to avoid my family by going into my closet and reading, reading everything, entering the world of words, words that eventually captured my pain and diverted it into something with which I could better understand myself ... theory is personal, words are personal, words are pain. Even these words that I so reluctantly type are words of privilege, circumstance, resistance to not be like my mother, not be like my brother. I escaped both fates, yet I embody the resistance to both, the phallic and the symbolic Mother. I identify with both. I flow fluidly between the self and other, and am left staggering between the two.

There are so many things that amaze me about my brother ... even now. Yet as I was transcribing tapes he had left, I found myself angry with him. He said, 'I didn't agree with my mother's way of doing things ... and I chose to leave. I wasn't comfortable with her rules and it was my choice not to stay there ... Being a runaway at thirteen, I experienced a lot of street life. But, I always thought I could do it my own way and that I could make my own mistakes. I feel that I'm a strong person because of it.'

Mark took complete responsibility for what he did, not for what happened to him. I cannot believe this! I do not want to. He left me cassettes that record what he felt and thought at the end of his life, and in one of them he talks about New Orleans as if he loved it there. He mentions that it was his choice to leave home – that he was not 'comfortable' with her 'rules'? He speaks of these 'rules' as if there were allowances, as if there were little or no fear, as if he had never written 'I will not forget to unload the dishwasher' 20,000 times. How can he love the place of our childhood, of his prostitution? How can he take control of the passive voice, turning it into the active, demonstrating his decision? He even states that he was thirteen, not fourteen, when he ran away from home. More than this, he talks of forgiving my mother! Forgiving her? I have had reinvented JFK dreams of gunning her down in her First Baptist Church. I created her death while living in South America. All my friends there would ask me about my family, and I once tried to say, 'No hablo con mi madre, ella esta loca.' But they simply looked at me as if craziness and cruelty were not sufficient excuses to break that eternal cordus umbilicus, so I soon learned to create accidents, worldwide tragedies. 'My mother died on the Avianca flight from Caracas,' I say. They look astonished. I go into further detail, explaining the wrecked body of the jet, the burned bodies, and finally, my mother, charred to the bone, screaming out for help. I always get too engrossed in the details of her death ... to the point of pleasure. I soon realize that the family is looking at me in horror because I am smiling. Mark was able to demystify our mother, to refer to her by name, 'Sheila,' and after finding his natural mother, to replace her with his newly found, newly born mother. My brother was able to create his mother, his sexuality, his race, his life, his death. I saw Mark dying because of the situation we were put into. I simply do not see choices, only recourses, desperate necessities. My brother, however, empowered himself with the ability to act and not to be acted upon; even if it meant forgiving my mother, accepting and authoring his sexuality, his race, and the physical manifestation of AIDS. My brother was able to accept what I reject, what I loathe ...

Just as we cannot accept the monolithic construction of truth, of the *visible*, neither can we accept any monolithic representation of the *invisible*. We cannot understand difference as singular but must recognize the plurality of voices, bodies, and lives that intersect, move, and shift. For many of us know how the invisible has a curious way of inhabiting a very large, a very crowded, a very homogeneous, and a far too often accepted *closet*. Autobiography is the interactive terrain for the polyphony of individual utterances, a multitude of minority voices that cannot be aggregated into one identity, one easily acceptable or dismissible whole. Autobiography is the absolute space of difference whereby the autobiographer, the simultaneous subject and object of her own discourse, uses language to reformulate not only her own experience but also the experience of others. The mimetic faculty engenders, according to Taussig, a 'terrifically ambiguous power ... to represent the world' as well as the power 'to falsify, mask, and pose' (1993, 42–3). Autobiography could therefore be viewed as the act of taking the 'indescribable' aspects of experience and evoking the discontinuities, the antagonisms, and the closure – of representing the difference within difference. No longer can we be strangers to our past, our sexuality, our race, our desire, ourselves. No longer can we be strangers to the voices of others. We are the other. Or, as Diamanda Galas's tattooed fingers read, 'We are all HIV+.'

Until Mark's death, I had a recurrent dream for more than two years: he and I are in his dark hospital room, he on his bed, and I on another bed pulled next to his. The tube running from his aorta is not hooked up to an IV but is attached to me, to my aorta. We touch each other's hands and stare at each other's bodies. I stopped having these dreams in February 1992. It was then that I learned of Mark's death. I had asked him not to tell anyone my phone number or address for fear that my mother would contact me again; thus, no one could reach me when Mark entered the hospital. Mark, delirious from the pain and drugs, thought I was in Africa, a place we talked of escaping to as children. I found out he had died and I was not there. However, his natural mother and I became acquainted after Mark's death and she described the whole scene to me:

Mark was very quiet that night. Then abruptly, a few hours before he left us, he sat up and drank apple juice and ate ice cream. He laughed and talked with us and all of a sudden, he got really quiet and reached out. There was nobody in the direction of his arm. I think he saw angels, the other side. Then he laid back down. Visiting hours were over and we told him we would come back tomorrow. He died a half hour later ... But you should be glad that you weren't there. He was wearing a diaper and every time they changed it they made us leave the room. They kept it dignified. He didn't want us to see him like that.

And so I was spared the absolute space of my brother's death. The shit. The diaper is the dignity, the space that separated my brother's death, his own death, from the rest. The shit is what the diaper covers up: the hidden narratives of family, racism, prostitution. They did not see the shit.

I had a different dream in June of that same year. It is like a film: Mark and I are in a room and I am holding him in my arms and he says, 'I'm going to die.' No, it is not over till the fat lady sings, I assure him. He replies, 'But she's singing.' Cut. A big, fat woman standing next to a mahogany piano, sings one note, strung out over several seconds, several lifetimes. Cut. I am holding my brother, lifeless. I scream over indefinite, immeasurable time. Cut.

My brother died of complications resulting from AIDS in February 1992. My brother died from complications resulting from our family, racism, and child prostitution in February 1992. The first is correct. The second is equally so. What is this autobiographical space for me? Is it where I cannot accept his death, the death that my brother accepted, the death that was his alone to construct, his autobiography? Is it where I reject the categorization of AIDS as a cause and instead locate it as a symptom of his death? Am I not attempting to alter his voice, to see the resemblances of our shared experience, to enter into his experiences, which I can really never know, to identify and name what was underneath his diaper, his narrative, his 'space of death,' the only thing separating his death as he wanted it, as he constructed it, from the death that I have just violently created for you, my own?

9 Transnational Identity Mappings in Andrea Levy's Fiction

ŞEBNEM TOPLU

As the world has attained a multiplicity of cultures coexisting within the same society, transnationalism has become one of the notions that describes the identity re/construction of diasporic, multicultural selves. As Steven Vertovec states, several disciplines describe the meanings, processes, scales, and methods of transnationalism in a wide variety of ways, suggesting several clusters or themes by way of 'disentangling' the term: transnationalism as a social morphology, as a type of consciousness, as a mode of cultural reproduction, as an avenue of capital, as a site of political engagement, and as a reconstruction of 'place or locality' (1999). Susheila Nasta, in her introduction to *Writing across Worlds*, maintains that 'writing has always been a form of cultural traveling, a means of transporting words into other worlds, of making crossings and forging connections between apparently conflicting worlds' (2004, 6). Regarding the transnationalism as a means of reconstructing the social and geographic space; the clash between the homeland and motherland, this chapter explores the rebuilding of multinational selves in England, focusing on family and identity mappings; that is, the transnational sensibilities of the protagonists in Andrea Levy's fiction.

Born to Jamaican parents in England, Andrea Levy is the author of *Every Light in the House Burnin'* (1994), *Never far from Nowhere* (1996), *Fruit of the Lemon* (1999), and *Small Island* (2004). Like the work of many other second-generation multicultural British writers, Levy's first three novels delineate the hybridity and identity crises of Jamaican-English multicultural personae that arise because of their dark skin colour and cultural origins. The Jamaican families Levy depicts are of two successive generations: the diasporic parents who arrived in England in the

1950s, the so-called *Windrush* generation,[1] and their sons and daughters. Despite their immigrant parents' struggle to survive, and their
own constant attempts to be considered as British-born citizens, Andrea
Levy's young female protagonists are not exempt from racial prejudice
and hostility, which create the context for their own form of transnational sensibility, of living on shifting borders. With the exception of
Small Island, Levy's books give voice mainly to young adult protagonists who experience both internal conflicts with their transnational,
diasporic parents and external tension created by the host society. Levy
shifts her style in her last novel, *Small Island*, which is narrated poly-
vocally by Jamaican and English couples without children, the former
epitomizing the survival of immigrant Jamaicans in London during
and after the Second World War. Regarding postimperial, multicultural
Britain, James Procter argues that there are crucial differences in the
etymologies of 'black' in the United States and the United Kingdom,
because in the United States the term has 'conventionally referred to a
particular "racial" community (African-American)' (2003, 5) whereas in
the British context '"black" has been translated as a political rather than
racial category' (2003, 6). As Jim Pines defines it, in terms of filmic discourse over the 1980s, black Britishness represents 'a complex set of
relations ... which are not necessarily structured as binary oppositions
– e.g., black or British – but rather relations which are much more subtle
and complex in their construction' (2001, 63). Within this context,
Procter notes that 'any analysis of postwar Britain needs to give careful
consideration, not just to the terms "black" and "British," but to the
complex relationship between them' (2003, 5), a position that I believe
describes the ambivalence of transnational identities.

Within the complex relations of multicultural society, family, especially black parents, play an essential role in the child's adaptation to
the host culture. At the same time, miscegenation operates in a diverse
and more complex pattern that requires analysis beyond the scope of
this essay. Asserting the significance of the family in his 'The Negro and
Psychopathology' ([1956] 2004), Frantz Fanon contends that in Europe
the idea of family represents a certain fashion in which the world presents itself to the child. Fanon contends that there are close connections
between the structure of the family and the structure of the nation, and
hence the family is a miniature of the nation. Because children emerge
as the 'shadow' of their parents, they find themselves among the same
laws, the same principles, and the same values. In Fanon's equation, a
'normal' child who has grown up in a 'normal' family will be a 'normal'

man' and 'there is no disproportion between the life of the family and the life of the nation' (202). Nevertheless, Fanon adds that we observe the opposite in 'the man of color': a 'normal Negro child, having grown up within a normal family, will become abnormal on the slightest contact with the white world' (202–3). This significant analysis may help to clarify the inner tension of the transnational identities that exist within the spaces between questions and answers. Fanon supports his argument by giving examples from Freud's psychoanalytic theories of psychic traumas repressed in the unconscious and applies them to the case of the black man in colonized countries where 'a drama [has been] enacted everyday' (203). Consequently, Fanon claims that as long as he remains among his own people, the 'little' black 'follows very nearly the course as the little white,' but if he goes to Europe, he will 're-appraise his lot' (203). Fanon states that the 'Negro' will feel 'different from the other people' because he is 'made inferior' (205) and has to choose between his family and European society; 'the individual who climbs up into society – white and civilized – tends to reject his family – black and savage – on the plane of imagination' (205) and so the schema becomes

Family   Individual ← → Society

It is possible to regard Fanon's contention as parallel to the notion of transnationalism in the sense of the reconstruction of self along with the reconstruction of space in an alien culture: having to adapt both the self and its perception of society. In this sense, the position of the diasporic individuals – in other words, the location of transnational parents in Britain and their yearning for their British-born children to adapt to the mother country yet simultaneously maintain their Jamaican culture – is a highly complicated and problematic phenomenon. Consequently, the ambivalence of identity specific to the generation of 'coloured' children in multicultural Britain contains deep complexities during the conceptualization of their identities, which inevitably lack fixity compared to those of their diasporic parents.

The linearity of history is in reverse in Levy's last novel. *Small Island* projects the early diasporic life in 1950s through the black protagonists Hortense and Gilbert. Hortense is raised in Jamaica by relatives, never meeting her black Jamaican mother or her white English father. As a colonized British subject, she becomes a teacher and longs to go to England and have a better life. Gilbert is a black Jamaican. He admires a Royal Air Force show parade in Jamaica and, obeying the call of the

Mother Country (England), joins up to fight Hitler. He is stationed at Falmouth, England, and instead of training as a pilot becomes a truck driver. While he wears an air force uniform, however, he finds that he is not much discriminated against for being black. When the war ends he is released from the army and returns to Jamaica, but he longs to return to England. Hortense offers to give him the money to return as a civilian, on condition that he marry her and send for her after he settles down. Gilbert accepts the deal and goes to London, where he realizes bitterly that life is completely different for a black civilian. Much like the characters in Samuel Selvon's *The Lonely Londoners* (1956), the Jamaicans in this novel form a community and try to support each other. The only white person to give Gilbert a home is Queenie Bligh, who met him in England during the war when he was an officer and needs to rent her rooms to immigrant Jamaicans to survive the postwar years because her husband, Bernard, is missing in India. While Gilbert tries to cope with odd jobs and a filthy room, his wife, Hortense, arrives with fresh hopes, only to be shocked by decrepit London after the Blitz. Levy projects in Hortense's colonized Englishness a mock evocation of empire: first her perfect English, the received pronunciation, is not comprehensible for the common English; second her manners and the way she dresses (very properly with white gloves and a hat) are an ironic and appalling signifier of mimicry for beholders. That Hortense is a clear outsider, however, becomes evident from the fact that she is not allowed to teach despite her Jamaican British school diploma. In the end, their desperate situation is somewhat ameliorated by the addition of a black adopted baby (Queenie's illegitimate child by another black RAF officer), and a better home to live in by the help of Gilbert's Jamaican friend Winston.

Levy in a sense creates what I would like to call a 'mock-transnationalism.' Jamaican culture is a mixture of the British culture imposed by the colonizer, (which eradicated the indigenous past in terms of language, education, and religion) and remaining indigenous elements such as types of food. The single Jamaican cultural artefact that Gilbert yearns for during his RAF years is the spicy food, a marker of transnational feeling because language, education, and culture have become a mimicry of British culture. Gilbert humorously points out,

> This was war. There was hardship I prepared for – bullet, bomb and casual death – but not for the persecution of living without curried shrimp or pepper-pot soup. I was not ready, I was not trained to eat food that was prepared in a pan of boiling water, the sole purpose of which was to rid it

of taste and texture. How the English built empires when their armies marched on nothing but mush should be one of the wonders of the world. I thought it would be combat that would make me regret having volunteered, not boiled-up potatoes, boiled-up vegetables – grey and limp on the plate like they had been eaten once before. Why the English come to cook everything by this method? Lucky they kept that boiling business as their national secret and did not insist that the people of their colonies stop frying and spicing their food. (Levy 2004, 125–6)

Gilbert's genuine transnational criticism of English food is eradicated by Levy in the following chapters, however, whereas Hortense's mock transnational very perfect English language and appearance is pursued throughout. Gilbert adapts to England as a civilian, and shortly after Hortense arrives, he asks her to cook egg and chips. When she fails to know what chips are and cooks something inedible, they have a row, which ironically reveals that Gilbert has finally got used to the English food he has detested, yet, on the other hand, also discloses that although Jamaica was colonized in every other cultural way, the food has remained genuine. Apart from the food, though, throughout the fiction, the husband and wife's genuine transnational feeling is projected through their understanding of one another's feelings and frustrations, and through their unity in the struggle against hardship and discrimination.

In her debut novel, *Every Light in the House Burnin'*, Levy's narrator, Angela, is the fourth child of the Jamaican Jacobs family. Her narration shifts between her childhood memories as an eleven-year-old and her impressions as a young graduate of art college, projecting ambivalence toward her siblings and mother in general and her father in particular. In Levy's second novel, *Never far from Nowhere*, she gives alternating voices to two sisters, Vivien and Olive, three years apart in age and distinctly different colours. Fatherless at an early age, the narrative evolves from the sisters' coming of age and generational conflict with their single mother. Their colour difference and the related racial discrimination tear apart the lives of the sisters, causing them to take divergent approaches to life. Olive, who is darker, leaves school, marries an Irish immigrant worker while five months pregnant, divorces shortly thereafter, lives as a single mother with her daughter, Amy, is abused by racism, and finally lives as a prostitute. Vivien, the much lighter in colour, receives her A levels, becomes a successful art student, and is accepted by white middle-class English society. Levy follows the same trend in *Fruit of the Lemon*, in which she gives voice to Faith

Jackson, also an art school graduate, who leaves her parents' home, works at the BBC, and lives with her white friends, believing herself to be one of them. Her acceptance by society is revealed by and large as a false assumption, which leads Faith to an identity crisis in the first half of the novel and results in her journey to Jamaica in the second half. Similarly, Vivien receives a degree and adapts to the society but achieves only financial security instead of true happiness.

Before mapping family relations in Levy's fiction, I note a recurring theme in the novels that deserves attention: majoring in art. Levy reveals her ironic choice with the comment of Faith's art teacher at the degree show in *Fruit of the Lemon*: 'Your work has an ethnicity which shines through ... A sort of African or South American feel which is obviously part of you. Don't you find that exciting, Faith?' to which Faith remarks, 'As I was born and bred in Haringey I could only suppose that I had some sort of collective unconscious that was coming from my slave ancestry' (31). Levy's selection of the word 'slave' instead of 'black' is likewise ironic and is testimony to Faith's awareness of the racialized category in which her teacher's comment places her. At the same time, Levy's characters' accomplishments in the British educational system serve as a sign of their assimilation to British culture. As far as education in general is concerned, Chris Jenks notes that children at school are equipped with 'thought styles, manners, sensitivities and patterns of relevance and relation that ensure a re-production of their class position and the ideological framework' and that societies 'almost inevitably reproduce their structures of hierarchy and power through the process of the development of self' (1996, 44). As a result, 'education serves to transform the cultural heritage into a common individual unconscious' (Bourdieu and Passeron 1977, 192–5). Hence, the English educational background of Levy's protagonists in part builds their adaptation to the English society, while their Jamaican parental background contrasts with this national identity formation.

The title of *Every Light in the House Burnin'* refers to a constant complaint by the father of the family: that the family members leave the lights on in rooms when no one is in them. His pronunciation of 'burnin'' signifies the colonized's borrowed mother tongue, although the phrase itself signifies paternal authority and poverty. Angela initiates her narration by introducing her father, describing his patriarchal position in the Jacobs family within the context of their poverty in Britain and their contrasting traditional Jamaican attitude: 'My dad once drank six cups of tea and ate six buttered rolls ... to avoid them being wasted' (Levy 1994, 1). This incident happens in a motorway café when Angela is eleven; it is their first holiday and they cannot afford any extra expense. The father insists on having tea and rolls that nobody else wants, so he has to eat them all, revealing the traditional attitude toward wasting food in this simple act of patriarchy and poverty that parallels the title of the work. As Homi Bhabha notes in 'DissemiNation,' 'The scraps, patches, and rags of daily life must be repeatedly turned into the signs of a national culture, while the very act of the narrative performance interpolates a growing circle of national subjects' (1990, 297). Starting with poverty, which is the transnational sign of being Jamaican in England, the narration proceeds with Jamaican patriarchal values. 'My dad was a man – most dads are,' narrates Angela. 'But my dad had been taught or was shown or picked up that a man was certain things and a woman was others ... He was head of a family – a breadwinner' (Levy 1994, 2).

Winston Jacobs, the father in *Every Light in the House Burnin'*, arrives in England in 1948 on the SS *Empire Windrush* and docks in Tilbury with high hopes of making a better living in the mother country, along with around 500 other Jamaican immigrants. Procter notes that the episode of the ship now highlights the 'historicity' of the migrants, supplying them with an 'iconic status that has helped make them part of the dominant imagery of black Britain' in the late twentieth and early twenty-first centuries (2003, 202–3). In fact, the parents in all three novels belong to the *Windrush* generation of the 1950s, and Levy ends her sequence with *Small Island*, a unique exploration of that decade. Winston works at the post office. His wife, Beryl, joins him in his one room six months after he arrives. She is a teacher, but her Jamaican certificate is not accepted so she sews at home until all her children are grown up and then goes back to college to receive a valid diploma. In *Never far from Nowhere*, the father, Newton Charles, is a bus ticket collector, then a mechanic, and the mother, Rose, serves meals at the local school and tea at the hospital. In *Fruit of the Lemon*, Faith's father, Wade Jackson, is a building labourer, and her mother, Mildred, is a nurse. Susheila Nasta (1995, 48–9) points out that following the Second World War, 40,000 West Indians immigrated to Britain in search of employment. Originally invited by the Labour government to solve the immediate labour crisis, these islanders moved to Britain expecting to improve their standard of living, but many were disappointed.

Bhabha discusses the significance of the *Empire Windrush* more critically in *The Location of Culture*, discussing the outcome while analysing

Handsworth Songs, a film made by the Black Audio and Film Collective during the uprisings of 1985 in the Handsworth district of Birmingham. Shot in the midst of the uprising, Bhabha notes, the film is

> haunted by two moments: the arrival of the migrant population in the 1950s, and the emergence of a black British peoples in the diaspora ... Between the moments of the migrants' arrival and the minorities' emergence spans the filmic time of a continual displacement of narrative ... Two memories repeat incessantly to translate the living perplexity of history into the time of migration: first the arrival of the ship laden with immigrants from the ex-colonies, just stepping off the boat, always just emerging – as in the fantasmatic scenario of Freud's family romance – into the land where the streets are paved with gold. This is followed by another image of the perplexity and power of an emergent peoples, caught in the shot of a dreadlocked Rastafarian cutting a swathe through a posse of policemen during the uprising ... a dangerous repetition ... the edge of human life that translates what will come next and what has gone before in the writing of History ... The discourse of minority reveals the insurmountable ambivalence that structures the *equivocal* movement of historical time. How does one encounter the past as an anteriority that continually introduces an otherness and alterity into the present? How does one then narrate the present as a form of contemporaneity that is neither punctual nor synchronous? (1994, 155–7, emphasis in original)

Bhabha's observation pertains to Levy's work in that it theorizes immigration in a time–space context.

After their landing, black people not only experienced racial discrimination but likewise were considered as the cause of housing problems for whites. According to Susan Smith, large proportions of the existing housing stock had been damaged or destroyed during the Second World War, and because of the resulting shortage in the decades that followed black households were denied their fair share of housing and the general problems of accommodation prominently attributed to black immigration (1989, 51). That situation forms part of the family problems delineated in Levy's fiction. The Jacobs family in *Every Light in the House Burnin'* has four children, three within one year of each other: two girls, Yvonne and Patricia, then a boy, John, and four years later, Angela. Two children share a small room each and Angela notes, 'The council gave my mum and dad a flat – a temporary flat on an old thirties red brick council estate. They said it was just until they found somewhere more suitable, but that was before I was born and I lived there until I was twenty-one' (Levy 1994, 7). In *Never far from Nowhere*, when the older narrator, Olive, marries Peter, he has to move into her house because they cannot get a house from the council. Even when their baby is born the family has to go on living in the only room Olive has had since childhood. When Peter leaves Olive for another woman, she cannot get a house for herself and her baby for a long time, and when she does she cannot afford it but ends up back at her mother's. In *Fruit of the Lemon*, Levy likewise mentions the old council house the family had to live in and the boxes that the parents always kept as a sign of the constant removal process, signifying the ambivalence of displacement and homelessness. When the family is finally offered a bigger and better place it is on the outskirts of London, isolated and ironically after all the children have grown up and moved away. In *Small Island*, Queenie offers Hortense and Gilbert the shelter of a very small room when Gilbert who had nowhere else to go. Procter points out that postwar, postcolonial migration to England in the 1950s and '60s amounted to more than 'the abandonment of "home," or to an ontological condition of 'homelessness' (2003, 4); it also involved a 'desperate territorial struggle *for* home within the context of housing shortages and the overtly racialised "colour bar" surrounding domestic space' (4). Thus, Procter argues, housing did not emerge 'out of the blue as a primary signifier in early postwar black British writing, but during a period of acute housing shortages in which the dwelling had established itself as a key arena of racial contestation' (22).

Levy characterizes parents in the diaspora as poor, displaced, lonely, and disillusioned, hated by the society in which they find themselves yet unwilling to disclose their disillusionment and loneliness to their children. The reason they do not want to go back is another outcome of colonization. Immigration to Britain offered the prospect of a new life unthreatened by flood, famine, or the miserable poverty that was their country's legacy from imperial rule. In the British West Indies, the cost of living had almost doubled during the war, and thus it was to Britain that young men and women escaped from high unemployment and low wages (Fryer 1984, 373–4). In Levy's fiction, the diasporic parents do not choose to talk about Jamaica to their children so that their British-born children can adapt or get assimilated and thus become accepted: 'He [Angela's father] never talked about his family or his life in Jamaica. He seemed only to exist in one plane of time – the present' (Levy 1994, 3). It is also noteworthy that Angela's parents do not use their names: 'My dad called my mum "Mum" and my mum called my dad "Dad." I was about ten years old before I knew their actual names ... My dad didn't like anyone to know his name. It was another *secret*' (3, emphasis added), like his position at the post office. The mother also keeps secrets, especially hiding her true feelings, creating a space of inclusion in the society for her children. Modelling the parents' secrecy, the siblings form their secrets, too: 'My brother lived in a secret world. He went out and nobody knew where he went or who he went with' (15). Moreover, 'My sisters were a bit of a mystery to me. They were teenagers, much older than me and they lived in a world of their own, which was in their bedroom' (20). The parents' denial of their cultural background also excludes close relatives. The children are informed of the existence of their father's sister, Doreen, only shortly before her brief visit. Doreen lives in Jamaica with her Scottish husband, Andrew. The visit covers barely an hour, quite brief considering the closeness of kin and the distance of time, yet the encounter is ironic in its revelation that Doreen has a more comfortable life in Jamaica than her brother has in England. While she and her husband say how much they enjoy living in Jamaica, with a big house, a car, and money to travel, Beryl has to lie to keep up appearances. 'Well, I have everything I need just here' (126), she says, at which moment very dramatically the lights go off. Without two shillings to put in the metre, they must borrow from Andrew. Another incident of familial secrecy is revealed by when Winston goes away for a few days. He goes to Leicester to his identical twin's funeral, and it is the first time he has acknowledged having a brother. The secrecy of the family shocks Angela, but her father points out, 'You can't let these things bother you' (237). Likewise, when Angela's father has cancer, Beryl conceals the truth from both Angela and Winston himself. A suspicious Angela finally discovers the truth in a letter that her mother writes to her, though they see each other quite frequently. When Angela proposes that Beryl reveal his condition to Winston, she says, 'He'd just go downhill much quicker and I don't think I could cope with that' (86). This is the only time the mother and the twenty-year-old daughter talk overtly, so Angela feels irritated: 'Her emotion and honesty embarrassed me. It was new between us' (86). These incidents demonstrate how much immigrants suffer and try to conceal their feelings even from their own children, supporting Fanon's claim that immigrants sacrifice the family in choosing the society, but despite their desperate desire to adapt to a hostile country they belong nowhere.

The parents in *Never far from Nowhere* and *Fruit of the Lemon* similarly prefer not to talk about their feelings or their Jamaican origin. In *Never far from Nowhere*, when Olive decides to go and live in Jamaica with her daughter, her mother tells Vivien, 'I tell her [Olive] she doesn't know what she talking about. She belong here. She born here. It's all she know. I tell her she doesn't know what it like in Jamaica' (1996, 280). In *Fruit of the Lemon*, the sense of something missing, the sense of the cultural and historical void of the family is finally exposed when Faith has an identity crisis and her parents relent by sending her to stay with her aunt in Jamaica.

Denial of origins creates problems for the children who live displaced in an oppressive society to which they cannot really feel they belong. The ambivalence of living at the margins of both cultures causes tension that the young people try to transcend, belonging nowhere. As a British-born writer, Levy delineates the experiences of second-generation immigrants and the transnational sensibilities that occur in separate spaces and realities (secrets versus truth). As Laura Hall states, the two worlds cannot be separated into discrete entities but are 'inextricably interwoven' (1995, 91). This situation does not disprove Fanon's contention that individuals privilege society over family; on the contrary, it discloses the complexity of the transnational situation. The black person privileges belonging to white society over his or her black family, so this blending of cultures is not of equal proportions. Transnational sensibility is complex because it may arise from an individual choice to live in another country, or more often, from the choice of transnational/immigrant parents, whose children then have to struggle to be accepted by both society and their parents, since it is not easy to deny the parents totally. This complexity may explain why Levy focuses on immigrant parents' disillusionment and harsh survival conditions, as exemplified in her most recent novel, *Small Island*.

When they introduce family members, Levy's narrators focus on colour differences between the siblings as an ironic legacy of alterity. Bill Ashcroft, Gareth Griffiths, and Helen Tiffin suggest that

in the Caribbean, the European imperial enterprise ensured that the worst features of colonialism throughout the globe would all be combined in one region: the virtual annihilation of the native population of Caribs and Arawaks, the plundering and internecine piracy amongst the European powers; the deracination and atrocities of the slave trade and plantation slavery, and the subsequent systems of indenture which stranded Chinese and Indians in the Caribbean ... From the early days of slavery, cultural crash and miscegenation formed the brutal texture of Caribbean life. (2002, 144)

Hence, the lighter shades of black that Levy's protagonists yearn for is the outcome of slavery and miscegenation not only of black and white – the colonized and the colonizer – but also of races such as Indian and Chinese.

In *Every Light in the House Burnin'*, Angela's only brother, John, carries colonization as a birthmark: 'a red, fuzzy head of hair that people would stare at in the street. "It's the Scottish in you," my mum would say to him but she never explained where the Scottish came from' (Levy 1994, 15). The elder sister Patricia has skin darker than anyone else in the family and her features are 'fine and more European. Sometimes she looked like she didn't belong to us' (21). When Angela and John are children and are told by their 'friends' in the neighbourhood to go back to where they came from, their colour is projected as a prominent form of denial by their mother, whose first reaction is to take no notice of the taunts directed at her children. It is the first time the narrator comments, 'But we're different – we're coloured,' to which her mother replies, 'Look child ... You born here. That's what matter ... You're not black and you're not white. That's what we are – we're not black and we're not white.' 'What are we then?' her brother asks. 'Cha child – you're just you – you born here – you just tell them to mind their business' (59) repeats the mother, helplessly focusing on the lighter shade of blackness, hoping it matters. The father reinforces her approach with 'Yes... take no notice. You come from here. You don't let them worry you' (59), in an effort to keep the diasporic boundaries at an extremely limited point in his house and work place. In the face of the explicit racism shown by the neighbourhood children and against the systemic, largely unspoken racial connotations of the English, the only thing the parents advise their children to do is to ignore racism, because that is the only thing either the grown ups or the children can do.

Another impact of colonization on mock-transnational identities is their visible hybridity, apparent by shades of colour, which they believe to be crucial in the sense that a lighter shade of black is a sign of Englishness. It is a cultural phenomenon that although white English people see only black people and do not discriminate between, for example, black people originating from Jamaica and brown people originating from India, colonized blacks consider darker or lighter shades very important. Ironically, of course, a lighter shade is proof of miscegenation. It is also one of the significant causes of sibling rivalry in *Never far from Nowhere*. Levy allows her narrator Vivien to disclose right away that her parents are from Jamaica and give the family lineage, explaining that the mother's great-grandmother was a slave, but in her freedom married a man descended from Scottish farmers. Thus Vivien's mother has fair skin with 'strong African features' (Levy 1996, 2). Her father's mother, on the other hand, was part Spanish and part African and married a man of North African descent. This mosaic leaves a legacy to the children: Vivien, with fair skin and black, wavy hair, and Olive with black skin, 'a head of tight frizzy hair streaked with red and green eyes' (2). As well as experiencing societal oppression, Olive also suffers from within, starting with her mother's teasing in childhood. Olive's narration begins with her mother' calling her the black sheep of the family, cynically adding, 'Although she knew that she and my dad were not the only people who came over here from Jamaica in the fifties, she liked to think that because they were fair-skinned they were the only decent people who came. The only ones with a "bit of class." And she believed that the English would recognize this' (7). Rose's naïve belief in the merits of a lighter shade of black and her complaints about black people in England are a pathetic outcome of colonization, of hybridity arising from carrying British blood instead of being pure Jamaican black, in addition to cultural hybridity. When old enough, Olive tries to confront her mother: '"I'm black," I used to say, when I was old enough to butt in.' The mother replies 'Don't be silly, Olive, you're not coloured.' 'No, mum, I'm black.' 'No Olive, you're not black, and that's enough of this stupidness.' 'Well, I'm not white, I have to be something.' 'You're not white and you're not black – you're you,' she would say' (7), repeating Angela's mother's discourse. Olive is Levy's only protagonist who wants to be accepted as black and wants her own daughter Amy to know that she is black, although her father was Irish and she has very pale skin. Confronting her mother, Olive points to the ambivalence of denial: 'No, I grew up confused – she's [Olive's daughter] growing up black ... I tell her she's black. It's a political statement, not just a fact' (8).

This discourse on visible hybridity is an ironic metaphor of cultural hybridity that, as Nasta puts it, has been useful 'as a conceptual and critical tool' (2002, 178). Nasta points out that in the 1980s, contemporary literary theorists and cultural critics were keen to stress the transformative potential for Britain's black and Asian 'minorities' of living in a hybrid context, thus 'not only creating a new space for agency at the interstices of the nation's borders, but a space where formerly antagonistic and polarized versions of cultural identity could be realigned and negotiated' (2002, 178). She adds that 'hybridity,' whether we accept contemporary definitions of it or not, 'can take many forms and be expressed through a variety of different narrative solutions' (179). Consequently, 'in employing "hybridity" indiscriminately as a universal concept, there is a danger of failing to recognize that the particular histories of specific writers and their individual locations determine the nature of the way they write whether inside or outside the hybrid space' (180).

In *Fruit of the Lemon*, narrator Faith Jackson's parents conceal knowledge of their homeland, like Vivien and Olive's desperate parents. The sense of hope and optimism in belonging to England articulated by Faith's parents is an archetypal motif within the immigrant genre, though interestingly it is counterbalanced by Faith's elder brother, Carl, who chides Faith about her anglicized lifestyle and her futile attempts to be fully like the English, although she has never been to Jamaica and she was born into English culture. As a result, denying her colour and Jamaican origin by choosing to be friends only with the white English and sharing a house only with whites, leads Faith to a nervous breakdown. When she witnesses an assault on a black woman and the woman is helped by her white housemate Simon, Faith believes Simon is 'different,' yet her housemates, including Simon, start joking about the incident after overcoming the shock. This finally forces Faith to acknowledge the fact of her alterity. The self-denial of her blackness reaches a climax: she does not leave her room for days. Conversely, all she sees is 'a black girl lying in bed. I covered the mirror with a bath towel. I didn't want to be black anymore. I just wanted to live. The other mirror in the room I covered with a tee-shirt. *Voilà!* I was no longer black' (160). Finally, Levy applies a different strategy and Faith's parents convince her to visit her Aunt Coral in Jamaica. Faith begins her trip as an English girl, criticizing everything she observes, from people's clothing to the 'chaotic' city generally, just like an outsider. However, when her Aunt Coral tells her the bitter life stories of each member of her family, Faith gradually realizes that she is of Jamaican origin, a transformation mirrored in her shift from British outlook to Jamaican style.[2] This is exemplified in her shift from casual clothes, such as jeans and t-shirts, to her eventual embrace of Jamaican dress and a Jamaican style of tying up her hair when accompanying her aunt to church.

Levy's discourse in this novel diverges from her previous paths, describing a journey through which the character of Faith is enabled to reconstruct her true background as she learns about Jamaica, and in so doing forms a positive transnational identity instead of pretending she is truly British.

The narrator's relation with her father is the basic theme in *Every Light in the House Burnin'*. Sadly, Angela's childhood memories are mostly concerned with violence, such as her father beating all his children with his belt, or at least chasing them with a shoe in hand and shouting. Even after they grow up, Angela's sisters, Patricia and Yvonne, are threatened with beating when they come home late. When Angela brings home her first boyfriend as a teenager, her father scares him away by shouting 'Who is this? Who are you?' (Levy 1994, 207). Angela also counters with violence. This is the only time she screams 'I hate you' (208) and compares her father with the British: 'Why did I have to be born to him? Other dads were nice in their jeans and open necked shirts. They smiled at boyfriends and even offered them beer. But my dad, in his grey suit trousers from a time gone by – but my dad, he had to shout' (208). Thus the ambivalence of transnational identity is unequivocally disclosed in both the parents' and the children's attitude. The father wants to keep his old-fashioned grey trousers and Jamaican sense of patriarchy; he refuses to act like an English father, and his transnational behaviour causes disillusionment for a daughter who wants to have an English father, although she is aware that being black precludes the possibility of being truly English. Despite a ruthless portrayal of the father, Levy also shows his strong emotional bond with the cat, implying that the affection he is supposed to bestow on his children he gives instead the cat. The only time he is seen to cry is when the cat dies, revealing his affectionate side, his best kept secret.

Because parental violence is not exclusive to fathers, it is not possible to claim that it carries patriarchal overtones. Perhaps violence in Levy's fiction is a sign of the parents' disillusionment, paradoxically projected as their anxiety about bringing up the kind of children they believe will be respected by and assimilated into society. Levy makes it clear that Jamaican background is not so much a source of violent behaviour as cause of the characters' frustration in the sense of provoking the racism they experience. In *Never far from Nowhere*, Olive goes to grammar school as the only black student. Her friends make jokes about 'wogs or coons and then say "Sorry Olive, I don't mean you, you're all right"' (Levy 1996, 26). She hates the school, works as a shop assistant, and starts going to night clubs. When her father becomes ill, she cannot stand to see him sitting in a chair coughing all day and she justifies her dislike by remembering that when she was very young he used to chase her and hit her with his slipper, sometimes because she had spilled or lost something, but sometimes for no reason she could understand. Moreover, after her father's death her mother likewise chases Olive round the flat because she comes home late at night: 'It was driving me mad. I'd stay out later and later in the hope that she'd be in bed or at least too tired to fight. I dreaded coming home ... When I thought of my mum all I saw was this big contorted angry face with slit eyes, fat cheeks and mouth open with a pink tongue flapping furiously. That's all I could see' (39). Constant distress is something Olive remembers from her childhood years, too, as the following sad statement indicates: 'I couldn't remember what she looked like when she smiled, and as for laughing – no – just a childhood memory' (39). Her mother's anxiety is proven to be justified, though it does not justify her violence: Olive marries when she is five months pregnant, and her husband eventually leaves her.

In *Fruit of the Lemon*, narrator Faith does not imply any family violence, only complains about the strict rules: 'I had lived at home all through my art college life ... [a]nd for four years I had had to juggle late-night parties, sit-ins and randy boyfriends, with 1940s Caribbean strictures' (1999, 16). Levy here diversifies her narrative approach with humour, and *Fruit of the Lemon* does not carry the bitter overtones of the previous two novels, although she does portray the tension of racism in society and gender discrimination of Faith's parents between herself and her brother, Carl, who is free to act as he likes.

In *Every Light in the House Burnin'* describes a striking contrast: when Angela's father is young, he uses violence to discipline his children, anxious to see them grow up and adjust, but when he is old and feeble, he is afraid of dying. Then the roles reverse, and Angela, seemingly British and educated with a college degree, tries to arrange special care for her father. At this point, racial discrimination shows itself most deliberately. Angela realizes that no matter what her education or who her white, educated friends are, her father is treated intolerably either at home or in the hospital by doctors and nurses alike until he dies. Angela talks about her anger in a violent fantasy when a nurse calls her father 'Old man Jacobs': 'I could no longer speak. I picked up this woman by her throat and held her up against the wall and slapped her. I screamed at her, "Don't call my dad, 'Old man Jacobs' – my dad is not your plaything, not your annoyance."' I let her fall to the floor and then I picked her up again and threw her against the opposite wall and I kicked her and kicked her while she was down' (Levy 1994, 153).

In his last hours, Winston Jacobs keeps screaming 'Lazarus help me get it out,' and 'Oh God, Lazarus, please help me' (241). Lazarus refers to two separate figures who appear in the New Testament. One is the Lazarus of Jesus' parable, which appears solely in Luke 16:19–31, and the other is the Lazarus of the miracle recounted in John 11:41–4. If we consider that Levy implies the Lazarus in Luke, Winston's scream becomes ironic. The rich man who does not help the beggar signifies England, and the beggar Lazarus, laid at the rich man's gate and full of sores, desiring to be fed with the crumbs that fell from the rich man's table, signifies Winston. Lazarus is rewarded in heaven, whereas the rich man goes to hell. The father dies after screaming for Lazarus for a day. When the hospital phones Angela and her mother to say that he is dying, Angela wants to arrive after he is dead because she is embarrassed by his cries. The nurse declares that she called a rabbi to help him, pointing to the name Jacobs and Winston's cries for Lazarus as the reason, even though he belonged to the Church of England. The situation exposes a double irony: England is insensible to the cries of the black and the misunderstanding between cultures continues after death. Levy ends the tragedy with Angela's remark, '"They got you a rabbi, Dad," I said. "God knows where you'll be now," I smiled' (248), suggesting that her father's state of alienation becomes eternal. Angela's shame at her father's cries in pain might be considered a sign of her belonging to British culture or an ironic reflection of the Jamaican side of the family's secret codes: the exposure of emotions. As Hanif Kureishi once put it in an interview, 'People think that I'm caught between two cultures, but I'm not. I'm British; I can make it in England. It's my father who's caught. He can't make it' (Pally 1986, 53).

In *Every Light in the House Burnin'*, Angela's eldest sister Patricia marries when she is eighteen and pregnant by a white working-class man and starts living in Cardiff with her husband and son. Yvonne trains to become a nurse and goes to live in New Zealand. 'It was the furthest away she could get,' comments Angela (Levy 1994, 219). John travels all around Europe and Africa and lives in a kibbutz in Israel: 'He moved all the time' (219). Levy implies that Angela's siblings never visit their families again. Angela, the narrator, is the only child who goes to college. She moves out of her parents' home in the second year and helps them, especially while her father is suffering, visiting them very often.

Never far from Nowhere, on the other hand, ends with Olive's decision to go and live in Jamaica with her daughter and Vivien's decision to stay on at Canterbury Art College, leaving her mother, sister, and white, working-class boyfriend, Eddie, behind. As stated earlier, *Fruit of the Lemon* ends with Faith's journey to Jamaica, from where she returns fortified and reconciled with being black, and having a Jamaican origin while confidently asserting that she *is* British. Finally, *Small Island* ends with Hortense and Gilbert's settling down with an adopted black baby.

Thus, in Levy's fiction the protagonists do adapt, with the implication that they will survive in British society despite the racial prejudice they are aware of from the beginning. Vivien in *Never far from Nowhere* exemplifies this idea well:

> When I was young I used to look at my parents as they sat exhausted in chairs, ... and I used to think how lucky this country was to have them. How grateful people should be that they came here and did such responsible jobs. And how if they went back – if they went back to Jamaica – well, who knows what would happen to the buses, to the children or the new hospital wings. My parents helped this country, I thought. I thought it as I lay in bed at night. I thought it at school. I thought it walking down the street or playing in the flats. But when I was young, when I was still having my cheek pulled by passers-by and people winked at me on the tube, even then I knew that the English people hated us. (Levy 1996, 5)

Despite negative feelings, what Vivien voices also discloses that multicultural people do believe that by their transnationalism they add colour to British society, literally and metaphorically.

The ambivalent feelings of bitterness and longing prevail in transnational selves. As Catherine Hall comments, 'Imperial identities, made over centuries, are not easy to unravel. They live on in reworked forms in the postcolonial moment. This history demands our attention. If cultural identities are to be reconstructed and we are to learn to live with difference some memory work on empire is essential' (2001, 39). The fictional texts selected for discussion are not intended to define the enormous output of literary diaspora in Britain. As Nasta puts it, many suggestive correspondences exist across the fictional landscapes of the black and Asian diasporas in Britain. The central concerns of a number of black writers can be closely identified with those of a number of their Asian British contemporaries, but as Nasta importantly notes, while many of the writers have 'followed on form and share literary and cultural links with the earlier generation of writers, they now write Britain from within the racial dialectic of an Englishness that is their common home – the nation's inlaid other and yet endemically own history' (2002, 181).

Consequently, in the identity mapping of Levy's fiction, the term *transnationalism* is revealed as a means of reconstructing social and geographic space, and as the clash between the homeland and adopted land, and accordingly as the tension between the family and identity. Transnationalism in Levy's work so far is unequivocally pointed out from various angles, sometimes with bitterness, sometimes with humour.

PART THREE

Redefining Family

10 The Personal, the Political, and the Complexity of Identity: Some Thoughts on Mothering

MAY FRIEDMAN

My Big Fat Jewish Identity

The story is well known, of course: of racism within the mainstream feminist communities and sexism within minority communities. The very real struggles that are trapped beneath this academic observation, however, make it extraordinarily difficult to document the complexities of reconciling Judaism, including all its internal contradictions and identities, with progressive feminist ideas. When motherhood is added to this volatile mix, the challenge is overwhelming indeed. This challenge is also intensely personal and varies from mother to mother as women work at the intersections of various axes of difference. To get underneath this topic, then, is to begin to tell the story of my own complexity, my own specific intersectionality and the challenges and opportunities that I face.

I am an Iraqi Jewish feminist mother. It sounds like the beginning of a really bad joke: a mess of contradictions. Religion and feminism are often viewed as contradictory; Arab and Jewish identities are popularly seen as irreconcilable; Jews speak Yiddish and feminists are not mothers. And yet I am an Iraqi Jewish feminist mother in Toronto. If my identity is, as Stuart Hall (1998) suggests, always in production, then it is only my identification, my labels, that give me any notion of fixity. My identity, on the other hand, is the mediation and negotiation of those labels through the lens of my own self-view and the confused perceptions of others.

Although Iraqi Judaism is often mistaken as a hyphenated or hybridized identity, blending dual cultures, it is not. I am the daughter of two Iraqi Jewish parents, part of the formerly large, formerly vibrant community of Jews who lived in Babylon from 586 BCE to 1951. Unfortunately, most diasporic Jewish communities often set *mizrachi* (literally, Eastern) Jews apart. Growing up in Toronto, I had only a vague understanding of why the Judaism we practised at home or among other Iraqis bore merely a fleeting resemblance to the tunes, food, and practices of most Canadian (and, although unlabelled as such, European) Jews. When added to this the genuine hybridization of living in a family that immigrated twice within one generation, my Iraqi Jewish Canadian identity has generally resisted easy categorization. As I grew to adulthood and embraced feminism, the Iraqi and Jewish communities seemed less and less in tune with my own personal ideals. Yet within the progressive community, I was facing subtle and not-so-subtle instances of racism and anti-Semitism. Nonetheless, my personal multiplicity seemed reconcilable, albeit in an imperfect, unstable way. No, the real trouble began at a particular moment. The uneasy balance of my various roles and realms split apart with the addition of yet another title: mother.

As a mother, and as a feminist mother in particular, I want to help my children become their own people, to help them develop critical skills. Like most people, however, I also want to ensure that my children can appreciate and, I hope, maintain my own core values. As I watch my children grow, however, I cannot help but feel that something has to give. The core values that constitute my essential self are fundamentally contradictory. The only consistency between my different identities is an insistence on community, a difficult prescription to fulfil given that I am one of exactly three Iraqi Jewish feminists that I know of in North America. How do I raise my children immersed in their various communities when those communities appear to have no overlap at all?

Balabusta-Free: My Body of Knowledge

I gave birth. I am Jewish. Yet in all the fracture of identity that surrounds new parenthood, I could find no comfort in the role to which I would seem to be tailor-made, given the above statements: I am not a Jewish mother, that stereotype of the nagging, overprotective and overbearing maternal demon. To begin with, the stereotype of the neurotic Jewish mama toiling over a hot stove and urging her children to eat more has little to do with the reality of my busy, multifarious, frenetic life. Although far from perfect, our family is considerably more egalitarian than the caricature suggests. Furthermore, however, the Jewish mother crooning 'Ess, ess, mein kind!' in Yiddish has no place in my repertoire. My own mother croons 'Hayati! Gulbi!' using *her* mother tongue, Arabic, to call me her heart, her eyes.

The problem is not simply the stereotype, which undoubtedly alienates Jewish women, Arab and Eastern European alike. The deeper problem is that the Jewish community is as prone to racism as the feminist one. Thus, Ashkenazi (Eastern European) Jewish experiences are taken as the norm and stand in for all Jewish experiences in North America. For example, 'Oy vey, I'm kvelling over your kreplach. Did you make them with your shaine hentelach?' 'No, you putz, I bought them at Perl's' ... None of that has *anything* to do with me. Beyond the Jewish community, non-Jewish knowledge and perception of Jewish customs – including the words that have made it into the lexicon of standard English – reflect only Ashkenazi influences, as in *putz, shmuck,* and *shlong* (not incidentally, all words for penis). This is no place for an Iraqi Jewish feminist.

In 'United Jewish Feminist Front,' Loolwa Khazzoom, one of the Iraqi Jewish North American feminists mentioned above, writes words that vindicate my lifetime of feeling marginalized: 'As I came to understand ... "Jewish" meant "Ashkenazi." It did not mean my heritage, and it did not mean me. Any people and any traditions that were not from Northern Europe were, according to the messages of my childhood, not really Jewish' (2001, 168). The privileging of Ashkenazi experiences of Judaism is neither accidental nor innocent. Like the broader world, the Jewish community has fallen into a colonialist discourse that celebrates European attributes at the expense of others. As Ella Shohat, renowned feminist academic (and the other of the Iraqi Jewish feminists known to me) writes in *Taboo Memories, Diasporic Visions,* 'Eurocentric norms of scholarship established typically colonial relations that have taken a heavy toll on the representation of Arab-Jewish history and identity' (2006, 206).

If I feel alienated by the 'mainstream' (in other words, Ashkenazi) Jewish community, perhaps I had best raise my children with a thorough awareness of their Iraqi heritage by immersing them in Iraqi culture, cooking spicy *qibbeh* instead of bland matzoh balls. Having somehow birthed the world's lightest half-Iraqi children, I worry that because their Arab heritage is not written on their body as it is on mine, they will have no reason to learn about this part of their identities. I apply sunscreen to their white skin, gaze into their light eyes, and although my maternal instinct to protect them is somewhat relieved at their escape from some aspects of racism, I mourn their loss of Iraqi identity: Noah Friedman with the big blue eyes, Molly Friedman with the light brown hair. The stranger at the park says, 'Her eyes are *so green* – but your hair is *so curly!*' – their easy assimilation into the mainstream Jewish community sets them apart from me and eradicates an exceptional community that is dying out. Under these circumstances, perhaps I must commit myself to a thorough involvement with the Iraqi Jewish community in order to help my children remain true to their roots?

My children's Ashkenazi father – not to mention their Yiddish-speaking bubie and zadie – might be justifiably discomfited were my children's Iraqi identity to usurp their Ashkenazi selves. Although Ashkenazi Judaism is unquestionably taken as the norm, my in-laws are nonetheless the children of Holocaust survivors, both born in displaced persons camps in Europe after the war. Transmission of their unique customs and mores is therefore no less essential to them than to my Iraqi parents. Beyond the specifics of our family, however, they, along with many other Jews, might be wary were my children to learn Arabic. To most North American Jews (my Arab Canadian parents included, ironically), Jews are the *opposite* of Arabs, our sworn enemies. In fact, I feel this anti-Arab sentiment most strongly within the Iraqi Jewish community. They have internalized the message that in order to pass as Jewish, they must subdue their Arabness. As a result, they are truly hateful with respect to other (read: non-Jewish, read: Muslim) Arabs. Learning Arabic is *not* the done thing. Of course, the fact that *we* are Arabs and *we* speak Arabic is conveniently left out ... as is the fact that I am embodied as an Arab woman, that my appearance speaks loudly and is worthy of ongoing comment as I go through the world. Out with my children, asked the question, suspiciously, 'Are they *yours?*' – how can I forget that I am Iraqi? And what are the implications for future babies? My Arabness, ephemeral in many respects, is certainly present in my genes. What if those genes assert themselves in future children? What are the implications for our families if the next child is honey brown instead of milk white?

Thank You, O Lord, for Making Me a Feminist

If the story written on my body tells me to raise my kids Iraqi, my heart and my conscience swing the debate to other realms. It is vitally important to me to raise my children in an environment that is as free of hate as possible, that is queer positive, that takes a flexible and open-minded position on both gender and sex. This is part of my transnational sensibility: a focus on liminality and responsiveness that is the opposite of the proscriptive environment of my own upbringing. The Iraqi Jews I have encountered, perhaps responding to the racism they feel from the mainstream Jewish community, do not respond well to notions of liminality, nor of equality on the basis of race, sex, or, really, anything else. On the basis of gender, a step into the Iraqi Jewish synagogue in Toronto is a step back to the 1950s, where the women take care of the babies and gossip while the men get on with the serious business of praying. The tunes are heartbreakingly lovely and familiar, but the overall experience of attending my family's house of worship is spiritually bankrupt. I want Noah and Molly to grow up with an awareness of *all* of their Jewish heritage, but I cannot imagine doing so at the expense of exposing them to extreme sexism, to further racism, to hateful and closed-minded views.

If I listen to my heart, perhaps I must seek out a home within the progressive Jewish community? Writing in *Listen Up: Voices from the Next Feminist Generation*, Robin M. Neidorf argues that 'Jewish feminists of my generation have the advantages of existing alternatives. We have models of Jewish communities that are not traditionally observant yet continue to call themselves Jewish. We have grown up with the powerful reality of women rabbis. We have celebrated our Bat Mitzvahs without the pressure of being the first in our congregation to do so' (1995, 217).

Indeed, my son now attends the city's only progressive Jewish day school. We seem to have finally found a progressive synagogue. Yet I am uneasy. I am a young Jewish feminist, yet my reality is not represented in Neidorf's confident exposition. Undoubtedly, the Judaism we encounter within progressive settings will be more easily reconciled with my feminist values. But it will not be *my* Judaism. My daughter's Bat Mitzvah will occur, but it will not be with the Iraqis, where young women are still not permitted to approach the Torah. My son will learn to speak Hebrew with a Yiddish inflection; he will giggle at my parents' accent. More important, a rich and ancient tradition will end with me. But to stay in the Iraqi synagogue, with its total absence of children's services (a not-so-subtle implication that young parents – let's face it, young mothers – need not bother attending), with its bored and boring women's section, with its liberal sprinkling of bling and its even more generous level of gossip about the bling wearers, with its ill-disguised patriarchy and *hate* – to do that is simply not conscionable.

It is possible that in a progressive context, more attention will be paid to diversity and our family's various traditions will be honoured. I remain unconvinced. In the online magazine *Solidarity*, Ella Shohat writes about North American responses to her intersected identity: 'Americans are often amazed to discover the existentially nauseating or charmingly exotic possibilities of such a syncretic identity. I recall a well-established colleague who despite my elaborate lessons on the history of Arab Jews, still had trouble understanding that I was not a tragic anomaly – for instance, the daughter of an Arab (Palestinian) and an Israeli (European Jew)' (2003, n.p.).

My experiences have been consistent with Shohat's: that in progressive circles, at best, my Iraqi Jewish heritage is eagerly embraced and consumed, but not necessarily honoured. At worst, my inbox is flooded with anti-Semitic or racist email, or both. Certainly, at the very least, whether I am consumed or condemned, my Jewishness and my Arabness are viewed as dissonant. Within feminist and leftist circles, there is little room for an Arab Jew with a complicated critique of Israel. Faced with the discomfort that my multiplicity provokes, it is tempting to believe that if only I could abandon my Arab identity, I could find the perfect feminist Jewish community.

Many other feminists have already considered the difficulties inherent in combining Judaism with feminism. Certainly, I found that my inauguration into the world of Jewish motherhood seriously challenged my ability to maintain any level of egalitarianism. As a veteran mother of eight days' duration, I attended my son's circumcision, where I remained upstairs calming the baby before the ceremony and quietly nursing him alone afterward. The 120 invited guests did not see me. There is no photographic evidence of my presence at my son's initiation into the Jewish community. This, despite the Ashkenazi *mohel*, and the copious amounts of lox and blintzes eagerly served up at my parents' home that morning. Clearly, a simple abandonment of Iraqi Judaism will not overcome the challenges of blending these disparate identities. Nonetheless, the incoherence of my alienation presents a new set of challenges, a uniquely transnational setting for the age-old story that resists traditional solutions.

Fundamentally, there are a number of tensions between feminism and Judaism. Although several Jewish women were integrally involved in the evolution of the women's liberation movement (for example, Betty Friedan and Gloria Steinem), there is nonetheless a great deal of discomfort and anti-Semitism within the women's movement to this day. Judaism, like many religions, is seen as irreconcilable with feminism, and anyone who attempts to maintain a religious identity may be viewed as simply a dupe of patriarchy. There is obviously some truth to this. Judaism does not attempt to hide its patriarchal roots, as evidenced by the oft-cited morning prayer recited by all religious Jewish men: 'Thank you, O Lord, for not making me a woman.' Iraqi is written on my body; feminism is in my heart. Why not jettison Judaism in order to simplify the equation?

My commitment to Jewish identity does not stem exclusively from my simple desire to transmit my history and culture to my offspring. Rather, it has a more sinister motivation: when my children encounter anti-Semitism, as they inevitably will, I want them to have a broader context for their Jewish heritage than simply as something worthy of hatred. When they understand that by not celebrating Christmas, we are unmistakably other, I want my children to have something to embrace rather than the uneasiness of simply not fitting in. Is this paranoia on my part? Am I simply neurotically anticipating future horrors unnecessarily, thus ensuring that I finally *do* fit into that Jewish mother stereotype? It is certainly possible, yet my children have four grandparents who were fully integrated into their respective nations but had to escape life-threatening persecution within their lifetimes. As Linda Stone Fish writes, 'The fear of anti-Semitism is externally driven and organized by actual or perceived threats and experiences, which may cause a high level of hypervigilance and overinvolvement in some Jewish mothers. The world is not a safe place, and we need to protect our children from violating experiences. If this fear is all we give our children of Judaism, however, it may leave them alienated from the richness that positive identification has to offer' (2000, 133).

Whether we choose to involve ourselves in the Jewish community or not, my kids will be made aware that they are different. We have a choice about whether to fill that identity with joy and vibrancy and messy contradictions or to leave it to our challengers to define.

Judith Plaskow, author of *Standing Again at Sinai: Judaism from a Feminist Perspective*, suggests that our only way of redeeming Judaism is by using feminist ideals to reconfigure it in a radical new way. Even Plaskow, however, admits that her motivation is born more of a sense of longing for a cohesive home and less from an optimism regarding the potential blending of feminism and Judaism: 'For me, the move toward embracing a whole Jewish/feminist identity did not grow out of my conviction that Judaism is "redeemable," but out of my sense that sundering Judaism and feminism would mean sundering my being' (1991, xiii). Chana Rothman, writing about the struggle of reconciling her presence in the Jewish and queer communities, gives us a more stark and upsetting option: 'Confronted with the ignorance of so many queers about Jewish culture – masked in "Happy Holidays" or "How do you pronounce that?" – I have felt so isolated trying to be my Jewish self that I can barely let my voice rise up to the surface. I'm always pushing it down, closing my mouth, stripping my identity to its leanest politic so I can be part of a community I want so badly to call home' (1997, 32).

In our search for home, do we not often follow Rothman's model and, in the mode of Cinderella's stepsisters, simply lop off those pieces of ourselves that do not easily fit together? In other words, if a blending of progressive, Jewish. and Iraqi politics is so difficult, then perhaps the option that remains is simply to pick one? As Plaskow writes, however, 'I am not a Jew in the synagogue and a feminist in the world. I am a Jewish feminist and a feminist Jew in every moment of my life' (1991, ix). I do not know how to erase or minimize my various identities, nor do I want to. In parenting, however, I am forced to choose: the sexist Iraqi synagogue or the progressive Ashkenazi school. The feminist, queer-friendly daycare (with Santa on the walls) or the homophobic Jewish nursery. I fear that I must cultivate social conscience at the expense of Jewish involvement and that the rare setting that blends both erases my ethnicity, my community, my family of origin.

Conclusion

As I raise my young children, I aim, like all parents, to balance competing claims on their emerging identities. In so doing, however, I am teaching them a valuable lesson about their various communities. Jews have never doubted the power of a good argument, nor the positive aspects of thoroughly exploring more than one point of view; the entire Talmud is essentially one long argument. Likewise, the women's movement has been paved more by divergent opinions than by homogeneity. And, boy, you should hear those Iraqis argue. In my struggle with my internal contradictions, then, I am being true to myself and to my communities, communities that are characterized more by disorder than by stability. I am living my transnational sensibility in my parenting, my skin, and my daily interrogation of my messy contradictions.

As I struggled to gather my thoughts in order to write this chapter, I complained to my partner, 'It's too much! I don't know where to start! Two competing identities, okay! But *three* – this is impossible. How can I write a succinct and coherent paper about my chaotic, mixed-up identity?'

'Why don't you just leave something out?' he asked. I suppose that is the heart of the problem. If I could leave something out, my dilemma would cease to exist, but so would some essential part of my identity. My situation, though unique and personal, raises some questions about the whole notion of coherent identity.

Although my struggle for coherence has its moments of pain and alienation, I believe that my inability to clearly answer the question 'Where are you from?' may, in fact, be a gift. My children, with all their hyphens, and with all the challenges of maintaining and nourishing their seemingly disparate and contradictory parts, are monuments to transnationalism. They do not know it, but they threaten fixed identities in ways that are potentially radical and exciting. As I watch my bright and lively young son, my curious and sturdy small daughter, as I see them begin to create their own place in the world, I am hopeful that our efforts to live within the contradictions will provide a fruitful approach to the challenge of multiple identities, one that will see this hybridity as a gift and an opportunity rather than a burden to bear.

11 Mothers on the Move: Experiences of Indonesian Women Migrant Workers

THERESA W. DEVASAHAYAM AND
NOOR ABDUL RAHMAN

> I do regret leaving my family to earn a living overseas. This is because it will be inevitable that my children will not feel close and bonded with me. It is only natural for them to be close and bonded to the one who has taken over the task of caring for them and attending to their daily needs. Therefore I always pray that if my children have their own children, they are not pushed into this situation where they have no choice but to choose this path [of migrating] to earn a living.[1]
>
> (Suwarni, forty-two, married with two children, twenty-three and seventeen)

In the last three last decades, Asia has seen growing numbers of women traversing national borders around the world to find waged work in affluent countries (DeWind and Holdaway 2005; Ehrenreich and Hochschild 2002; Huguet 2003; Huguet and Punpuing 2005; Piper 2004; UNESCAP 2008). The database for 2000–5 of the Economic and Social Commission for the Asia Pacific records more than 700,000 women from Indonesia, the Philippines, and Sri Lanka engaged in waged work abroad in 2005 (UNESCAP 2008). While in the past men have resorted to leaving the home and even country in search of wages, now women have sought this route for similar reasons. From Indonesia alone, demographic estimates in mid-2006 point to a total of around 2.7 million Indonesians working overseas, mainly women in the domestic work sector (Hugo 2007).

Migrating for work for many of these women, however, is fraught with tensions and contradictions. The words of Indonesian foreign domestic worker (FDW) Suwarni, above, strongly suggest that many of these women, particularly those who are mothers, have found themselves in a curious bind: although they gain financial empowerment in their work and help to lift their families out of poverty, invariably they are forced to suffer strain on familial ties and the mother–child bond. Suwarni's story is moving. Her deepest regret is that her sojourn in Singapore has resulted in the weakening of her family unit: her husband took on a mistress, and her sons have refused to acknowledge her as their mother for most of their childhood. Despite being able to pay off her family's debt, support her children through school, finance her son's marriage, and build two houses (one for her son and one for her and her husband), Suwarni strongly feels that being an FDW is not an ideal means of fulfilling a mother's responsibilities to her family. She is incapable of engaging in the direct nurturing and caregiving that she values as important in strengthening the mother–child bond and creating the family unit. Moreover, she views herself as having compromised her identity as an 'ideal woman,' as she admits to being 'the one to blame' for the divisions that have emerged in her marriage and family.

Narratives like Suwarni's abound among married women migrant workers. Their experiences indicate that the 'cult of domesticity' continues to be strong in their lives irrespective of their becoming wage earners and helping to sustain their families. In other words, the breadwinner ideology of the man as the main wage earner in the family and the woman as relegated to the private sphere, recognized primarily for her reproductive function and her role as nurturer and caregiver, has seen a shift only to the extent that women now engage in waged work. They do so, however, without relinquishing the mother role.

Over the past decades, feminists have challenged monolithic notions of the family (Collier and Yanagisako 1987), highlighting that the boundaries between the private and the public are illusory because mothering takes place in both domains equally. The stories of women migrant workers reflect this point vividly. That these women find themselves having to negotiate their social identities as mothers while physically absent from their families because of waged work adds another dimension to feminist assertions in the literature on migration, underscoring the role of female migrants as individual workers rather than as political subjects caught in a web of cultural, political, and economic complexities (Nagar et al. 2002). But how do women migrants construct their identity and negotiate their role as mothers at a distance? Furthermore, how do they view their new identities as workers?

Liberal feminists have asserted that gender equality can only be achieved through the re-patterning of the patriarchal and sexist division of labour when women move into waged employment (Bem 1993; Friedan 1963; Lorber 1994; Rhode 1997; Schaeffer 2001), thereby creating shifts in the meaning of motherhood when such women take on the role of worker and, in many instances, of the family breadwinner. In exploring the social and economic complexities that Indonesian women migrants encounter, this chapter shows how the conclusion that waged employment is an empowering experience for women (putting them on equal footing with men) is simplistic. It is crucial to consider the positionality of these women in terms of the cultural ideologies that guide their social behaviour. In other words, we seek to discover 'the historicized particularity of their relationship' to an '"authentic" form ... of tradition, [and] local structures of domination' (Grewal and Kaplan 1994, 17). The experiences that women migrants voice clearly reveal that they have contested patriarchal values by finding empowerment in their role as financial providers in the family; however, they fall short in 'performing woman/mother' roles that are in keeping with the prescribed interactions of daily life, as their efforts are curtailed because they are not physically present with their children (Butler 1990, 1993). Ultimately, they feel that they have not lived up to the cultural expectations of being 'good' mothers.' From a feminist perspective, it seems that these women are trapped in a patriarchal ideology that decentres the power they could ideally have held in and beyond the family because they are burdened by familial commitments and thus unable to compete on par with men in the workforce. Instead, it appears from their narratives that they derive meaning from their role as breadwinners as long as their role as physical carers is not jeopardized. At the core of their experiences as transnational mothers and workers lies tension and yet resolution. Finding themselves at the 'border' in their everyday lived experiences – being at once transnational mothers and transnational workers – has led these women to create a transnational sensibility of their seemingly conflicting identities. Thus, the feminist idea that waged work is a social leveller between the sexes may be contested because it does not necessarily apply to the migrant experience of Indonesian women. The governing premise of this theoretical framework dismisses the possibility of cultural differences in constructing the varied identities of women.

Narratives from ten Indonesian female domestic workers, mainly poorly educated and from the rural areas, provide the ethnographic material for this chapter.[2] Over three months, we conducted interviews lasting one to two hours each at a local mosque in Singapore where the women often went for religious and English-language instruction. The selection of interviewees was not random, however, as they were already known to Noor Abdul Rahman from prior intensive research on domestic workers, and her familiarity with them contributed greatly to their ease and openness during the interview process. Information was collected in Indonesian and later translated. In addition, we collected life histories that proved useful in helping us to understand the background of the ten women.

Working Abroad

Most Indonesian women taking jobs as domestic workers head to Saudi Arabia and Malaysia, while the remaining migration flows to Singapore and Hong Kong. Hugo (2002) points out that the vast majority of Indonesian foreign domestic workers hail from Java, particularly west Java. The prospect of working abroad is not problem free even though the women leave the country through official channels of labour migration. They often arrive in Singapore unaware of their employment rights and tend to fall victim to abuse easily. Furthermore, it is common to find women who do not know where or from whom to seek help (Abdul Rahman 2003). In 2006, the Singapore government installed a standardized contract to improve the employment conditions of domestic workers, such as guaranteeing access to a regular day off. A review conducted in 2008 by local media of the real effects of the contract in changing employment conditions showed that many employers still resist the idea of granting domestic workers regular rest days and have found ways to evade the requirement (Lin 2008). Moreover, many physical abuses occur in the domestic realm, invisible to the eyes of the public, increasing the vulnerability of these women (Huang and Yeoh 1996; Yeoh, Huang, and Devasahayam 2004). Only if abuse comes to the attention of the relevant government authorities will the penal code take effect and employers be prosecuted. As well, Indonesian women are susceptible to unfavourable labour conditions even before arriving in Singapore, as Sidney Jones perceptively comments: 'Exploitation and abuse of migrants [begins] before the migrant ever sets foot abroad' (2000, 39). The would-be migrants are forced to deal with a gamut of officials from agents to trainers who can be quick to siphon off a substantial fee for the services they provide. The problem of abuse and exploitation can be attributed largely to the fact that laws in Indonesia tend to be poorly implemented to protect the rights of these women.

In spite of the pitfalls of working abroad and the possible hardships, FDWs continue to arrive in Singapore. Despite the risks outlined above, these married women still choose to work abroad. Moreover, they do so even though they are fully aware that they will be physically distanced from their spouses and children and that local constructions of motherhood remain, demanding that the migrant continue to be the primary caregiver regardless of the new context in which she finds herself (Sunindyo 1996).

State and Social Constructions of the Mother Role

In Indonesia under the New Order, women are regarded as a vital force in the development of the country for their part in ensuring social stability and reducing the birth rate. Government officials often reiterate women's lead in the performance of reproductive duties. Their roles as good wives and mothers, and most of all as educators of the younger generation, although culturally assigned as well, are regarded in official discourse to be the most important ones women perform. While both men and women are expected to be responsible for the welfare of their families, communities, and businesses, the prevailing gender ideology emphasized by state discourse means that men have access to greater power and prestige. By contrast, the tasks that women execute are seen as mundane and practical, and are often unrecognized and unrewarded. In the same context, the husband is recognized as the head of the family and assigned the role of breadwinner. Although colonial and postindependence regimes subscribed to such a discourse, the ideology was vigorously institutionalized during Suharto's regime through the activities of two key state institutions, the Family Welfare Movement (PKK) and Dharmawanita, which were also the largest and most powerful women's organizations during that era (Brenner 1995; Parawansa 2002; Wolf 1992). The activities organized by these two organizations were founded on the ideals of 'state Ibuism,' or state maternalism, under which the primary functions of women were recognized as producers of the nation's future generations, loyal companions to their husbands, mothers and educators of children, managers of households, and useful members of society (Sen 1998; Wolf 1992).

The activities of the PKK and Dharmawanita propagated and helped to reinforce women's roles and identities in the domestic sphere, obscuring and overlooking their roles and identities as workers, that is, as either paid employees or unpaid family labour. However, in seeking international legitimacy, Indonesia under the Suharto regime was quite active in engaging in the international discourse of women's rights. In 1978, it observed the United Nations declaration of the Decade for Women (1975–85) by setting up the Ministry for the Role of Women, whose mission was to help women manage their dual roles in the domestic and public spheres (Parawansa 2002). From then on, the official discourse on women shifted from an ideal of woman as primarily mother and wife to one of woman as contributor not only to the family but also to national economic development (Sen 1998, 43). Thus, *peran ganda*, or dual role, became the buzzword in the official discourse of the New Order regime.

In response to criticism from Indonesian feminists who were concerned about the impact of *peran ganda* on the actual workload of women, the Broad Guidelines on State Policy (GBHN) were amended, recognizing the dual role of both men and women and emphasizing their shared responsibility in the domestic sphere, especially with regard to the education and 'cultural and philosophical guidance of children' (Sen 1998, 45). However, the physical labour involved in raising a family and maintaining a household was largely left out of the process of redefining gender equality, much to the disadvantage of working-class women in both urban and rural settings, who could not afford hired help. There has been no major paradigmatic shift in the post-Suharto era in the official discourse on the roles and identities of women. Largely, efforts have been channelled along the same path, promoting a more equitable treatment of women in the family, society, and nation (Parawansa 2002).

Despite shifting official discourses espousing greater gender equity and shared responsibility in the domestic realm, research has shown that women dominate in matters relating to the family both as primary caregivers performing the bulk of domestic responsibilities and as managers of the household finances, with many playing the role of breadwinners (Brenner 1995; Gertz 1961 and Jay 1969 cited in Wolf 2000; Hart 1986 and Mather 1985 cited in Wolf 1992; Saptari 2000). Brenner (1995) argues that women dominate in matters relating to the family because of widespread acceptance of the nature of the sexes, which governs the expectations that men and women have of themselves. Brenner's ethnographic explorations in Solo, central Java, among the merchant community revealed that women believe 'they have naturally stronger bonds with their offspring than their husbands which leads them to take the burden of securing their descendants' futures more heavily on their own shoulders' (1995, 36).

It is also widely believed that women are more able to control their desires, or *nafsu*, relative to men and hence are more suited for the job of managing the family's purse strings and ensuring that income goes toward the welfare of the family in order to improve the its social status in the long run. Men are believed to be more likely to squander the household money on their 'uncontrollable desires' and indulge in extramarital affairs purely to fulfil their personal desires (Brenner 1995). Brenner's research also shows that even if women engaged in seemingly self-centred, ascetic practices such as praying and fasting, they always did so for the 'benefit of their children and future descendants' (36). And if merchant women seemed to give in to their sexual desires, predominantly they did so for the sake of ensuring their family's material resources and benefits. Therefore, Brenner's work clearly shows the dominant role women play in the domestic and public spheres and, more important, how widely held beliefs about the innate qualities of women and men contribute to cultural practices. It must be noted, however, that Brenner's work and that of others such as Gertz (1961) and Jay (1969) (cited in Wolf 1992) focuses on portraying women's responsibility toward the family with regard to managing and securing financial resources. Our research, on the other hand, highlights another dimension of women's responsibility: their role as primary caregivers and nurturers in the family and the resulting conflicts they face when they take on the role of breadwinner.

In spite of the tensions these women experience, they did not dispute the notion that as mothers they should play a central role in the upbringing of children. They saw the defining characteristic of the mother role as close proximity to their children in order to be actively involved in their upbringing. Furthermore, they see this role as quintessentially a woman's rather than a man's, and therefore transfer this role to other female relatives rather than to their husbands. They elaborated these ideas as follows:

Q   Have you ever regretted your decision to go overseas in order to
     build a house for your family and to save enough for your child's
     future?
A   Yes, I do regret it at times, especially when I was having problems
     with my husband. Moreover, a mother is the one who should be
     responsible for the child's development. A mother is the one who

should shower the child with love by being with him and taking care of his every need. A mother is also the one who should be with him all the time. But when I think about money and how my husband and I cannot afford to give our child a decent future, I have no choice but to be apart from him and my husband. I am determined to go home to them once I have enough savings so that I can be with them to take care of them. (Mirsenah, twenty-seven, married with a son, six)

Q   You were an entrepreneur in Indonesia and later came here to Singapore to work when your business failed. You have always played the role of breadwinner in the family and left the childminding to your husband. Do you have any regrets embracing this role?

A   Well sometimes I do cry when I'm on my own. I am sad that even though I am able to support my daughters up to university because I work in Singapore, I feel that I have not carried out my responsibilities as a mother fully. I mean, look at my elder daughter. When she got married she arranged everything herself. I just gave her the money and when I got there all the preparations have been done. I had no part to play in it except to be there and provide the money for it. I also think that because I was not able to play mother to them, that's why they have become so independent and don't need me to take care of them. But if I did not come here, I don't think I would be able to send them to school. (Mira, forty-seven, married with two daughters, twenty-six and twenty-two)

The above quotations show the importance that women place on being able to carry out the role of primary caregivers and nurturers to their children. Mirsenah echoed that employment is tied to the ability to shower the child with affection and love, embodied in the responsibility of having to take care of the child personally. Mira referred to the power to make decisions and to actively organize a major event in a child's life as characteristic of 'good mothering.' Both Mirsenah and Mira strongly indicated that although they were able to fulfil the role as breadwinner and contributor toward the economic needs of their children, they had a sense of regret and dissatisfaction in not being able to carry out the caring work of a mother directly. Javanese women expect not only to strive for their families' needs in terms of securing their economic well-being but also to nurture and care for their children. Thus, an ideological contradiction arises when cultural notions of 'good mothering' in the Indonesian context assumes that mothers should be in close proximity to their children. Most of the women in our sample echoed this idea.

For the Sake of Our Children: Why We Work Abroad

Labour patterns across the world show that women take on jobs that enable them to balance their roles as workers and caregivers. As a consequence, many educated, middle-class women enter the service industry or professions that supposedly capitalize on their nurturing capacity, such as teaching or nursing. Women lower down the educational hierarchy encounter similar stereotypes, as they are often linked to jobs socially and symbolically perceived to be 'domestic,' 'nurturing,' and thus 'feminine.' Evidence from Indonesia reinforces this point, as the vast majority of these women have minimal education and low skills (Hugo 2002, 164–5). For them, the lure of working abroad stems from the lack of waged work in the villages and the thriving demand for domestic work in the receiving economies. Furthermore, the salaries these women earn abroad are comparable to those earned by women with higher education in their own countries. Thus, working abroad for most FDWs signifies an economic survival strategy and an obvious route to upward mobility (UNESCAP 2008).

While the main incentive for working abroad is financial success, the decision is often determined by the urgency of meeting the needs of their children. In explicating data collected by Raharto, Hugo, Romdiati, and Bandiyono (1999) on respondents leaving East Flores for temporary work overseas, Hugo (2002), states that female migrants are more likely than males to cite family-related causes for migration, although there is a striking difference between married and unmarried women. The latter are conditioned to move to escape family constraints, while the former are driven by financial needs.

All the women interviewed emphasized that the driving force to take up work overseas is *merubah nasib* (to change one's destiny). Generally this phrase refers to attempts to break out of the cycle of poverty that they and preceding generations have been caught in, characterized by lack of decent housing and education, early marriage, hand-to-mouth existence, and limited occupational choice. The interviewees said their main aim was to earn enough money to build a house rather than live with extended kin. A few had failed businesses and were forced to take up work overseas to service their debts. The divorcees also cited providing for children's daily needs and educational goals as the main reasons why they decided to move.

Generally, our interviews revealed that overseas work for these women is their only choice if they wanted to further their goals to *merubah nasib*. Some women became FDWs because their husbands had failed to find work to support the family. Married women also said that they decided on this path only after their husbands had failed to secure work overseas. One woman has always been the breadwinner in the family as an entrepreneur because her husband was much older than she and was not able to find suitable work. Another FDW and her husband had mutually decided that she would attempt to secure work overseas as a strategy to seek financial security; she insisted that she be the one to work abroad although her husband suggested that they both seek work in Malaysia so that they could be together. She later mentioned that her objection to her husband's proposal stemmed from a fear that if he increased his spending power, she would stand a greater risk of losing him to another woman, thereby placing their marriage in jeopardy. Yet another respondent indicated that she took the onus to go overseas in order to be able to build a house because her husband was not able to secure regular work. This, she thought, stemmed partly from his laziness and partly from his overdependence on his parents.

Without the opportunity to work as unskilled contract workers overseas, the poor and uneducated in Indonesia would not be able to afford basic needs such as housing and education for their children:

Q   If you did not bite the bullet and come here to work, would you be able to afford to send your son to school with you working alongside your husband in Indonesia?

A   To tell you the truth, no. There is no income security in Indonesia. Most times we earn only enough to feed ourselves. At times we may also bring home too little to even buy food for the day! Furthermore we are both from poor families ... At least landowners are able to plant their own food or even sell the fruits of their harvest in a good year. But we are both poor ... We don't have any land ... nothing ... Therefore we both have to work even though [it means] just to feed ourselves. (Mirsenah)

Q   Would you be able to continue supporting your daughters through school if you had continued working in Jakarta as a shop assistant?

A   No. Well, if you talk about food we seem to have enough, praise to
    Allah. My mother owns some land and what we eat mostly comes
    from our own garden. The cash income earned from the extra
    harvest also supplements our daily cooking needs such as purchas-
    ing cooking oil and other stuff we need to buy. But we just get by
    and there are no extras for anything else. My elder daughter is now
    in secondary school and she needs Rp 300,000 every month for her
    transport, pocket money, and fees. In Jakarta I was earning Rp 300,000
    as a shop assistant! What about her sister? Therefore, if I did not take
    the initiative to come here, I would never be able to afford to send
    both of them to school. (Suwarti, thirty, divorced with two daugh-
    ters, fifteen and eleven)

Characterized by high unemployment and underemployment and lack
of competitiveness in the international labour market, Indonesia's economy has pushed women to take on the role of breadwinners even if it
entails being separated from their families. In addition, the revelation by
one of our respondents concurs with Brenner's (1995) observation of an
accepted belief that Javanese men are more likely to give in to their *nafsu*
when they have money, which means that they are often unsuitable as
economic power holders and breadwinners. FDW Mirsenah shows that
transnational mothers, on the other hand, negotiate good mothering by
remaining focused on the family and not succumbing to their desires or
nafsu, especially when it comes to spending their wages. For her, at-
taining financial autonomy is bound up with serving her family's needs
rather than with self-interest. Despite their varying reasons for working
abroad, all of the women expressed very strong sentiments of altruism
relating to their children as the focus of their sojourn:

Q   Given that you are physically separated from your family, how in
    your opinion can you become a 'good mother'?
A   I know that a good mother is one who is also able to be with her
    family and to take care of them. But given the situation that I need to
    be away from them in order to secure their future, I must make sure
    that I uphold my family's good name. I must make sure that I do not
    forget them after I have earned lots of money and just do as I please.
    I must always make sure that I do not tarnish their reputation and
    also my husband's dignity. I must remember that I am here for my
    family's sake, to save money for them and not to waste money on
    unimportant things. (Mirsenah)

FDW Suwarni noted that she was even more determined to continue working overseas as an act of sacrifice for her children and her future grandchildren after tasting the bitter pill of separation from them. Suwarni recalled the painful times she went through when she first arrived and her intense loneliness as a result of missing her children and husband. She described the emotional mix of deep disappointment, immense guilt, and hurt she felt when she returned home for a vacation after serving her first contract, only to learn that her husband had taken on a mistress and her young children would not acknowledge her, refusing even to sleep in the same house. Although Suwarni's relations with her husband and sons have been on the mend over the years, she highlighted that going overseas entails immense pain and sacrifice for a wife and a mother, especially as she may be forced to face conflicts that threaten the unity of the family. However, she also realizes that the poor and desperate in Indonesia often have very limited options if they are to *merubah nasib*:

Q   Now that you have been here for thirteen years and have almost achieved everything that you aimed for, what are your future goals?

A   When I finally go home I am determined to rebuild my relationship with my husband. I think it is enough that I am the one who makes this sacrifice. I want to make sure first that neither of my children nor my grandchildren have to go through a life like mine. I want to make sure that they will not be poor so that they will not be compelled to choose this route. (Suwarni)

Our findings make it clear that the impetus for temporary migration is primarily to fulfil familial needs, valued as the primary responsibility of a Javanese woman. For these women, migrating for the 'other' is tantamount to fulfilling a sense of self that is perceived as ideal, since the mother role is their most significant one. Moreover, because they find the experience of being physically apart from their families difficult, even painful, they are adamant that the sacrifices they have had to make in terms of working abroad form a pattern they do not wish repeated in the succeeding generations. In this sense, women do 'take the burden of securing their descendants' futures more heavily on their own shoulders' (Brenner 1995, 36). However, given current economic conditions, these Javanese mothers are forced to compromise and sometimes risk their roles and identities as 'good mothers' in the process.

With the Help of Others: Negotiating the Mother Role away from Home

The absence of the woman from home means that the work of mothering has to be transferred to a surrogate mother, a woman who lives in close proximity to the child. The women interviewed commonly said that they sought the help of family members at home and communicated with them regularly to receive updates on their children's development and to help with their surveillance and discipline. In fact, they believed that the support of family back home was central in ensuring that their children did not go astray or become susceptible to bad influence:

Q   Do you worry that your daughter may become undisciplined because of your absence?

A   So far, praise to Allah, I have never had that problem. My family helped me a lot in ensuring that she always has good spiritual instruction. I have many siblings, seven of them, so they also play a role in bringing up my daughter in the sense of giving her good advice and acting as role models. I am happy that every time I remind her not to forget her prayers, she says 'Yes mama I know that if I am [too] lazy to pray then my mind will not be at peace.' (Sri, forty-four, divorced and remarried with one daughter, eighteen)

Others with children below the age of five noted that their husbands and babysitters played a key role in familiarizing their children with them. Mirsenah noted that her husband used to show their then two-year-old son her photograph. She noted that this was useful because her son was at first 'shy' to come near her when she arrived back in the village; however, he warmed up to her after a few days. Suwarni noted that her son started to accept her more easily on becoming a teenager and entering secondary school because his guardian, also a relative, repeatedly advised him to acknowledge her as his mother. Thus, transnational mothers rely on the strength of the family support at home, a crucial network for their efforts in negotiating 'good mothering' from a distance and maintaining their identities as mothers.

Research shows that Javanese mothers have always worked creatively to tap into the networks of kin, family, and friends for child minding when they are away at work (Saptari 2000; Wolf 1992). These networks may be both intra- and inter-household, based on relationships of reciprocity and obligation. In accordance with cultural norms, women come home in the evening, procure food, cook, serve, and take over the work of child minding.[3] The connection of the mother role with these activities starts when a woman breastfeeds her child. As the child grows older, physical interaction between child and mother is also necessary for the production of kinship, as women give of themselves through cooking and distributing food (cf Carsten 1997; Devasahayam 2001). Hence, these activities are meaningful not simply as physical tasks but rather as a social means through which kinship is (re)produced at the everyday level, as a child learns to associate these activities with the mother role. However, physical separation means that this practice must be transferred to surrogate mothers, thereby weakening the mother–child bond. For Javanese women, gender and, in turn, the mother role can be achieved only through what Butler refers to as 'performativity': ways in which bodies repetitively perform themselves not just as 'feminine' juxtaposed against 'masculine' but as 'mothers' in opposition to 'fathers' (1990, 24–5; 1993, 12–13). As such, if a woman is unable to fulfil this role, she experiences a great deal of anxiety:

Q   When you decided to come here, weren't you worried that it might strain your relationship with your husband?

A   Well, not really because we both have promised to stay faithful. Anyway, we live so near our families and the mosque so if he does anything funny I will know straight away. I am more worried about my daughter. I am most worried that she will not identify me as her mother, you know, with me being so far away and not being able to take care of her. So when I went home the last time for a break I was really anxious that she would not identify me as her mother because that would break my heart. (Aminah, twenty-six, married with a daughter, three.)

While Aminah, is all too aware of the 'threat' that she faces in losing her 'mother' identity, which she values highly, Siti and Suwarni poignantly illustrate the real impact of separation on the mother–child relationship:

Q   How is your relationship with your child considering that you have been away for seven years and were able to spend only one month with him within that span of time?

A   I left when he was about six ... Of course we don't have a close relationship! When I came back from Malaysia after serving the three-year contract he would not even come near me, let alone let me kiss him. Although he knows I am his mother, his actions show that he doesn't acknowledge me as his mother. I felt really sad and hurt as he does not respond to me when I call him. He kept sticking to my sister-in-law, who takes care of him while I'm away. He calls her 'mother.' He even refused to sleep in my house when I was there but instead continued sleeping at her house. (Siti, thirty-three, married with a son, thirteen)

Q In your thirteen years here how often do you go back to the village?

A It depends. The first time I went home was after serving two years. Then again after four years and then again after five years! Each time I came home, my sons had grown up. They did not want to come near me. When I first rang them from Singapore they refused to speak to me. When I was home they called me 'aunty.' They did not identify me as their mother. Once, they even asked their babysitter, a neighbour who is also a relative, who I was. She explained that I was their mother and that I lived there. They did not believe her and said our mother is away and she's not coming back. I cried and cried the whole time I was back then. I guess that's what happens when you leave your children when they are still young. (Suwarni)

The fear of losing their kinship identity as mothers in the eyes of their children was the greatest concern of these FDWs. They were fully aware that the distance between them had incapacitated them from fully playing the mother role as culturally prescribed. In the cases of Suwarni and Siti, it is clear that a woman's identity as mother is inextricable from its performative roles. The deep disappointment and sadness they strongly feel suggests the high value they put on their success in strengthening and maintaining social and kin relations while seeking financial empowerment for their families. Caught in this dilemma, these transnational mothers rationalized their separation from their children in terms of the urgency of meeting the needs of the latter. Moreover, they deliberately made this situation known to their children in order to reaffirm their position as mothers.

Tuti and Suwatri also suggest that transnational mothers run the risk of being construed as 'bad mothers' by their children because the separation means abandoning culturally prescribed mothering roles:

Q Before you left for Singapore, did you explain to your children why you were leaving?

A   Yes of course ... I told them I am leaving for Singapore to earn money
so that they both can go to school. Then they asked 'How long, ma?'
I said 'Maybe two years. If I have saved enough I will come back.' So
when I returned for vacation after two years, the elder one told me
'Mama, I want to continue schooling until STM.'[4] So I told him, 'In
that case, I am here for a short break only ... I will have to go back
again to earn more money for you.' So they accepted the fact that
their mother is away for their sake and they did not hold it against
me. (Tuti, thirty-five, married with two sons, fourteen and seven)

Q   How do you communicate with your daughters?
A   I write to them. I want them to know and understand that although
I am very far away from them, I have not forgotten about them and
only think about making money. I constantly remind them I am here
in Singapore for their sake. I remind them that if I am not here and
we are not apart, it would be impossible to see them through school.
So they understand. (Suwarti)

Doing What I Can: Forms of Mothering at a Distance

Although Javanese women have always played a central role in securing their families' financial needs, 'good mothering' is not limited to
seeking financial empowerment for the family by cleverly managing
resources or becoming the primary breadwinner. It is shown that as
good mothers, women are not only expected but also place expectations on themselves to carry out the primary caregiver role in the family.
As separation presents a conflict to transnational mothers in their efforts to be 'good mothers,' our interviews reveal that they have devised
various means of fulfilling that role from a distance:

Q   When you are here, how do you carry out your role in bringing up
your children? Don't you think it's a conflict because you are
separated from them?
A   Well, I keep in constant touch, through letters, telephone calls and
these days by sending text messages (SMS).[5] Bringing up the
children is indeed a mother's responsibility but if I remain at home,
what happens to their future? My husband is not responsible and I
don't think he can afford to send his children to school. So over here,
I always make sure that I pray for their well-being. They also pray
for me. The SMS never stops flowing. I call them at least three times

every month so that I can bridge the distance between us. I feel that even though I'm far from them, I do not relinquish my duties as a mother in giving my children a proper upbringing. I think this is a must and it is compulsory just like the five prayers to a Muslim. I always tell them that I am here not to distance myself from them or run away from them and not because I don't love them. I always remind them that as a family, all three of us should not be dependent on anyone but ourselves. I do those things in order not to abandon my duties as a mother. (Ratna, thirty-eight, divorced with two children, twenty and seventeen)

Sustaining communication with the family, and especially with the children, is thus central to carrying out the mother role. It is a way to demonstrate that they do not discharge themselves from their nurturing role. Telephone calls, letters, and SMS strengthen familial ties and mother–child bonding not only because they enable expressions of love but also because they allow the mother to give advice and keep up to date with her children's development and progress and vice versa. Ratna noted in her interview that technology such as SMS and the telephone makes it possible for her children and her to be more spontaneous in communicating with each other than they can be through letters. Our interviews revealed these forms of communication to be common practice among transnational mothers in negotiating the mother role given the separation of time and space from their children.

Conversely, irregular communication can certainly severely strain the mother–child relationship as Siti and Suwarni illustrate. Suwarni admitted that it was very difficult for her to communicate and express herself because she could not contain her emotions when writing letters or speaking with her family on the telephone. The situation was made difficult because she had to call someone else to connect her to her family. Siti noted a similar situation. She felt uneasy that she had to call her neighbour in order to speak to her son or husband. She admitted that she seldom calls because she does not want to inconvenience her neighbour. Moreover, she does not receive support from home in her efforts to communicate as her husband never phones or writes to her unless he needs monetary help. The inability of these transnational mothers to overcome the communication barrier had a severe impact on their mother–child relationship, culminating in the refusal of their children to acknowledge them as mothers when they returned for vacations. The situation only seemed to improve over the years as their children gained the maturity to understand their mothers' prolonged absences.

Transnational mothers invest a lot of hard work to carry out the mother role from a distance. This stems from a fear of losing their kinship status as mothers as a result of not being able to carry out the activities associated with that role. Since direct caregiving and nurturing are held up as core values of 'good mothering' in the Javanese context, transnational mothers seek every possible means to negotiate time and distance in order to fulfil their mother role. Clearly, many of these women have found success in furnishing their families with material gains otherwise unattainable, yet ultimately most express various degrees of regret and guilt over not being able to fulfil their caring and nurturing roles as they would have desired:

> I never fail to think of them at night after work, especially when I have just received a letter from my daughter telling me about her progress and all. I will write 'Reni ... you are now grown up and able to think ... I missed so much of your childhood ... I feel really unfortunate and regret that I am not able to be with you and watch you grow ...' and then I will just start to cry by myself. (Suwarti)

Conclusion

The ambition of liberal feminists to eliminate gender as an organizing principle in the distribution of social 'goods' by invoking universal rules in the pursuit of equality is a tall order (Lorber 2000, 2001). The ideal situation, they argue, is to treat each individual as a free moral agent, choosing a lifestyle most suitable to her or him, and to ensure that the choice is respected by others in the family as well as society at large. An analysis that emphasizes agency is consistent with the dominant ethos of societies in which 'self' and 'other' are conceptually and socially distinct, and the self is granted ascendancy over the other.

Stripping 'difference' from the person in the Indonesian context is a near impossibility as the self, although existentially and epistemologically distinct, is relational to the other. It is for this reason that it is relevant to take into account cultural notions of 'good mothering' as they come into play in the lives of Indonesian women – whether on their home ground or in the overseas context. Becoming financial providers has empowered them socially, but whether they feel this to be of the greatest value to them at the personal level is highly nuanced. Whether working abroad or near home, for these women, empowerment is also wrapped up with the cultural values attached to family and kin relationships. Those who have chosen to work away from their families have had to pay a price, experiencing social disempowerment (as construed by having kin relations strained) at the expense of being financially empowered.

In *The Cultural Contradictions of Motherhood*, Sharon Hays argues that the ideology of mothering, emphasizing women's sacrificial tendencies in how they lavish copious amounts of time, energy, and resources on children, characterizes middle- and upper-class women in the United States. In Hays's own words, a mother must

> recognize and conscientiously respond to all the child's needs and desires, and to every stage of the child's emotional and intellectual development. This means that a mother must acquire detailed knowledge of what the experts consider proper child development, and then spend a good deal of time and money attempting to foster it … [T]his is an emotionally taxing job as well, since the essential foundation for proper child development is love and affection. In sum, the methods of appropriate child rearing are construed as *child-centered, expert-guided, emotionally absorbing, labor-intensive and financially expensive*. (1996, 8, emphasis in original)

In Hays's analysis, working-class women are spared from this hegemonic mothering paradigm because they are not able to afford it financially. Although Indonesian women who find low-paid jobs in countries such as Singapore do not necessarily purchase material goods and services such as ballet and piano lessons and high-quality childcare for their children, it is obvious that they do not focus on their own needs to justify their desire to work. These mothers frame their engagement in the labour market in terms of family needs, with their children being at the centre of their efforts, as may be the case for middle- and upper-class women in the United States, if we accept Hays's argument.

Returning to the question presented earlier in the discussion, we may ask whether FDWs are denied identities of personhood outside the experience of mothering because they first feel called to the mother role according to cultural norms. The answer invokes a prevalent stereotype. While women are presented with opportunities to realize self through wage employment, it is always difficult for them to separate the self from the other because of local constructions of personhood. Hence, whether becoming financially capable is essential to gender empowerment and the construction of a personal and independent identity for these women, conversations with FDWs reveal that by and large they experience self-fulfilment and actualization but never at the expense of creating stable kin relations. But given that they are separated from their families, their intentions and efforts in caring for and nurturing their children are fraught with difficulty and uncertainty. Clutching on to an ideology, as constructed by local cultural norms, that defines them as 'good women' only when they are 'good mothers' has become a point of contention for many of them – a site of insecurity that would have never emerged had they found decent employment in their homeland rather than abroad.

12 From Changowitz to Bailey Wong: Mixed Heritage and Transnational Families in Gish Jen's Fiction

LAN DONG

Gish Jen has earned her position in contemporary American literature through her acclaimed short stories and novels. Most of her short fiction, including early publications in various literary journals and in the collection *Who's Irish* (1999), explores the issues of identity, family, and the multi-ethnic environment in contemporary America. The main characters of her debut novel, *Typical American* (1991), as a familial unit and as individuals who migrated from China in the 1930s, attempt to build a space both within and outside their family residence in America. Such a 'homing' process is intertwined with a negotiation of gender relations between the family members (Dong 2004, 67). Both the opening sentence – 'It's an American story' (Jen 1992, 3) – and the title of the book raise the question of what being American really means.[1] The question 'Who is American?' remains a frequent theme in Jen's literary works. In particular, her novels, *Mona in the Promised Land* (1996) and *The Love Wife* (2004) both involve compelling stories of mixed heritage and transnational families.

The field of transnational studies has been viewed as a fragmented and emerging area that lacks a well-defined theoretical framework and a coherent analytical approach (Portes, Guarnizo, and Landolt 1999, 218–19; Yeoh, Willis, and Fakhri 2003, 207–8, 215). Yet in mapping the terrain of transnationality, such key concepts as identity, diaspora, community, and nation have attracted considerable scholarly attention that is of a cohesive nature (Brah 1996; Huang, Teo, and Yeoh 2000; Rouse 1995; Smith 2001; Yeoh, Willis, and Fakhri 2003). In terms of identity politics, contemporary discussions frequently note the increasingly prominent multi-ethnic and interethnic relations in the United States. In particular, some critics have addressed the inevitable interaction between different racial and ethnic groups in their respective processes of identity construction in present-day America (Hune 1991; Lipsitz 2001; Okihiro 1991). Beginning in the 1990s, scholars in Asian American studies have noted and articulated the need to widen the traditional focus within national boundaries to a transnational framework as a result of globalization, 'a process that [has] denied the centrality of the nation-state' (Lee and Shibusawa 2005, vii). Following these theoretical and critical leads and paying particular attention to the transnational sensibility reflected in family dynamics, this essay examines how the identities of the characters in Gish Jen's novels, *Mona in the Promised Land* and *The Love Wife*, are contested in their interracial and transnational encounters. They display Jen's 'continual exploration of the complex issues of identity, racism, and the multi-ethnic environment in the contemporary United States' (Dong 2008, 475). These novels are of particular significance in the study of transnationalism because they shift the focus of attention from immigrants to American-born generations and from ethnic minorities to Caucasian Americans and people of mixed heritage. A number of critics and scholars have discussed transnationalism within the framework of diaspora (Ang 2003; Thorpe 2005; Yeoh, Willis, and Fakhri 2003). Gish Jen's fiction portrays the issue of the transnational in the context of American families. Her characters, no matter what nationality, ethnicity, and gender they are, present differing ways of growing up transnational and pose a challenge to the reader's understanding of being American.

When discussing the implications of the word *transnational*, Vera Mackie points to the tension associated with the term, 'which always keeps the "national" firmly in focus' (2001, 184). In Gish Jen's fiction, the entanglement of the transnational, national, racial, and ethnic is frequently cast in the spotlight as she utilizes a witty style to tell the stories of the Changowitzs and the Bailey Wongs. The protagonist Mona Changowitz constructs her distinctive identity through negotiating between Chinese-ness, American-ness, and Jewish-ness; the character of Janie Bailey Wong (known by her nickname, Blondie) struggles to find her own position between Chinese-ness, American-ness, and whiteness. In Gish Jen's works, 'American identity as a diversity that is acquired and constructed rather than inherited and "natural"' appears repeatedly (Partridge 2005, 243).

One 'melty January morning' in Scarshill, New York, Mona Chang becomes Jewish: 'Through a sheet, three witnesses listen solemnly to the dunk. She chants her Shema Israel. She burns her special four-stranded candle. Her three witnesses sign neatly her nice framable certificate. And in this way, she becomes Mona-also-known-as-Ruth, a more or less genuine Catholic Chinese Jew' (Jen 1997, 44). If this Mona-turning-from-Chinese-to-Jewish presents a challenge to the reader's understanding of what it means to be ethnic American, then the story of the Bailey Wong family pushes the boundaries further to question the meaning of being white American in a transnational family. Janie, the main character, cannot help but notice the different hair colours and skin tones in her family, which includes a Caucasian mother, a Chinese American father, two adopted daughters of Asian heritage, a biological son who is blonde, and a Chinese nanny. Janie describes her family as an odd mixture of heads of black hair with just two heads of blonde: 'Any passerby would have thought ... that I was visiting with my son, Bailey ... Watching in the mirror, it seemed to me that the Wongs owned the space, and that you could see it in the way they gestured back and forth to one another' (Jen 2004, 245–6). As these examples suggest, in Jen's fictional world, the Changowitzs and the Bailey Wongs reshape their identities and their transnational families, and in the process redefine what it means to be American.

In *Mona in the Promised Land*, the teenaged protagonist Mona searches for her identity as a young minority woman by engaging with people of different nationalities, races, and ethnicities and converting to Judaism. As Chinese American writer Amy Tan remarks, in this novel 'Gish Jen bravely skewers what we *think* we mean by assimilation, cultural diversity and the uniquely American right to forge a new identity and then patent it. Not only that, now I finally know why Chinese mothers are like Jewish mothers' (Jen 1997, fly page, emphasis in original). Indeed, set in the late 1960s and '70s, the novel presents multiethnicity and mixed heritage as facts of life rather than as abstract concepts. The story traces a searching process in which Mona transforms from a member of the Chinese American Chang household to one of the Changowitzs, a transnational family of Jewish, German, Chinese, and American heritage.

The story starts by introducing the Changs: 'There they are, nice Chinese family – father, mother, two born-here girls' (Jen 1997, 3). Both parents, Ralph and Helen, are first-generation immigrants from China. Their ultimate goal seems to be sending their girls, Callie and Mona, to Ivy League colleges. In terms of the social environment, the story begins in 1968, when 'the blushing dawn of ethnic awareness has yet to pink up their inky suburban night' and 'they're the New Jews, after all, a model minority and Great American Success. They know they belong in the promised land' (3). In that year, Mona is in sixth grade and her family has just moved to a new house in Scarshill, New York, a neighbourhood predominantly 'rich and Jewish' (3). These lines reveal three unavoidable aspects of Mona's identity formation: she is American by birth; she has Chinese ancestry from her parents; and with her family, she settles down in a Jewish community. For Mona, these factors are intertwined with one another even before she realizes how complex her reality will become. In Ien Ang's conception, hybridity is 'a concept that confronts and problematises boundaries, although it does not erase them. As such, hybridity always implies an unsettling of identities' (2003, 149). In Gish Jen's story, such hybridity, both emotional and ideological, applies to the social and communal context as well as to Mona's personal experience. The writer, with the insight to centre the story on her young protagonist's search for a self that befits her cultural identity, prompts her readers to contemplate what being American really means. The novel thus engages the affinity between Chinese Americans and Jewish Americans during Mona's coming of age.

As a teenager, Mona is inevitably confronted with her identity among her family, her teachers, her schoolmates, and their parents. To forget that she is Chinese is ironically easy and hard at once for Mona: 'It is easy because by her lonesome she in fact often does. Out in the world of other people, though, Mona has people like Miss Feeble to keep the subject shiny' (Jen 1997, 32). The fact that she is perceived as Chinese makes her (and her sister, Callie) feel like a 'permanent exchange student in school.' It also makes Mona a phenomenon for a while among the sixth graders. Whether to confirm her cultural origins or to enjoy the attention afforded to her because of her 'difference,' Mona sometimes performs so-called Chinese customs in front of her peers: mysticizing Chinese cuisine, asserting that Chinese people eat living monkey brains, declaring that she has no need to use deodorant, pretending that she knows how to practise karate and how to get pregnant with tea, and even showing off the few Chinese words she knows in Shanghai dialect. On the one hand, her Chinese-ness is a crucial method of distinguishing herself from the other American teens in school. On the other hand, she uses Chinese-ness to differentiate herself from her first-generation parents as well: she identifies herself as a *Chinese American* and labels her parents as *immigrants* from China, even though she is aware that her parents would never use the word 'immigrant' to describe themselves.

If the fact that Mona becomes a phenomenon as a Chinese American is more or less owing to the cultural heritage she receives from her parents and to her innately distinct physical features, she attracts more attention later in the novel as the result of a self-conscious choice to convert to Judaism. Earlier, Mona 'got confirmed in the Catholic Church, but she did it the way you were supposed to' (Jen 1997, 32). Yet she has never been a practising Catholic and has not given it much thought. In her high school years, Judaism is almost a fashion among her peers. After her best friend, Barbara Gugelstein, converts to Judaism, Mona considers Judaism and the issue of choosing one's religion and belonging seriously. Because of her personal situation as an ethnic American, Mona frequently feels herself to be 'a stranger in a strange land' with a 'home away from home' (33). In this sense, one can argue that her conversion may be a way of her searching for belonging as well as a sign of adolescent rebellion. Before she thinks of converting and talking to Rabbi Horowitz, Mona first straightens out the idea of a 'switch,' which is the main point of Jen's novel. The ability of some people to transform from what they were before to what they are now originates from the fact that *All over the world, people have their own cultures. That's what they learned in social studies'* (18, emphasis in original). At the age of sixteen, however, Mona experiences her inaugural celebratory Jewish ceremony without her family being present, or informed. This act of becoming Jewish is as much a religious choice for Mona as it is a cultural change. After becoming a Chinese Jew, she feels herself being treated as the 'official mascot,' a 'phenomenon,' and 'a kind of Jewish Yoko Ono' (32, 63, 223). In Mona's eyes, converting to Judaism is therefore a way of realizing the idea of being American. As such, Chinese-ness, American-ness, and Jewish-ness are integrated into her identity construction.

By way of conversion, Mona claims her Jewish-ness through religious belonging and her American-ness through actualizing the idea of being an American living in a 'free country.' Mona's choice is at odds with a monolithic understanding of racial categories: 'Racial categories obviously do not exist outside cultural and spatial contexts, but are thoroughly framed by and within it' (Ang 1994, 9). As a matter of course, Mona's action also violates her parents' conception of a well-behaved Chinese daughter. In several ensuing discussions and debates with her mother regarding her conversion, Mona elaborates on the conjunction between American-ness and Jewish-ness in her identity construction:

'That's enough Jewish,' she [Helen] says. 'Forget about services. Not funny anymore. You know where all the trouble started? All the trouble started from you become Jewish.'

'Mom,' Mona says. 'It's a free country. I can go to temple if I want. In fact, if I wanted to, I could go to a mosque ...'

'Forget about free country,' she says.

'What do you mean? This is America. I can remember what I want, I can be what I want, I can ... It's a free country, I can talk however I want. It's my right.'

'Free country! Right! In this house, no such thing!'

'That's exactly the problem! Everywhere else is America, but in this house it's China!'

'That's right! No America here! In this house, children listen to parents!' (Jen 1997, 248, 250)

In Mona's interpretation, the act of becoming Jewish could be taken as a part or an embodiment of being American, in light of the free choice it offers for her individuality. Yet Helen can accept her daughter being American, but not Jewish.

Mona's embrace of her Jewish-ness brings in another character, who plays a crucial role in the book's plot development as well as in Mona's life: Seth Mandel, an American-born Jew of German heritage. This shortish, bright-eyed, pony-tailed guy with big, broad shoulders becomes Mona's boyfriend, partner, and eventually husband. Their relationship further complicates Mona's process of identity construction. The book ends with the birth of the Changowitzs, a newly forged American family of three. It is the day before Mona and Seth's wedding as well as the one-year birthday party for their biracial daughter, Io. Mona and her Aunt Theresa are discussing the possibility of her name change after the marriage:

And what about her name? Should she change it in this wedding tomorrow?

'To Mandel?' says Theresa, surprised. 'No more women's lib? Mona Mandel. Mona Mandel.' She tries it out. 'It sounds very nice. Like a river.'

'No, no. To Changowitz,' says Mona. 'I was thinking that Seth would change his name to match.'

'You could,' says Theresa bravely. 'Though what about Io? Will she become Changowitz too?'

'Of course,' says Mona. (Jen 1997, 303)

According to Trinh Minh-ha, 'naming is part of the human rituals of incorporation' (1989, 54), Mona's naming strategy confirms her self-consciously constructed identity as a Jewish American woman of Chinese origin. She adds the suffix -owitz, usually associated with Eastern European Jews, to her Chinese surname, Chang, to coin a new family name, Changowitz, for herself, her husband-to-be, Seth Mandel, and their daughter, Io. This process of self-realization exemplifies her way of avoiding being 'unnamed,' which is 'less human than the inhuman or sub-human' (54). Mona's naming strategy highlights the self-chosen identity of this particular family to be Jewish American of German and Chinese heritage and defines the meaning of being American in a unique way. The hybrid nature of Changowitz is the very representation of Mona's coming of age with a self-constructed cultural self. Mona's idea of changing the whole family into this newly minted name also indicates a reconstruction of her husband's identity and defines their mixed-race daughter, Io, in this new American family.

Through her humorous, multidimensional protagonist Mona, Gish Jen explores the entanglement of Jewish, Chinese, and American identities. Jen's literary investigation of multi-ethnic America and transnational families does not stop at the interaction between Chinese and Jewish American identities. In her next novel, *The Love Wife*, Jen adds another question to the discussion of identity through the character of Janie: what does it mean to be Caucasian American in an era when the key concepts of race and ethnicity appear so widely in popular and scholarly publications? Moreover, when people repeatedly talk about issues of minorities, how does the so-called majority represent its identity and how do people of mixed heritage reshape whiteness in American families?

If Mona's identity pursuit is entangled with interracial relationships and ends with the formation of a transnational family of her own, then the Bailey Wong family in *The Love Wife* takes a transnational stance on its first appearance in the story. The issue of identity is contested through the family life of Janie Bailey, a Caucasian woman in her forties. She is the wife of Carnegie Wong, a Chinese American man; and the mother of two Asian girls, fifteen-year-old Lizzy, adopted in the United States, and nine-year-old Wendy, adopted from China, and of a biological biracial son, thirteen-month-old Ellison (nicknamed Bailey). This self-chosen and self-made family, as their neighbour Mitchell proclaims, is the *'new American family'* and is viewed as 'unnatural' by

Janie's Chinese mother-in-law, Mama Wong (Jen 2004, 3, emphasis in original). To make their family life even more complicated, a new nanny, Lin Lan, joins the household from China, in response to Mama Wong's will.

It is true that the characters in Jen's works are often 'captured in moments of transition, as they try to make sense of their past and anticipate the future' (Heung 1999, 41). Yet for the Bailey Wongs, leading an everyday life in a transnational family proves to be a particularly difficult struggle for adults and children alike. In this family, Janie, the only Caucasian member, frequently feels like an outsider, a guest, an ethnic minority, and somebody with the wrong skin colour. The two girls need to figure out where they belong. Lizzy is bothered by the fact that nobody knows her exact heritage because she was an abandoned newborn. Her birth parents did not leave a note, and all people can tell from her physical features is that she is probably of Asian heritage. Wendy considers herself a second choice because her parents adopted her after their failed attempts to have a child of their own. For Janie and the Bailey Wong children, the family house becomes a transnational space and their daily life is a site filled with cultural and racial differences.

The narrative starts in 1999, on the day Lin Lan arrives. Janie and Carnegie have been married for fifteen years and live in a nice town outside Boston with their children. Mama Wong has died after fighting Alzheimer's disease for years. The story portrays the changes in the Bailey Wong family routine triggered by the Chinese-ness symbolized in Lin Lan, while also recollecting the couple's childhoods and marriage. The first moment when Janie sees the 'fresh-off-the-plane' Lin Lan, Lizzy, and Wendy standing together at the airport, Janie thinks 'they seemed, despite their differences, a set. Was that racist? Like kitchen canisters, I thought. S-M-L' (Jen 2004, 16). This initial impression, perhaps a mother's instinct, turns out to be a prelude to the division of the family along racial lines: the Wongs (Chinese) versus the Baileys (white). Clifford Geertz has proposed that we now live in a globalized world with 'a gradual spectrum of mixed-up differences' (1988, 148). Not only does the Bailey Wong family appear to be a perfect representative of such a spectrum, but the narrative structure of this novel also reflects a 'mixed-up soup du jour' nature (Jen 2004, 8). All members of the family except for baby Ellison, who is too young to talk, are equally important narrators; they all tell stories about their family from different perspectives and through the use of different languages

(English and Chinese). Often the reader will find several narrators on a single page, differentiated by their names in capital letters in front of their narratives. On hearing the voices that vary by age, gender, and relation to other family members, the reader learns about the family dynamics from different points of view, looks at events from differing perspectives, and comprehends the personality of each character as well as the relationships among them. Such a distinctive organization helps to demonstrate the multiracial and transnational environment of the novel.

Commenting on *The Love Wife* in a book review, Carol Anshaw remarks, 'There is weight to the way Jen deals with cultural chasms, with the identity issues inherent in race and affiliation, abandonment and adoption' (2004, 9). In particular, Janie's dilemma over Chinese-ness and American-ness warrants a careful examination of her position as a white American in a transnational family of mixed heritage. If, for Mona, Chinese-ness, as 'an imposed identity,' needs to be reconstructed so that she can be 'inescapably Chinese by *descent*' yet 'only sometimes Chinese by *consent*' (Ang 1994, 9, 18, emphasis in original), then for Janie, whether she can integrate Chinese-ness into her identity construction remains a question. When Janie was growing up, the Bailey family 'always hosted exchange students' (Jen 2004, 6).[2] She has studied Mandarin in college and participated in a summer intensive Chinese program in Hong Kong in order to learn more about the language and culture. Before the arrival of their Chinese nanny, Lin Lan, Janie is the only one in the family who speaks Chinese. When Carnegie, Janie, and Lizzy go to Wuji City in China to adopt Wendy, it is Janie who takes the role of a translator. Nevertheless, can she really claim Chinese-ness with 'those blue blue eyes and that blond blond hair and those pink pink lips' (8)? In the eyes of her Chinese mother-in-law, Mama Wong, this is not even a legitimate question. The nickname Mama Wong gives Janie, 'Blondie,' sets up her position as being excluded from Chinese-ness. In contrast, even though Carnegie does not speak Chinese and has little knowledge about Chinese culture before Mama Wong dies, he inherits Chinese-ness 'naturally' simply because his parents are Chinese from China. In the novel, Janie cannot help but question herself: how does she become the person who cannot admit how hard she has found the trip to China to adopt Wendy and who has to be more careful when addressing issues of race and cultural heritage than everybody else in her family (132)? When it comes to claiming Chinese-ness, why is she disfranchised? Here the reader may ask: can

Caucasian Americans adopt ethnic identities as much as immigrants adopt American-ness? How does the rising number of people of mixed heritage and transnational families affect the way we define the meaning of white American?

After Lin Lan's arrival, the daughters Lizzy and Wendy develop strong interests in their Chinese heritage and start to embrace Chinese language, food, tradition, and history, ignoring that Lizzy's heritage might not be Chinese at all. Even though the girls' new China mania is encouraged and welcomed in the Bailey Wong family, the mother–daughter relationships seem to deteriorate as a result. The more Chinese-ness the children adopt from Lin Lan, the more distance Janie feels from them. Very soon, Lizzy and Wendy prefer to hang out with Lin Lan, enjoy the Chinese snacks and stories she supplies, and spend more and more time in her apartment above the garage-née-barn.

In terms of physical appearance, Janie has but one ally in the family: her and Carnegie's biracial son. Getting pregnant at the age of forty-three, Janie gives birth to a 'bright, brassy King-Midas-couldn't-have-made-him-blonder blond' boy, who has 'Virgin Mary blue' eyes (Jen 2004, 154). As if to match his mother's nickname, Ellison is called 'Bailey' in the family. Even Janie has to admit that baby Bailey Wong looks like her:

> I watched Bailey for bits of Carnegie and myself and our families ... He had Carnegie's tilt eyes, and bridgeless nose, and perfect ears. From birth, though he had my light hair and, for a while, my blue eyes – things that somehow mattered more. He was left-handed like my father and, like my father, from birth a full sail. The more I looked at him, the more I saw bits of my grandparents and parents, and all my brothers and sisters. (Jen 2004, 156)

Although Ellison eventually turns brown-eyed like his father, he is still too blonde to pass as a 'mixed-up soup du jour' (8). Were Ellison to resemble Carnegie, would he be a Wong more than a Bailey? Here the reader is invited to give a second thought to the meanings of mixed heritage. Janie's parents and grandparents may have come from different countries, she herself may be German American or Scotch-Irish American, and Ellison is obviously biracial. But, as Lizzy explicates, 'It doesn't matter as much because you're white ... Nobody wonders where you're from, nobody asks you' (213). The demarcation between the Wongs and the Baileys is intensified by the arrival of the blonde

Ellison and the Chinese Lin Lan who, as the novel later reveals, is Mama Wong's daughter from her previous marriage. This household seems to fall into two halves that separate from each other day by day: the Chinese and the white. When Carnegie and Janie decide to separate at the end of the novel, the family splits along the racial lines: Janie moves out of the family house into a cottage, taking Ellison with her because he is too young to have shared custody, while the girls stay with Carnegie and Lin Lan and visit their mother half the time.

One of the artistic features of Gish Jen's writing is that her stories are full of unexpected twists. Jen opens *The Love Wife* with Mama Wong's comments on the Bailey Wongs as 'unnatural' and 'not real' (2004, 3, 4). Compared to Janie and their children, Carnegie seems to be less troubled and confused about his identity. Toward the end of the novel, the Bailey Wongs finally receive from a relative in Hong Kong the Wong family book that Mama Wong has left to Wendy. This three-volume, soft-covered book adds more complexity to the family: Carnegie is not Mama Wong's biological son. Rather, she adopted him in the United States. It leaves the reader to wonder: does this make Carnegie less Chinese than he used to be because he is not a real Wong? Dale Raben calls *The Love Wife* 'a truly intimate portrayal of *a typical American family*'s year of tribulation, confusion, love, and self-discovery' (2004, 68, emphasis added). In her mosaic narratives, Jen leaves the reader to figure out what *a typical American family* means and in what ways Carnegie and Janie's family fits into that category.

In *Mona in the Promised Land*, Gish Jen contributes to the ongoing discussion of 'the complexities and uncertainties associated with the label "Chinese American"' through the birth of a mixed family, the Changowitzs' (Dong 2006, 20). Given that *Mona in the Promised Land* sheds light on issues of identity, mixed heritage, and transnational family, the novel is thus a 'timely and original ... probing of the basic assumptions about identity' for an era in which identity politics take central stage (Heung 1996, 25). In *The Love Wife*, Jen sets the blonde American wife and mother Janie in a more conflictual spotlight and challenges the reader to reconsider the question, 'Who is American?' Mona's journey of discovering the meaning of being American is closely tied to realizing what it means to become Chinese, Jewish, and American at the same time, while Janie's search for her position among her husband, children, mother-in-law, and nanny calls for further contemplation of the meaning of being white in a multiracial family. Yahlin Chang may not be accurate in observing that Gish Jen 'dissolves cultural and ethnic conflicts in the acid of comedy' (1996, 56). Instead, Jen's portrayals of 'cultural and ethnic conflicts' in her characters' everyday family life focus more on the differing strategies that emerge in the members' efforts to define themselves. In this sense, Jen, in her fictional world, continues to explore the multiplicity and complexity within individual identity in contemporary United States.

13 Tug of War: The Gender Dynamics of Parenting in a Bi/Transnational Family

KATRIN KRIŽ AND UDAY MANANDHAR

This chapter contributes to the literature on gender in transnational families by highlighting the effect of bi/transnationality on gender roles in parenting in one family in which three generations live together for extended periods. A bi/transnational family is one in which the partners in a couple hail from different continents and have migrated to a third. We analyse the impact of bi/transnationality from the perspective of a professional, middle-class, dual-earner Austro-Nepali couple living in a metropolitan area in the northeastern United States.

This chapter builds on a theoretical paradigm that Ella Shohat (1998) has called 'the transnational imaginary.' This paradigm originates in an intellectual awareness in recent feminist thought of the transnational movements of people. During the past decade, feminist theorizing has incorporated the consequences of a globalizing world as well as post-modern critiques of essentialist subjectivity. One major assumption behind this recent feminist theorizing, which we call transnational feminism here, is the connection between people across continents. For instance, Shohat emphasizes the hybrid nature of communities in a world characterized by the movement of people, goods, and images. The multicultural feminist stance embraced by Shohat acknowledges that there are 'tensions and overlappings that take place "within" and "between" cultures, ethnicities, and nations' (1998, 1). Shohat proposes a feminist paradigm in which transnationalism plays a major role: 'a relational analysis of co-implicated histories, cultures, and identities' that transcends ideas limited to nations, areas, and regions (46).

Another major theoretical underpinning of transnational feminism used here is the assumption of the multiple and negotiated nature of identity. Multicultural feminism seeks to avoid the Eurocentrist assumptions of Western liberal feminism and acknowledges that there may be numerous voices within social groups (Shohat 1998). Transnational feminism also explicitly acknowledges diasporic subjectivity and identity construction. For instance, Inderpal Grewal's 1994 essay on two autobiographies, Sara Suleri's *Meatless Days* and Gloria E. Anzaldúa's *Borderlands/La Frontera*, emphasizes the heterogeneous, negotiated, and fluid subjectivity of women. Grewal's analysis takes into consideration the different constructions of women by social class, caste, and so forth, as well as constructions by social roles such as wife and mother.

This chapter extends current sociological literature on the gendered dynamics of parenting in middle-class transnational families in the United States, which has focused on mothering in couples in which partners have the same country of origin. For instance, Seungsook Moon's 2003 study analyses the mothering approaches of middle-class Korean immigrant families in the United States. Moon found that in dual-earner families in which mothers share parenting responsibilities with other female family members in the household, an unequal gendered division of labour in parenting is not likely to change. Moon argues that the presence of mothers or mothers-in-law allows mothers to pursue training and continue full-time employment but also undermines fathers' parenting involvement by decreasing the urgency with which women wish to negotiate the division of labour with their partners (857).

This chapter, which draws on our personal experience during the first year of our daughter Uma's life, demonstrates that the presence of grandmothers from different cultural backgrounds may pull a couple's ideas on gender further apart, resulting in a cultural tug of war. The text reveals the fluid, negotiated character of gender roles in transnational families, which is an effect of bi/transnationality as well as transgenerationality. The methodological starting point is a transnational sensibility that acknowledges the possibility of fluid, hybrid, and contested identities. The first-person format speaks to this transnational sensibility because it opens up a narrative space in which questions and answers can coexist.

First, the chapter delineates the authors' differing gendered expectations with regard to parenting by presenting both our voices, one after the other. The different paragraphs illustrate the cultural frames of reference with regard to parenting and our respective reactions to the other parent's child rearing. We then explore each other's views and Katrin's attempts to resist and negotiate a gender dynamics of parenting that champions the mother as the primary caregiver who does 'intensive parenting.' We conclude by arguing that in a transnational family, binationality combined with transgenerationality may result in a tug of war of competing positions on gender and parenting.

Our Family Backgrounds

Individual and cultural backgrounds influence parents' ideas about their responsibilities as mothers and fathers. Uma's mother, who grew up in a middle-class transgenerational family in Austria in which women were employed, conceives of motherhood as connected to maternal employment. She considers herself a feminist and is most concerned with dividing parenting responsibilities equally. Her views are influenced by the views of her mother, a feminist from a working-class background who thinks that women's identities should be built not solely on their social roles as mothers and workers but also as breadwinners and workers. Uma's father, whose middle-class Nepali parents were alternately absent from the home while he was a young child, and who was in the care of one parent or relatives for extended periods, is most concerned with spending quality time with his daughter and giving her as much attention as possible. This type of parenting overlaps with an approach known as 'intensive mothering' – an ideal embraced by black and white middle-class couples in the United States today (Hays 1996; Lareau 2002). Our parenting identities differ because of our individual backgrounds.

Uma's Mother

My approach to parenting our daughter, Uma (a pseudonym), stems from my family background. I grew up in Austria, nurtured by parents with a class-conscious, feminist perspective that valued maternal employment. When I was a child, I was surrounded by a working mother, a middle-class grandmother who was still employed, and a working-class grandmother who had been in the labour force for long periods of her life. My mother's thinking about parenting grew out of her personal response to the disempowering gender roles prevalent in Austria in the early 1960s. Her ideas about gender were also rooted in her relationship with my father and her experience as the youngest child in four, raised by a single, working-class mother. My mother made sure that my two brothers and I had the same opportunities, regardless of our gender.

Both my parents were raised by single mothers who worked outside the home to sustain their families. My maternal grandmother's husband died of cancer when my mother was eight years old and my grandmother had just turned forty. To make ends meet, my grandmother initially worked in a factory that produced paper packaging. My father's mother, who was estranged from her husband, worked as a secretary and accountant in the construction company owned by her younger brother until she was eighty years old. My mother started working as a teacher when I was in primary school. I was always proud of my mother's and grandmothers' having jobs, and I think having a job is an important part of a mother's life.

Uma's Father

My approach to fatherhood and response to Kati's ways of rearing Uma seem to be based on my upbringing. I was brought up in rather difficult circumstances in Nepal. My parents always appeared to be short of money; there were three children and we lived in a one-bedroom apartment. For many months of the year one or both of my parents were not present in the household because they were pursuing their studies abroad or were posted in various parts of the country as a result of their jobs. In spite of these difficulties, my parents tried very hard to give us all the love we needed, along with the freedom to be children. Because of this background I feel a great need to be present and available for Uma as often as I can. Likewise I feel the need to provide Uma with the love and attention she deserves without laying down too many rules.

Gender and Parenting: 'Affenliebe' versus 'Fulfilling Baby's Wishes'

During Katrin's maternity leave and in the nine months following, our different parenting approaches became a source of tension and negotiations when she returned to work and her mother flew in from Austria to care for Uma for one month. When Katrin was on maternity leave, her role as full-time mother and the Uday's role as full-time earner were clearly defined, and Katrin therefore expected to be involved in Uma's care to a larger extent than Uday. However, when she returned to work, she felt that the demands of his childrearing approach, which had been perfectly compatible with full-time, stay-at-home motherhood, became incompatible with her reality as a full-time worker.

The presence of the maternal grandmother in the home also affected how we built our respective identities as parents. Katrin's focus on the importance of an equal division of labour in parenting was sharpened by re-entry into the labour market and the arrival of her mother. Uday's sense of parental devotion to and self-sacrifice for the baby was heightened at the same time that his actual involvement with the baby decreased because of the grandmother's push for (overdue) home renovations, which corresponded to her understanding of a man's identity as a builder (but not necessarily as a father actively engaged in child rearing).

Uma's Mother

When I returned to full-time work in the winter, my mother flew in from Austria to take care of Uma for one month. Then Uday's parents, who hail from Nepal, lived with us and took care of Uma for five months. My mother subsequently returned to take care of Uma for another two months before Uma started daycare in the fall.

When our baby was born, I had lived with my husband (in the United States, the United Kingdom, and continental Europe) for twelve years, and we had established a fairly traditional gendered division of labour in the household. I did more cooking and cleaning, whereas Uday paid the bills, fixed the car, did repairs on the house, and mowed the lawn. When we were talking about having a baby, I always insisted that I would have a baby (and a full-time job) only if I could count on him to share parenting responsibilities equally.

In the first month after Uma's birth, my mother stayed with us and helped run the household and take care of Uma, giving me time to rest during the day. After her departure, Uday and I were on our own for two months, even though we received a lot of help from our friends, who went grocery shopping for us and delivered countless meals. In those two months, I took care of Uma during the day while Uday was at work. When Uday returned from work, he shared parenting responsibilities with me, fed Uma, comforted her, put her to sleep on his chest, and got up at night to help me feed and diaper her. We did not always agree on parenting approaches then. For instance, I wanted to move Uma out of our bedroom and into her own room to sleep when she was six weeks old, whereas Uday preferred for her to sleep with us. However, these differences did not result in discussions about the fairness or unfairness of our gendered division of labour in parenting. I felt that we carried the burden of caring equally because I worked at home while Uday was working in his job, and at night we were both frequently awake taking care of Uma.

However, when I returned to work, our different opinions on parenting took on gendered overtones. From my perspective, I worked as hard as Uday during the day and felt that we should share caring for Uma equally in the evenings and nights, when it was our time (and not my mother's) to care for Uma. However, my mother, who had returned to take care of Uma for one month, had asked Uday to finish (much-needed) house renovations, which meant that it became my sole responsibility to put Uma to sleep in the evening.

When I returned to work, Uma went to bed around 9:30 p.m. and woke up around 5:00 a.m. When I was on maternity leave, we had made it a habit to put her to sleep by singing to her and rocking her, a process that took between one and two hours every evening. After I returned to work, the evening was the time of day when I felt most exhausted, and I therefore wanted Uday to be as involved with Uma as I was. In an email to one of my best friends I explained why I hadn't picked up the phone when she had called the previous evening:

> I was trying to put Uma to sleep for about an hour and she kept waking up and crying and crying ... I think I sang 'Twinkle Twinkle' about ten times before switching to 'Guten Abend, gute Nacht.' Next time I'll have to reel in Uday's help earlier. He was working on the closet. When he finally came upstairs and put Uma on his chest at around 9:30, I was SO exhausted I fell asleep within a second.

My mother, who found that Uday's expectations of me as a mother were unnecessarily high (spending two hours putting a child to sleep was unnecessary, in her eyes), frequently told him and me that she considered his behaviour toward Uma 'hysterical' and a serious case of 'Affenliebe.' This term literally translates into 'monkey's love' in German and makes one envision a monkey baby hanging on its mother's belly, an image that distances the listener. 'Affenliebe' has a negative connotation and refers to a kind of motherly love that is overbearing and does not give a child room to develop an autonomous identity.

I then felt that Uday's approach, which had not bothered me when I was on maternity leave, placed the burden of child rearing solely on me: I was supposed to be responsive to the child to the point of self-sacrifice while Uday was renovating our home. I felt that Uday's parenting approach was no longer compatible with my reality as a mother who was also a full-time worker. As I no longer had the energy to take one to two hours to soothe Uma into sleeping. I wanted to teach Uma to put herself to sleep. This process, which involved letting Uma cry for short periods, met with fierce resistance from Uday, who felt that as parents we needed to give our all to make Uma comfortable and happy. I felt that that was not the motherhood journey I had signed up for. After all, I had booked the comfortable cabin on the sun deck of a cruise liner, not the dirty cot in the galleys of the *Bounty*.

Uma's Father

My reaction to Kati's childrearing approach was one of disbelief and the desire to remind her that Uma was just a baby. Uma needed to express her wishes in the ways she knew, usually by crying, and I as a parent would try to fulfil her wishes the best way I knew and understood how.

Uma's Mother

When my whole upper body started to ache from carrying Uma around in the evening so I could comfort her while she was falling asleep, I knew that Uday and I needed to change our parenting practices. I engaged Uday in a discussion about parenting at least once a week and said that I didn't think it was fair that I was doing all the rocking and singing while he was working on house renovations. Uday, on the other hand, felt that I needed to 'work harder' at comforting Uma. Whereas I focused on the gendered division of parenting labour, he emphasized our different approaches to parenting.

Uma's Father

Kati's focus on gender equality in child rearing appeared to me to affect her vision of 'reality' on the ground: our newly purchased, dilapidated home. For several hours each day, I worked on the renovations after coming home from work. I did this partly to please Kati, who was getting increasingly frustrated with the state of the house, especially all the parts that were still in dire need of repair. In addition, the pressure to complete the renovations increased when Kati's mother came from Austria.

I also felt that the introduction of Kati's mother to the family increased the tension in the household as she would openly take sides when Kati and I had disagreements about ways to deal with raising Uma. This was very stressful for me as my own mother never interfered in our matters when she was visiting. The presence of Kati's mother put a great stress on Kati's and my relationship, which in turn appeared to affect the way we dealt with Uma and her upbringing.

Gender Negotiations

Katrin mother sought to reduce the burden of a mothering approach that was time intensive as well as energy intensive. Her strategies depended on whether her mother or Uday's parents were present. When her mother was living with them, encouraged by her mother, Katrin attempted to change Uday's behaviour to achieve a more equal gendered division of labour in parenting. He resisted these attempts, which led to tensions. When his parents were living with the couple, she no longer sought to change his behaviour but tried to reduce her care work by involving her in-laws in parenting and by changing the baby's sleeping routines. The mother's strategies decreased tension but did not increase Uday's willingness to share parenting responsibilities equally. This willingness did, however, increase once grandparents were no longer living with the couple. The situational and fluid nature of gender identity, gendered practices, and negotiations over parenting approaches depended on who was present in the household at a given time.

Uma's Mother

In hindsight, I can see that I employed various tactics to decrease my care-related burden once I returned to work. When my mother was living with us, I sought to achieve a more equitable division of labour between Uday and me by asking him to share caring responsibilities for Uma. This did not actually change our division of labour but it did increase the tension between us. Once my mother had left and Uday's parents lived with us, I changed my tactics from 'active resistance.' For instance, one strategy I employed was to change Uma's behaviour by teaching her to put herself to sleep in the evening instead of rocking her for a couple of hours. I also validated my parenting approach by thinking 'poor mother!' to myself every time Uday or his family members referred to Uma as 'poor baby' as a result of my child-rearing practices, such as when they heard Uma cry while falling asleep. I also started asking my parents-in-law for help take care of Uma on weekends while Uday was working on the house or in the yard and I was working on my research. Although these tactics did not challenge or change our division of labour in parenting because they relied on Uday's parents and not his own care involvement, they did decrease the tensions between us.

When our respective parents left after Uma started daycare, Uday and I still engaged in discussions about parenting approaches, but it became easier to negotiate our way out of our individual approaches without our parents' presence. It was easier because the power dynamics between us had been restored at the same time as we were forced to cooperate because of the absence of grandparents.

Uma's Father

After our parents left, we both appeared to find our bearings and come up with more pragmatic methods of dealing with Uma. We did not simply give in to what we were used to from our own cultures and backgrounds. Even though we still had disagreements over parenting approaches, we were more pragmatic and open to negotiation over the things we should be doing for Uma.

Tug of War: Transgenerationality and Bi/transnational Families

In what ways does transgenerationality affect gendered identities in bi/transnational families? This chapter shows that people's sense of self is deeply affected by the people with whom they closely interact. In our case, the presence of grandmothers in the home affected our spousal negotiations over gender roles in parenting. Parental bi/transnationality, in combination with transgenerationality, turned parental negotiations over care responsibilities into a veritable tug of war that pulled our ideological positions further apart. Gender identities are fluid and context dependent – a fact established by feminist research on 'borderland' children, children of white mothers and black fathers in Britain. This research has shown that mothers of borderland children experience a shifting 'double consciousness,' which results from shifting people's reactions to them at times when they are and are not with their black children (Ifekwunigwe 1998).

Our autobiographical account shows that the impact of the previous generation on parenting identities and negotiations depends on the degree of grandmothers' feminist consciousness and their willingness to interfere in family matters. The presence of an Austrian grandmother who got involved in our discussions on parenting not only heightened our conflicts by increasing Katrin's willingness to openly challenge an unequal gendered division of labour but also strengthened Uday's resistance to becoming more involved with child rearing, ultimately entrenching an unequal division of labour. The presence of a Nepali grandmother who kept out of spousal negotiations over parenting also failed to actively promote gender equality in parenting. However, her assumption of some mothering responsibilities greatly relieved Katrin's caring tasks and reduced our tensions. Here, the irony lies in the fact that, in practical terms, the contribution of the Nepali grandmother, based on the tradition of the devoted mother, helped Katrin more than the egalitarian approach of her own mother.

Previous research has shown that the presence of female relatives in middle-class transnational families does not generally challenge an unequal gendered division of labour in parenting among dual-earner couples because mothers feel less pressure to negotiate parenting responsibilities with their spouses when other women help carry their domestic burdens (Moon 2003). Moon's study showed that 'the husbands of the younger immigrant women became more involved in mothering in the absence of their own mothers or their wives' mothers and reduced their involvement in mothering in the presence of such female relatives' (851). Our experiences also suggest that the absence of female relatives may increase fathers' involvement in parenting. In addition, the impact of the presence of female relatives on a mother's willingness to resist an unequal distribution of parenting responsibilities depends on the feminist consciousness of the female relative as well as the feminist consciousness of the mother, which may be strengthened with a feminist relative in the home. The presence of a feminist grandmother may also decrease a father's willingness to get involved in parenting. Therefore, the presence of a feminist grandmother may not have a positive short-term effect. It may, however, have a positive long-term effect by raising both partners' consciousness of gender equality in parenting. This heightened feminist consciousness may affect their parenting once grandmothers have left.

This chapter also demonstrates that a mother may deploy different strategies to reduce childcare-related burdens. In the presence of a feminist grandmother, a mother may start negotiations with the father. In the presence of a more traditional grandmother, a feminist mother may rely on the older woman for mothering help or seek to change the baby's behaviour to facilitate mothering, or both. The evidence in this chapter points to multiple gendered practices that are context dependent.

We further argue that the cultural and policy environment in which bi/transnational, transgenerational families live can also affect the outcome of a father's parenting involvement and a mother's willingness to negotiate with the father. In middle-class bi/transnational families living in the United States, the outcome of dual-earner couples' negotiations over parenting responsibilities is undoubtedly affected by the presence of a dominant cultural ideology of mothering that advocates that (middle-class) mothers spend most of their time and energy on their children. The presence of this 'ideology of intensive mothering' (Hays 1996) and the absence of a dominant cultural ideology positing that dual-earner couples should share parenting responsibilities equally tilt their negotiations in the father's direction and introduce practical contradictions for full-time mother-earners like Katrin. At the same time, the policy environment in the United States, which favours privatized childcare options, makes it more likely that grandmothers will be substantially involved in raising children, especially in low-income families.

Conclusion

This chapter extends previous research on the gendered dynamics of parenting in transnational, transgenerational families by taking into account the impact of both bi/transnationality and transgenerationality on gendered parental identities and practices. It supports previous sociological research on parenting in transnational families by showing that middle-class transnational couples with children may be less likely to share parenting responsibilities equally when grandmothers are present in the home who are willing to act as substitute mothers and engage in intensive parenting. The presence of grandmothers profoundly affects parents' understandings of themselves as parents. In bi/transnational, transgenerational families, parental gender identities and childrearing approaches are fluid and depend on the gender views and practices of the adults living in the household at a given time.

Notes and Acknowledgments

Introduction

1 See the various effects of globalization as discussed in, among others, Appadurai 1996; Jameson and Miyoshi 1998; Sassen 1998.

2 A by no means exhaustive list of works that theorize the subject is Grewal 2005; Grewal and Kaplan 1994; Hannerz 1996; Khagram and Levitt 2008; Mohanty 2003; Narayan and Harding 2000; Ong 1999; Schiller, Basch, and Blanc-Szanton 1992.

3 Writing about transgender studies, Bernice Hausman admits that she 'can't imagine being a feminist now without thinking through categories made available by queer theory – its attack on heteronormativity, its emphasis on performativity versus essence, its insistent denaturalization of sexuality' (2001, 466–7).

4 This is often expressed as 'But where are you *really* from?' a question that Amritjit Singh and Peter Schmidt (2000, 7) take as a starting point for their analysis of U.S. cultural plurality. In the United States, to Singh and Schmidt, this question implies that the person who is asked it cannot possibly, in the cultural imagination of what it means to be American, belong to – hence, be from – the United States.

5 Ulrich Beck writes in *What Is Globalization?*

> One constant feature is the overturning of the central premises of the first modernity: namely, the idea that *we live and act in the self-enclosed spaces of national states and their respective national societies*. Globalization means that borders becomes markedly less relevant to everyday behaviour in the various dimensions of economics, information, ecology, technology, cross-cultural conflict and civil society. It points to

something not understood and hard to understand yet at the same time familiar, which is charging everyone to adapt and respond in various ways. (2002, 20)

6 In the introduction to their collection of essays *Minor Transnationalism*, Françoise Lionnet and Shu-mei Shih draw a distinction between transnationalism and globalization:

Whereas the global is, in our understanding, defined vis-à-vis a homogenous and dominant set of criteria, the transnational designates spaces and practices acted upon by border-crossing agents, be they dominant or marginal. The logic of globalization is centripetal and centrifugal at the same time and assumes a universal core or norm, which spreads out across the world while pulling into its vortex other forms of culture to be tested by its norm. It produces a hierarchy of subjects between the so-called universal and particular, with all the attendant problems of Eurocentric universalism. The transnational, on the contrary, can be conceived as a space of exchange and participation wherever processes of hybridization occur and where it is still possible for cultures to be produced and performed without necessary mediation by the center. (2005, 5)

7 Western humanism, in Mohanty's assertion, is largely engrossed in ethnocentric self-representations that emerge as a result of this comparison between the Third World woman's victimization by the patriarchal structures of her culture and First World women's authorial subjectivity:

Universal images of the Third World woman (the veiled woman, chaste virgin, etc.), images constructed from adding the 'Third World difference' to 'sexual difference,' are predicated upon (and hence obviously bring into sharper focus) assumptions about Western women as secular, liberated, and having control over their own lives. (2003, 42)

8 There is an ongoing debate about the applicability of transnational feminist theory to the race–gender nexus that shapes some women's lives. Eliza Noah eloquently summarizes this debate in the following way:

A certain postmodernist trend in academic feminist discourse called 'transnational feminism' seems so quickly to have replaced critiques by women of color, which argue for an intellectual and political incorporation of racial-gender diversity and its significance in shaping our respective communities. In other words, I learned that even as the labor and subjectivities of women of color continue to cross national boundaries, our experiences of racism, coloniality, and culture require us to prioritize 'feminist nationalist' movements – that is, work that addresses issues of sex and race. (2003, 133)

9 The question of how to write the self, a self that is always in flux and perhaps resists classification, becomes apparent in Caren Kaplan's concern 'whether or not autobiography is recoverable as a feminist writing strategy in the context of transnational affiliations' (1992, 116).

10 We are thinking here of 'literary gestures' in the sense of Rocío G. Davis and Sue-Im Lee's *Literary Gestures: The Aesthetic in Asian American Writing* (2006), a project of reading Asian American writing closely for its aesthetic and literary performances and not, as does much scholarship in ethnic American literature, for instance, primarily for depictions of cultural details and the social and material realities of specific ethnic communities. See also Elliott, Caton, and Rhyne 2002.

11 We mean text in Edward Said's definition as an 'event having a sensuous particularity as well as historical contingency,' a 'situation' (1983, 39).

12 Arjun Appadurai, for instance, delineates the limitations to theorizing the cultural diversity of the United States inherent in hyphenation (1993, 424)

13 For a discussion of family and power structures, see, for instance, Brennan 2004; Cole and Durham 2006; Devasahayam and Yeoh 2007; Ehrenreich and Hochschild 2002; Friedman and Calixte 2009; Hirsch 1997; Parreñas 2005; Schultermandl 2009; Zinn and Eitzen 1987.

14 In *Yearning: Race, Gender, and Cultural Politics* (1990), bell hooks, for instance, argues that African American women create, through their construction of a secure 'homeplace,' a 'site of resistance' for the cultural emancipation of their community. At the same time, transnational feminists use the trope of 'homeplace' as the location for diasporic cultures and their writers who do not fit into the paradigms of white mainstream feminism. See, for instance, Levitt and Waters 2002; and Martin and Mohanty 1986.

Chapter 1

Many thanks to the editors of this volume, May Friedman and Silvia Schultermandl, who helped to revise and edit this chapter and worked hard to make this publication possible; Luciana Martins, who kindly read an early draft and made helpful suggestions; Richard W. Wilkie, who taught me about humanistic geography; Patricia Marcus, my wife, for her patience and support; and my parents, Josette and Derrick Marcus, who were instrumental in providing vital information about Rio and my family. However, I am solely responsible for any content errors.

1 Transnational approaches look at how sociocultural interactions (such as occur over language, food, institutions) and financial interactions (such as monetary remittances) cross formal territories. The transnational focus refers to the diminished significance of national borders in the production and diffusion of ideas, objects and people, and by looking at processes by which individuals 'forge and sustain multi-stranded social, economic, and political relations that link together their societies of origin and settlement' (Basch, Schiller, and Sanzton-Blanc 1995, 6).

2 Tuan (1974) coined the term *topophilia* to describe 'love or attachment of place.' Johnston et al. elaborate: 'Another major form of *topophilia* is attachment to home place that can vary in scale from the nation to the home. Tuan suggests that such an attachment can be based upon memories, or pride of ownership or creation. Topophilia, therefore, is not only a response to place but actively produces places for people.' (2000, 840)

3 Imaginative geographies are 'representations of other places – of peoples and landscapes, cultures and "natures" – and of the ways in which these images reflect the desires, fantasies and preconceptions of their authors' (Johnston et al. 2000, 372).

4 The gaze I discuss here constitutes and conveys feelings evoked by me and by others, and thus belongs to a category of reminiscence par excellence.

5 From 1982 to 1985, I attended the American Graded School of São Paulo. To move from staunchly antiquated British educational system at that time – epitomized by the British School in Rio and St. Paul's School in São Paulo, one of the most prestigious private British schools in Latin America – to a more progressive environment at the American school was a very positive move for me.

6 The military dictatorship in Brazil lasted from 1964 to 1985.

7 A *carioca* is someone who was born and still lives in Rio de Janeiro.

Chapter 2

Dedicated to my family, past, present, and to come. May we eternally abide builders in the legacy of faith.

Chapter 3

1 Two early essays in diaspora studies discuss the myth of the homeland for immigrant communities in the United States with specific attention to the discursive and dialectical construction of cultural identification (Gilroy 1990–1; Safran 1991).

2 I am thinking here in particular of the reminiscences of Majaj's work with the scholarship of Chandra Talpade Mohanty (2003), Uma Narayan and Sandra Harding (2000), and Gayatri Chakravorty Spivak (1988).
3 Similarly, Cheryl Johnson-Odim, for instance, affirms that 'many Third World women feel that their self-defined needs are not addressed as priority items in the international feminist agenda, which does not address imperialism' (1991, 322).
4 For a detailed discussion of Said's interventions of oppositional and contrapuntal criticism, see Arac 1998.

Chapter 4

1 All the participants' names have been changed to protect their anonymity.
2 I am grateful to Vappu Tyyskä for this insightful comment.

Chapter 5

1 See Foucault 1986 on heterotopia, multilocality, and multiple lived experiences of space.

Chapter 6

I would like to thank Professor Sonja Bašić, Borislav Knežević, and Nikica Gilić for helpful suggestions and comments.
1 For a more extensive study of gender identities in transitional Croatian society, see in particular Leinert Novosel (1999), which contains a comprehensive summary in English and relevant bibliography.
2 My thanks to Nikica Gilić for pointing out this source.
3 In the U.S. context, see discussions on studies of the new South in *American Literature* 78, no. 4 (2006); on the Southwest see Saldívar 1997; for the new West, see Campbell 2000, and Limerick, 2000. Also, Appadurai (1996) offers an outline for this orientation into the field.
4 In two other films that have signalled the emergence of a new trend in Croatian film, *Blagajnica hoće ići na more* (*Cashier Wants to Go to the Seaside*, 2000) and *Fine mrtve djevojke* (*Fine Dead Girls*, 2002), both by Dalibor Matanić, there is a telling departure from the presupposed family norm. In the former, the cashier in question, who desires a summer holiday at the seaside, is a struggling single mother. In the latter, the focus is on a lesbian couple and moves toward a tragic dénouement but in the end also reinstalls the inevitable heterosexual family.

5 This generic mix is in itself a bit risky and quite difficult to balance. On one hand, the comic mode requires – and this is meant on a very general level – a disidentification between the viewer/reader and the characters, who are, according to the standard rhetorical dictum, worse than us. The melodramatic mode, on the other hand, requires – and manipulates – the viewer's or reader's constant emotional investment into and identification with the characters.

6 German-produced Westerns, the Winnetou films might be considered a regional (central European) and culturally specific variant of the Western, serving as a cinematographic transposition of the noble savage stereotype and deriving their force and vast popularity from the pseudo-Western vision of Karl May. Their lingering popularity and a teasing connection between consumer culture and alternative lifestyle, embodied in the figure of the imaginary 'Indian,' are seen in the 2009 opening of a tourist theme park at the Plitvice Lakes, one of the places where 'Winnetou' roamed. Several Winnetou films were shot on location in Croatia from 1965 to 1969, near or at locations relevant also for *What Is a Man*, a fact underscored by nostalgic evocations of bygone days and through the alternative masculinity that it spawns in one of the characters, Stanislav (Bojan Navojec), a local poet, ornithologist, ecologist, and war veteran.

7 I wonder whether the term *subjective shot* adequately captures the kind of auto-thematization going on in the film given that it principally implies a character's look, and so does not quite address Iva's secure sense of agency and control over what to notice and what to leave out. Something else is at stake here, too: it is not simply that Iva is looking around herself and noticing things but that as a person with the camera, in fact akin to the position of a director, she can, thanks to a handy and available technology, immediately translate her capacity to observe into film. So from the character as observer, a function highlighted by a subjective shot and thus still under the director's control, the audience moves to the sphere of an observer who is herself a director and so presents a presumably unmediated rendition of the content of her own looking, which is a much more powerful position. For further theoretical implications in distinguishing different narrative categories in film see Gilić 2004.

8 This model was debunked by Betty Friedan (1963), Angela Y. Davis (1983), and the second feminist wave; however, Nancy Cott's (1994) article testifies to its periodic resurgence in times of socio-economic crisis. See also Freedman 2002 (especially part 3); for the period up to the Civil War and the turn of the century in the United States, see Smith-Rosenberg 1986; for an historical overview, see Kerber and De Hart 1995.

Chapter 7

I owe immense debts to the people of Kankan, Guinea, for their kindness. Kader Kaba and Sékou Condé provided incomparable research assistance during this project.

1 I use the term *female genital cutting* here to orient the reader to the topic, but for the rest of the chapter I will use the term *excision*, the term most commonly used in French when this topic is discussed by indigenous scholars and activists.

2 Research for this study was conducted in the city of Kankan, Guinea, over eleven months during 2003 and included informal interviews, participant observation, and over seventy extensive oral life history interviews with return migrants and members of their households. Much of the data for the classifications I present in the second section of this chapter also come from a survey on 'good person behaviour' administered to 100 adult men and women between the ages of eighteen and seventy-five.

3 The centrality and construction of 'personhood' in African societies occupies nearly a century of anthropological investigation (Jackson and Karp 1990; Riesman 1986). Personhood includes two key aspects: the objective side, 'the distinctive qualities, capacities, and roles with which society endows a person'; and the subjective side, 'how the individual, as an actor, knows himself to be – or not to be the person he [or she] is expected to be in a given situation and status' (Fortes 1987, 251; also see Johnson 2000, 233n7).

4 The burgeoning literature on this topic since I first noted it in 1997 is immense, changing the status of the surgery from a 'traditional practice' to a 'human rights issue' and then to an issue of cultural identity, and back again. An important work for conceptualizing an ideology that structures the female body through cultural intervention is Janice Boddy's *Wombs and Alien Spirits* (1989). Shell-Duncan and Hernlund's edited volumes (2001, 2007) provide a number of interdisciplinary and divergent voices in the current debates surrounding the ongoing practice of female genital cutting in Africa. I continue to struggle with these debates in my teaching and as the mother of an ethnic Malinké daughter, born and raised in the United States. I am, of course, not alone in the personal demons that drive my scholarship on the body and Western feminism: see Gosselin 2000; Talle 2007.

5 A great deal of anxiety does exist in terms of these ceremonies, as they are technically illegal. Following one ceremony in 2003, I was followed by two older women. Though I was escorted by a local man, my research

assistant, Sékou Condé, they approached me and demanded that I give them the film from my camera with photos of the ceremony. I tried to explain digital photography, but the women became very upset with me and accused me of lying. Sékou did his best to mediate, and ultimately I erased the photos I had taken, but without the film in their hands, the women remained unconvinced. They demanded the camera itself. It was then that Sékou began to ask them why they were so upset, and they told him that a few years ago, a French woman who 'looked like me' had come to a ceremony in one of the *sous-préfectures*, and a few months later, they said that the families of the circumcised girls were fined and all who attended the ceremony were questioned by police and admonished not to attend such ceremonies in the future. Ultimately, another neighbour who knew me well came to my rescue and explained to the old women that I was a researcher who could be trusted not to get the people in trouble. It goes without saying that I have disguised the identities of everyone mentioned in this paper. International legal cases and asylum cases are also part of this international dialogue about FGC (Gosselin 2001; Johnson 2007; Piot 2007).

6 Tostan is a non-profit, community-led development organization based in Senegal, dedicated to 'educating and empowering Africans who have had little or no access to formal schooling' (Tostan 2009). Of particular interest to the group is the grassroots campaign to abandon female genital cutting. Recognizing that FGC is linked to marriage opportunities for women, Tostan developed a community-based response that places villagers in charge of the decisions about continuing the practice and does *not* require that FGC be eradicated in order to participate in the program (see Thomas 2001 for a discussion of the inefficacy of campaigns to end FGC). Since 1995, Tostan claims to have reduced the number of Fulani Senegalese communities practising FGC by half. As of 2007, Tostan had agents working with communities in Guinea, the Gambia, Guinea-Bissau, Mauritania, Mali, Djibouti, and Somalia.

7 At least in English and French, the word for education at home and education at school is the same (*éducation*). In Malinké, there is a linguistic differentiation between the education one receives in the home (*djodòn*) and that one receives at school (*kalan*, which literally means 'to read'). Implicit in this distinction is the emphasis on being a morally 'good' person, appropriately gendered, which can be learned only from an education in the home that involves the relational obligations to others within the household. In this context, Hawa was referring specifically to formal education, or *kalan*, underscored by the fact that throughout the earlier discussion regarding the circumcision of her children, she used the term *djodòn*. Like many of

my Malinké friends and informants, she makes a huge distinction between that which can be 'learned' with one's mind and that which must be incorporated through socialization with other 'persons' within the community.

Chapter 8

1 I refer to autobiography as a 'master narrative' of identity politics under which individual voices of *autobiography* are often, though not always, subsumed.

2 Susan Sontag's use of AIDS as a metaphor (1989) refers to the violence that occurs in the metaphorical packaging of this disease, which serves to increase the suffering of those inflicted by dehumanizing them and rendering them either 'victims' or 'survivors' while also creating unnecessary mass cultural anxiety within the general population.

3 According to West's *Annotated Mississippi Legal Code*, section 43-21-607, 'Child in need of supervision' means a child who has reached his seventh birthday and is in need of treatment or rehabilitation because the child:
   (i) Is habitually disobedient of reasonable and lawful commands of his parent, guardian or custodian and is ungovernable; or
   (ii) While being required to attend school, willfully and habitually violates the rules thereof or willfully and habitually absents himself therefrom; or
   (iii) Runs away from home without good cause; or
   (iv) Has committed a delinquent act or acts.

Chapter 9

1 The *Windrush* generation of West Indian immigrants in the late 1940s and '50s is named after the SS *Empire Windrush*, which docked at Tilbury in 1948. The African Caribbean and South Asian presence in Britain is the result of postwar migrations, as Britain's labour shortages were met by Jamaican and Trinidadian bus drivers, construction workers, hospital workers, and nurses (Hall 2001, 27).

2 To keep track of the family members, Levy puts a family tree in the novel that grows by the addition of each family member's story as Aunt Coral relates them, thus making Faith's rich background visible to the reader.

Chapter 11

1 Responses have been edited to ensure clarity. However, effort has been made to preserve the original meaning.

2 FDWs working in Singapore are from India, Indonesia, Myanmar, the Philippines, and Sri Lanka. Those from the Philippines tend to have much higher levels of education than those from the other countries. The majority have at least primary school education, whereas Filipinas have at least secondary school education and a considerable number have attended university. In order to ensure that foreign domestic workers are aware of their entitlements and of the labour provisions related to them, the Singapore government has mandated that all first-time FDW applicants have at least eight years of formal education and to be at least twenty-three years old.

3 Husbands usually help by doing their own washing and overseeing the education of the children.

4 STM is an institute of higher education, equivalent to a polytechnic in the British educational system.

5 SMS is the abbreviation for short message service, a very common form of communication because of its affordability.

Chapter 12

1 Marine Heung has pointed out Jen's effort to redefine 'the meaning of being American' in her review, 'Authentically Inauthentic' (1996, 25).

2 For a discussion of the distinction between descent and consent, see Werner Sollors's *Beyond Ethnicity: Consent and Descent in American Culture* (1986).

Chapter 13

We would like to thank Pamela Joshi, Christa Kelleher, Elspeth Slayter, and Nicholas Redel for their comments on earlier versions of this article.

References

Abdul Rahman, Noorashikin. 2003. 'Negotiating Power: A Case Study of Indonesian Foreign Domestic Workers in Singapore.' PhD diss., Curtin University of Technology. Curtin's Research Repository, http://adt.curtin.edu.au/theses.

Alarcón, Norma, Caren Kaplan, and Minoo Moallem. 1999. 'Introduction: Between Woman and Nation.' In *Between Woman and Nation: Nationalisms, Transnational Feminism, and the State*, ed. Caren Kaplan, Norma Alarcón, and Minoo Moallem, 1–16. Durham and London: Duke University Press.

Amireh, Amal, and Lisa Suhair Majaj, eds. 2000. *Going Global: The Transnational Reception of Third World Women Writers*. New York and London: Garland.

Anderson, Benedict. 1983. *Imagined Communities*. New York and London: Verso.

Ang, Ien. 1994. 'On Not Speaking Chinese: Postmodern Ethnicity and the Politics of Diaspora.' *New Formations* 24 (Winter): 1–18.

– 2003. 'Together-in-Difference: Beyond Diaspora, into Hybridity.' *Asian Studies Review* 27, no. 2: 142–54.

Anshaw, Carol. 2004. 'The 21st-Century Family.' *Women's Review of Books* 22, no. 2: 8–9.

Appadurai, Arjun. 1993. 'Patriotism and Its Futures.' *Public Culture* 5, no. 3: 411–29.

– 1996. *Modernity at Large: Cultural Dimensions of Globalization*. Minneapolis and London: University of Minnesota Press.

Arac, Jonathan. 1998. 'Criticism between Opposition and Counterpoint.' *boundary 2* 25, no. 2: 55–69.

Aračić, Pero, Josip Baloban, Stjepan Baloban, Željka Bišćan, Gordan Črpić, Goran Milas, Krunoslav Nikodem, Ivan Rimac, Ivan Štengl, and Siniša Zrinščak. 2005. *U potrazi za identitetom. Komparativna studija vrednota: Hrvatska i Europa*. Zagreb: Golden Marketing–Tehnička knjiga.

Ashcroft, Bill, Gareth Griffiths, and Helen Tiffin. 2002. *The Empire Writes Back: Theory and Practice in Post-Colonial Literatures*, 2nd ed. London and New York: Routledge.

Basch, Linda, Nina Glick Schiller, and Cristina Sanzton-Blanc. 1995. 'From Immigrant to Transmigrant: Theorizing Transnational Migration.' *Anthropological Quarterly* no. 6: 48–63.

Bayart, Jean-François. 1993. *The State in Africa: The Politics of the Belly*. New York: Longman.

Beck, Ulrich. 2000. *What Is Globalization?* Cambridge: Polity Press.

Bem, Sandra L. 1993. *The Lenses of Gender: Transforming Debates on Sexual Inequality*. New Haven: Yale University Press.

Benjamin, Walter. 1977. *The Origin of German Tragic Drama*. Trans. John Osborne. New York: Verso.

– 1986. 'Paris: Capital of the Nineteenth Century.' In *Reflections: Essays, Aphorisms, Autobiographical Writings*, ed. Walter Benjamin, 146–62. New York: Schocken Books.

Bhabha, Homi K. 1990. 'DissemiNation: Time, Narrative, and the Margins of the Modern Nation.' In *Nation and Narration*, ed. Homi K. Bhabha, 291–321. London and New York: Routledge.

– 1994. *The Location of Culture*. London and New York: Routledge.

Bledsoe, Caroline. 2002. *Contingent Lives: Fertility, Time, and Aging in West Africa*. Chicago: University of Chicago Press.

Boddy, Janice. 1989. *Wombs and Alien Spirits: Women, Men and the Zar Cult in Northern Sudan*. Madison: University of Wisconsin Press.

Bourdieu, Pierre, and Jean-Claude Passeron. 1977. *Reproduction in Education, Society and Culture*. London: Sage.

Brah, Avtar. 1996. *Cartographies of Diaspora: Contesting Identities*. London and New York: Routledge.

Brand, Sakia. 1998. 'Civil Law vs the Mandé Conception of Gendered Personhood: The Case of Bamako, Mali.' In *Negotiation and Social Space: A Gendered Analysis of Changing Kin and Security Networks in South Asia and Sub-Saharan Africa*, ed. Carla Risseeuw and Kamala Ganesh, 137–53. Walnut Creek, CA: AltaMira Press.

– 2001. *Mediating Means and Fate: A Socio-Political Analysis of Fertility and Demographic Change in Bamako, Mali*. Leiden: Brill.

Brennan, Denise. 2004. *What's Love Got to Do with It? Transnational Desires and Sex Tourism in the Dominican Republic*. Durham and London: Duke University Press.

Brenner, Suzanne A. 1995. 'Why Women Rule the Roost: Rethinking Javanese Ideologies of Gender and Self-Control.' In *Bewitching Women, Pious Men:*

Gender and Body Politics in Southeast Asia, ed. Aihwa Ong and Michael G. Peletz, 19–50. Berkeley: University of California Press.

Brettell, Caroline B. 2000. 'Theorizing Migration in Anthropology: The Social Construction of Networks, Identities, Communities and Globalscapes.' In *Migration Theory: Talking across Disciplines*, ed. Caroline B. Brettell and James F. Hollifield, 98–135. London and New York: Routledge.

Butler, Judith. 1990. *Gender Trouble: Feminism and the Subversion of Identity.* London and New York: Routledge.

– 1993. *Bodies That Matter: On the Discursive Limits of 'Sex.'* London and New York: Routledge.

Buttimer, Anne. 1976. 'Grasping the Dynamism of Lifeworld' *Annals of the Association of American Geographers* no. 66: 277–92.

Campbell, Neil. 2000. *The Cultures of the American New West.* Edinburgh: Edinburgh University Press.

Carsten, Janet. 1997. *The Heat of the Hearth: The Process of Kinship in a Malay Fishing Village Community.* Oxford: Clarendon.

Čegir, Tomislav. 2006. 'Emotivnost s pokrićem.' *Vijenac* 14, no. 310 (19 January), www.matica.hr/Vijenac/vijenac310.nsf/AllWebDocs/Film7.

César, Fillippe. 1974. 'Expectations and Reality: A Case Study of Return Migration from the United States to Southern Italy.' *International Migration Review* 8, no. 2: 245–62.

Chang, Yahlin. 1996. 'Again: Growing Up Absurd.' *Newsweek* 128, no. 3: 56.

Chavez, Leo. 1991. 'Outside the Imagined Community: Undocumented Settlers and Experiences of Incorporation.' *American Ethnologist* 18, no. 2: 257–78.

Chuh, Kandice. 2003. *Imagine Otherwise: On Asian Americanist Critique.* Durham and London: Duke University Press.

Čičak-Chand, Ružica, and Josip Kumpes, eds. 1998. *Etničnost, nacija, identitet: Hrvatska i Europa.* Zagreb: Institut za migracije i narodnosti, Naklada Jesenski i Turk, HSD.

Cole, Jennifer, and Deborah Durham, eds. 2006. *Generations and Globalization: Youth, Age, and Family in the New Economy.* Indianapolis: Indiana University Press.

Collier, Jane F., and Sylvia Yanagisako, eds. 1987. *Gender and Kinship: Essays Toward a Unified Analysis.* Stanford: Stanford University Press.

Collins, Patricia Hill. 1998. 'It's All in the Family: Intersections of Gender, Race, and Nation.' *Hypatia: A Journal of Feminist Philosophy* 13, no. 3: 62–82.

Cott, Nancy. 1994. 'The Modern Woman of the 1920s, American Style.' In *A History of Women in the West*, vol. 5, *Toward a Cultural Identity in the Twentieth Century*, ed. Françoise Thébaud, 76–91. Cambridge and London: The Belknap Press of Harvard University Press.

Csordas, Thomas. 1990. 'Embodiment as a Paradigm for Anthropology.' *Ethnos* 18: 5–47.

Darwin, Charles. [1909] 2000. *The Voyage of the Beagle*. With an introduction by H. James Birx. Amherst and New York: Prometheus Books.

Davis, Angela Y. 1983. *Women, Race and Class*. New York: Vintage.

Davis, Rocío G., and Sue-Im Lee, eds. 2006. *Literary Gestures: The Aesthetic in Asian American Writing*. Philadelphia: Temple University Press.

Delaney, Carol. 1990. 'The Hajj: Sacred and Secular.' *American Ethnologist* 17, no. 3: 513–30.

Delany, Samuel. 1988. *The Motion of Light in Water: Sex and Science Fiction Writing in the East Village, 1957–1965*. New York: Arbor House.

DeLillo, Don. 1991. *Mao II*. New York: Penguin Books.

Devasahayam, Theresa W. 2001. 'Consumed with Modernity and "Tradition": Food, Women, and Ethnicity in Changing Urban Malaysia.' PhD diss., Syracuse University.

Devasahayam, Theresa W., and Brenda S.A. Yeoh, eds. 2007. *Working and Mothering in Asia: Images, Ideologies and Identities*. Singapore: National University of Singapore Press.

DeWind, Josh, and Jennifer Holdaway. 2005. 'Internal and International Migration in Economic Development.' Paper presented at Fourth Coordination Meeting on International Migration, Population Division, Department of Economic and Social Affairs, United Nations Secretariat, New York, 26–27 October.

Dion, Karen, and Kenneth Dion. 2004. 'Gender, Immigrant Generation, and Ethnocultural Identity.' *Sex Roles* 50, no. 5/6: 347–55.

Dong, Lan. 2004. 'Gendered Home and Space for the Diaspora: Gish Jen's *Typical American*.' *thirdspace: a journal of feminist theory and culture* 4, no. 1: 66–86.

– 2006. 'Representing Cultural Uncertainty in *A Great Wall* and *Pushing Hands*.' *Interactions* 15, no. 2: 13–21.

– 2008. 'Gish Jen.' In *Encyclopedia of Asian American Literature*, ed. Guiyou Huang, 472–6. Westport, CT: Greenwood Press.

Driver, Felix, and Luciana Martins. 2002. 'Visual Histories: John Septimus Roe and the Art of Navigation, c. 1815–1830.' *History Workshop Journal* no. 54: 145–61.

Dubos, René. 1972. 'Of Persons, Places, and Nations.' In *A God Within*, ed. René Dubos, 87–110. New York: Charles Scribner's Sons.

Ehrenreich, Barbara, and Arlie Russell Hochschild, eds. 2002. *Global Woman: Nannies, Maids, and Sex Workers in the New Economy*. New York: Metropolitan Books.

Elia, Nada. 2006. 'Islamophobia and the "Privileging" of Arab American Women.' *NWSA Journal* 18, no. 3: 155–61.

Elliott, Emory, Louis Freitas Caton, and Jeffrey Rhyne, eds. 2002. *Aesthetics in a Multicultural Age*. Oxford: Oxford University Press.

Fadda-Conrey, Carol. 2006. 'Arab American Literature in the Ethnic Borderland: Cultural Intersections in Diana Abu-Jaber's *Crescent*.' *Multi-Ethnic Literature of the United States* 31, no. 4: 187–205.

Fanon, Frantz. [1956] 2004. 'The Negro and Psychopathology.' In *Identity: A Reader*, ed. Paul du Gay, Jessica Evans, and Peter Redman, 202–21. London: SAGE.

Feldman-Bianco, Bela. 1992. 'Multiple Layers of Time and Space: The Construction of Class, Ethnicity, and Nationalism among Portuguese Immigrants.' In *Towards a Transnational Perspective on Migration: Race, Class, Ethnicity and Nationalism Reconsidered*, ed. Nina Glick Schiller, Linda Basch, and Christina Blanc-Szanton, 145–74. New York: Annals of the New York Academy of Sciences.

Fetterley, Judith, and Marjorie Pryse. 2003. *Writing out of Place: Regionalism, Women, and American Literary Culture*. Urbana and Chicago: University of Illinois Press.

Fish, Linda Stone. 2000. 'My Journey toward Jewish Identification.' In *Jewish Mothers Tell Their Stories: Acts of Love and Courage*, ed. Rachel Josefowitz Siegel, Ellen Cole, and Susan Steinberg-Oren, 123–34. Binghamton, NY: Haworth Press.

Fortes, Meyer. 1987. 'The Concept of the Person.' In *Religion, Morality, and the Person: Essays on Tallensi Religion: Essays of Meyer Fortes*, ed. Jack Goody, 247–86. Cambridge: Cambridge University Press.

Foucault, Michel. 1972. *Histoire de la folie à l'âge classique*. Paris: Gallimard.

– 1980a. *The History of Sexuality*, vol. 1. New York: Vintage Books.

– 1980b. *Power/Knowledge: Selected Interviews and Other Writings, 1972–77*. New York: Pantheon Books.

– 1984. 'What Is an Author?' In *The Foucault Reader*, ed. Paul Rabinow, 101–20. New York: Pantheon Books.

– 1986. 'Of Other Spaces.' *Diacritics* 16: 22–7.

Freedman, Estelle B. 2002. *No Turning Back: The History of Feminism and the Future of Women*. New York: Ballantine Books.

Friedan, Betty. 1963. *The Feminine Mystique*. New York: Dell.

Friedman, May, and Shana L. Calixte, eds. 2009. *Mothering and Blogging: The Radical Act of the MommyBlog*. Toronto: Demeter Press.

Fryer, Peter. 1984. *Staying Power: The History of Black People in Britain*. London: Pluto Press.

Geertz, Clifford. 1988. *Works and Lives: The Anthropologist as Author*. Cambridge: Polity Press.

Geschiere, Peter. 1997. *The Modernity of Witchcraft: Politics and the Occult in Postcolonial Africa*. Charlottesville: University of Virginia Press.

Gilić, Nikica. 2004. 'Naratologija i Filmska Priča.' *Hrvatski Filmski Ljetopis* 37: 13–28.

Gilroy, Paul. 1990–1. 'It Ain't Where You're From, It's Where You're At ...' *Third Text* 13 (Winter): 3–16.

Glenn, Evelyn Nakano. 1999. 'The Social Construction and Institutionalization of Gender and Race: An Integrative Framework.' In *Revisioning Gender*, ed. Myra Marx Ferree, Judith Lorber, and Beth B. Hess, 3–42. Thousand Oaks, CA: Sage Publications.

Gosselin, Claudie. 2000. 'Feminism, Anthropology and the Politics of Excision in Mali: Global and Local Debates in a Postcolonial World.' *Anthropologica* 42, no. 1: 43–60.

– 2001. 'Handing over the Knife: Numu Women and the Campaign against Excision in Mali.' In *Female 'Circumcision' in Africa: Culture, Controversy and Change*, ed. Bettina Shell-Duncan and Ylva Hernlund, 193–213. Boulder, CO: Lynne Rienner Publishers.

Grewal, Inderpal. 1994. 'Autobiographic Subjects and Diasporic Locations: *Meatless Days* and *Borderlands*.' In *Scattered Hegemonies: Postmodernity and Transnational Feminist Practices*, ed. Inderpal Grewal and Caren Kaplan, 231–54. Minneapolis: University of Minnesota Press.

– 2005. *Transnational America: Feminisms, Diasporas, Neoliberalisms*. Durham and London: Duke University Press.

Grewal, Inderpal, and Caren Kaplan. 1992. 'Transnational Practices and Interdisciplinary Feminist Scholarship: Refiguring Women and Gender Studies.' In *Locating Feminism: The Politics of Women's Studies*, ed. Robyn Wiegman, 66–81. Durham and London: Duke University Press.

– 1994. 'Introduction: Transnational Feminist Practices and Questions of Postmodernity.' In *Scattered Hegemonies: Postmodernity and Transnational Feminist Practices*, ed. Inderpal Grewal and Caren Kaplan, 1–33. Minneapolis: University of Minnesota Press.

Grosz-Ngaté, Maria. 1989. 'Hidden Meanings: Explorations into a Bamanan Construction of Gender.' *Ethnology* 28: 167–83.

Gupta, Akhil, and James Ferguson. 1992. 'Beyond "Culture": Space, Identity and the Politics of Difference.' In *Culture, Power, and Place: Explorations in Critical Anthropology*, ed. Akhil Gupta and James Ferguson, 6–23. Durham and London: Duke University Press.

Hall, Catherine. 2001. 'British Cultural Identities and the Legacy of the Empire.' In *British Cultural Studies Geography, Nationality and Identity*, ed. David Morley and Kevin Robins, 27–39. Oxford: Oxford University Press.

Hall, Laura. 1995. 'New Nations, New Selves: The Novels of Timothy Mo and Kazuo Ishiguro.' In *Other Britain: Other British Contemporary Multicultural Fiction*, ed. Robert Lee, 90–110. London: Pluto Press.

Hall, Stuart. 1996. 'The Question of Cultural Identity.' In *Modernity: An Introduction to Modern Societies*, ed. Stuart Hall, David Held, Don Humbert, and Kenneth Thompson, 595–634. Oxford and Malden, MA: Blackwell.

– 1998. 'Cultural Identity and Diaspora.' In *Identity: Community, Culture, Difference*, ed. Jonathan Rutherford, 222–37. London: Lawrence and Wishart.

Handa, Amita. 2003. *Of Silk Saris and Mini-Skirts: South Asian Girls Walk the Tightrope of Culture*. Toronto: Women's Press.

Hannerz, Ulf. 1996. *Transnational Connections: Cultures, People, Places*. London and New York: Routledge.

Hassan, Salah D., and Marcy Jane Knopf-Newman. 2006. 'Introduction.' *Multi-Ethnic Literature of the United States* 31, no. 4: 3–13.

Hausman, Bernice L. 2001. 'Recent Transgender Theory.' *Feminist Studies* 27, no. 1: 465–90.

Hays, Sharon. 1996. *The Cultural Contradictions of Motherhood*. New Haven, CT: Yale University Press.

Hegel, Georg Wilhelm Friedrich. 1977. *Phenomenology of Spirit*. Trans. A.V. Miller. Oxford: Oxford University Press.

Hertz, Robert. 1960. *Death and the Right Hand*. Aberdeen: Cohen and West.

Heung, Marine. 1996. 'Authentically Inauthentic.' *Women's Review of Books* 13, no. 12: 25.

– 1999. 'Windows of Opportunity.' *Women's Review of Books* 16, nos. 10 and 11: 41.

Hill Collins, Patricia. 1998. 'It's All in the Family: Intersections of Gender, Race, and Nation.' *Hypatia: A Journal of Feminist Philosophy* 13, no. 3: 62–82.

Hirsch, Marianne. 1997. *Family Frames: Photography, Narrative, and Postmemory*. Cambridge, MA: Harvard University Press.

hooks, bell. 1990. *Yearning: Race, Gender, and Cultural Politics*. Boston: South End Press.

Hsu, Hsuan L. 2005. 'Literature and Regional Production.' *American Literary History* 17, no. 1: 36–69.

Huang, Shirlena, and Brenda S.A. Yeoh. 1996. 'Ties That Bind: State Policy and Migrant Female Domestic Helpers in Singapore.' *Geoforum* 27, no. 4: 479–96.

Huang, Shirlena, Peggy Teo, and Brenda Yeoh. 2000. 'Diasporic Subjects and Identity Negotiations: Women in and from Asia.' *Women's Studies International Forum* 23, no. 4: 391–8.

Hugo, Graeme. 2002. 'Women's International Labour Migration.' In *Women in Indonesia: Gender, Equity and Development*, ed. Kathryn Robinson and Sharon Bessel, 158–78. Singapore: Institute of Southeast Asian Studies.

– 2007. 'Indonesia's Labor Looks Abroad.' April. Migration Policy Institute, Country Profiles, www.migrationinformation.org/Profiles/display.cfm?id=594.

Huguet, Jerrold W. 2003. 'International Migration and Development: Opportunities and Challenges for Poverty Reduction.' In *Fifth Asian and Pacific Population Conference*, Asian Population Studies Series no. 158, 117–36. New York: United Nations.

Huguet, Jerrold W., and Sureeporn Punpuing. 2005. *International Migration in Thailand*. Bangkok: International Organization for Migration.

Hune, Shirley. 1991. 'Area Studies and Asian American Studies: Comparing Origins, Missions, and Frameworks.' In *Asian Americans: Comparative and Global Perspectives*, ed. Shirley Hune, Hyung-chan Kim, Stephen S. Fugita, and Amy Ling, 1–4. Pullman, WA: Washington State University Press.

Ifekwunigwe, Jayne O. 1998. 'Borderland Feminisms: Towards the Transgression of Unitary Transnational Feminisms.' *Gender and History* 10, no. 3: 553–7.

Jackson, Michael, and Ivan Karp. 1990. 'Introduction.' In *Personhood and Agency: The Experience of Self and Other in African Cultures*, ed. Michael Jackson and Ivan Karp, 15–30. Uppsala: Uppsala University Press.

Jameson, Frederick, and Masao Miyoshi. 1998. *The Cultures of Globalization*. Durham and London: Duke University Press.

Jansen, Clifford. 1988. *Italians in a Multicultural Canada*. Lewiston, NY: Edwin Mellen Press.

Jen, Gish. 1992. *Typical American*. New York: Plume.

– 1997. *Mona in the Promised Land*. New York: Vintage Books.

– 1999. *Who's Irish? Stories*. New York: Vintage Books.

– 2004. *The Love Wife*. New York: Vintage Books.

Jenks, Chris. 1996. *Childhood*. London and New York: Routledge.

Jiwani, Yasmin. 2001. *Intersecting Inequalities: Immigrant Women of Colour, Violence and Health Care*. Vancouver: BC Centre of Excellence for Women's Health, Vancouver Foundation.

Johnson, Michelle C. 2000. 'Being Mandinga, Being Muslim: Transnational Debates on Personhood and Religious Identity in Guinea-Bissau and Portugal.' PhD diss., University of Illinois at Urbana-Champaign.

- 2001. 'Becoming a Muslim, Becoming a Person: Female "Circumcision," Religious Identity, and Personhood in Guinea-Bissau.' In *Female Circumcision in Africa: Culture, Controversy, and Change*, ed. Bettina Shell-Duncan and Ylva Hernlund, 215–34. Boulder, CO: Lynne Rienner Publishers.
- 2007. 'Making Mandinga or Making Muslims? Debating Female Circumcision, Ethnicity, and Islam in Guinea-Bissau and Portugal.' In *Transcultural Bodies: Female Genital Cutting in Global Context*, ed. Bettina Shell-Duncan and Ylva Hernlund, 202–23. New Brunswick, NJ: Rutgers University Press.

Johnson-Odim, Cheryl. 1991. 'Common Themes, Different Contexts: Third World Women and Feminism.' In *Third World Women and the Politics of Feminism*, ed. Chandra Talpade Mohanty, Ann Russo, and Lourdes Torres, 314–27. Bloomington and Indianapolis: Indiana University Press.

Johnston, R.J., Derek Gregory, Geraldine Pratt, and Michael Watts. 2000. *The Dictionary of Human Geography*. 4th ed. Oxford and Malden, MA: Blackwell.

Jones, Sidney. 2000. *Making Money off Migrants: The Indonesian Exodus to Malaysia*. Hong Kong: Asia 2000; Wollongong, NSW: Centre for Asia Pacific Social Transformation Studies, University of Wollongong.

Kadi, Joanna. 1994. 'Introduction.' In *Food for Our Grandmothers: Writing by Arab-Americans and Arab-Canadian Feminists*, ed. Joanna Kadi, xiii-xx. Boston: South End Press.

Kaplan, Caren. 1992. 'Resisting Autobiography: Outlaw Genres and Transnational Feminist Subjects.' In *De/Colonizing the Subject: Politics and Gender in Women's Autobiographical Practice*, ed. Sidonie Smith and Julia Watson, 115–38. Minneapolis: University of Minnesota Press.
- 1994. 'The Politics of Location as Transnational Feminist Critical Practice.' In *Scattered Hegemonies: Postmodernity and Transnational Feminist Practices*, ed. Inderpal Grewal and Caren Kaplan, 137–52. Minneapolis: University of Minnesota Press.

Kaplan, E. Ann. 2000. 'Classical Hollywood Film and Melodrama.' In *American Cinema and Hollywood: Critical Approaches*, ed. John Hill and Pamela Church Gibson, 46–56. Oxford: Oxford University Press.

Kenny, Erin. 2005. '"A Log in Water Never Becomes a Crocodile": Practices of Return Migration and Intergenerational Gifting in West Africa.' PhD diss., University of Kentucky.

Kerber, Linda, and Jane Sharron De Hart, eds. 1995. *Women's America: Refocusing the Past*. New York: Oxford University Press.

Khagram Sanjeev, and Peggy Levitt, eds. 2008. *The Transnational Studies Reader: Intersections and Innovations*. London and New York: Routledge.

Khazzoom, Loolwa. 2001. 'United Jewish Feminist Front.' In *Yentl's Revenge: The Next Wave of Jewish Feminism*, ed. Danya Ruttenberg, 168–80. Seattle: Seal Press.

Kovačević, Sanja. 2001. 'The Patriarchal Worlds in Films by Zvonimir Berković.' *Moveast 5: International Film Periodical*, 63–92.

Kumar, Krishan. 2003. *The Making of English National Identity*. Cambridge: Cambridge University Press.

Lacan, Jacques. 1993. *The Psychoses*, ed. Jacques-Alain Miller. New York: Norton.

Laclau, Ernesto, and Chantal Mouffe. 1985. *Hegemony and Socialist Strategy: Towards a Radical Democratic Politics*. London: Verso.

Lareau, Annette. 2002. 'Invisible Inequality: Social Class and Childrearing in Black Families and White Families.' *American Sociological Review* 67, no. 5: 747–76.

Launay, Robert. 1995. 'The Power of Names: Illegitimacy in a Muslim Community in Côte d'Ivoire.' In *Situating Fertility: Anthropology and Demographic Inquiry*, ed. Susan Greenhalgh, 108–29. Cambridge: Cambridge University Press.

Lazreg, Marnia. 2000. 'The Triumphant Discourse of Global Feminism: Should Other Woman Be Known?' In *Going Global: The Transnational Reception of Third World Women Writers*, ed. Amal Amireh and Lisa Suhair Majaj, 29–8. New York: Garland Press.

Lee, Erika, and Naoko Shibusawa. 2005. 'Guest Editors' Introduction: What's Transnational Asian American History? Recent Trends and Challenges.' *Journal of Asian American Studies* 8, no. 3: vii–xvii.

Leinert Novosel, Smiljana. 1999. *Žena na pragu 21. Stoljeća: između majčinstva i profesije*. Zagreb: Ženska grupa TOD.

Levin, Elise. 2001. 'The Meaning of Menstrual Management in a High-Fertility Society: Guinea, West Africa.' In *Regulating Menstruation: Beliefs, Practices, Interpretations*, ed. Etienne van de Walle and Elisha P. Renne, 157–71. Chicago: University of Chicago Press.

Levitt, Peggy, and Mary Waters, eds. 2002. *The Changing Face of Home*. New York: Russell Sage Publications.

Levy, Andrea. 1994. *Every Light in the House Burnin'*. London: Headline Book Publishing.

– 1996. *Never far from Nowhere*. London: Headline Book Publishing.

– 1999. *Fruit of the Lemon*. London: Review.

– 2004. *Small Island*. London: Headline

Lim, Shirley Geok-lin. 2004. 'Where in the World Is Transnational Feminism?' *Tulsa Studies in Women's Literature* 23, no. 1: 7–12.

Limerick, Patricia Nelson. 2000. *Something in the Soil: Legacies and Reckonings in the New West*. New York: Norton.

Lin, Yanqin. 2008. '2 Years On, Employers Still Skirt Day-off Clause; Should There Be a Law to Get Employers to Comply?' *Today*, 25 April.

Lionnet, Françoise, and Shu-mei Shih, eds. 2005. *Minor Transnationalism*. Durham and London: Duke University Press.

Lipsitz, George. 2001. 'To Tell the Truth and Not Get Trapped: Why Interethnic Antiracism Matters Now.' In *Orientations: Mapping Studies in the Asian Diaspora*, ed. Kandice Chuh and Karen Shimakawa, 296–309. Durham and London: Duke University Press.

Livingstone, David N. 2003. *Putting Science in Its Place: Geographies of Scientific Knowledge*. Chicago: University of Chicago Press.

Long, Lynellen D., and Ellen Oxfeld. 2004. 'Introduction: An Ethnography of Return.' In *Coming Home? Refugees, Migrants, and Those Who Stayed Behind*, ed. Lynellen D. Long and Ellen Oxfeld, 1–15. Philadelphia: University of Pennsylvania Press.

Lorber, Judith. 1994. *Paradoxes of Gender*. New Haven, CT: Yale University Press.

– 2000. 'Using Gender to Undo Gender: A Feminist Degendering Movement.' *Feminist Theory* 1: 79–95.

– 2001. 'It's the 21st Century – Do You Know What Gender You Are?' *Advances in Gender Research* 5: 119–37.

– 2005. *Gender Inequality: Feminist Theory and Politics*, 3rd ed. Los Angeles: Roxbury Publishing.

Lott, Timothy. 2007. *Growing Up Catholic: The Pursuit of Truth from Tradition to Satisfaction*. Carol Springs, FL: Abundant Publishing.

Lowe, Lisa. 1991. *Immigrant Acts: On Asian American Cultural Politics*. Durham and London: Duke University Press.

Lyotard, Jean-François. 1984. *The Postmodern Condition*. Manchester: Manchester University Press.

Mackie, Vera. 2001. 'The Language of Globalization, Transnationality and Feminism.' *International Feminist Journal of Politics* 3, no. 2: 180–206.

Majaj, Lisa Suhair. 1992. 'Female Voices, Feminist Negotiations: An Experience Teaching Arab Women's Literature.' *Association for Middle Eastern Women's Studies Newsletter* 7, no. 3: 3–7.

– 1994a. 'Boundaries: Arab/American.' In *Food for Our Grandmothers: Writings by Arab-American and Arab-Canadian Feminists*, ed. Joanna Kadi, 65–86. Cambridge, MA: South End Press.

– 1994b. 'Claims.' The Synergy Foundation, www.synergyarts.org/poems/poem_Claims.htm.

- 1996. 'Arab American Literature and the Politics of Memory.' In *Memory and Cultural Politics: New Approaches to Ethnic American Literatures*, ed. Amritjit Singh, Joseph T. Skerrett Jr, and Robert Hogan, 266–90. Boston: Northeastern University Press.
- 1999. 'The Hyphenated Author: Emerging Genre of "Arab-American Literature" Poses Questions of Definition, Ethnicity and Art.' *Al Jadid Magazine* 26, no. 5.
- 2000. 'Arab Americans and the Meaning of Race.' In *Postcolonial Theory and the United States*, ed. Amritjit Singh and Peter Schmidt, 320–37. Jackson: University of Mississippi Press.
- 2003. 'Reel Bad Arabs.' Book review. *Cineaste* (Fall): 38–9.
- 2005. 'Of Stories and Storytellers.' *Saudi Aramco World* 56, no. 2 (March–April): 24–35.

Majaj, Lisa Suhair, and Amal Amireh. 2000. 'Introduction.' In *Going Global: The Transnational Reception of Third World Women Writers*, ed. Amal Amireh and Lisa Suhair Majaj, 1–25. New York: Garland Press.
- 2002. 'Preface: Situating Etel Adnan in a Literary Context.' In *Etel Adnan: Critical Essays on the Arab-American Writer and Artist*, ed. Lisa Suhair Majaj and Amal Amireh, 1–12. New York: McFarland Press.

Majaj, Lisa Suhair, Paula Sunderman, and Therese Saliba. 2002. 'Introduction.' In *Intersections: Gender, Nation and Community in Arab Women's Novels*, ed. Lisa Suhair Majaj, Paula Sunderman, and Therese Saliba, xvii–xxx. Syracuse, NY: Syracuse University Press.

Mani, Lata. 2003. 'Multiple Mediations: Feminist Scholarship in the Age of Multinational Reception.' In *Feminist Theory Reader*, ed. Carole Ruth McCann and Seung-Kyung Kim, 364–79. London and New York: Routledge.

Martin, Biddy, and Chandra Talpade Mohanty. 1986. 'Feminist Politics: What's Home Got to Do with It?' In *Feminist Studies/Critical Studies*, ed. Teresa de Lauretis, 191–212. Bloomington and Indianapolis: Indiana University Press.

Martins, Luciana de Lima. 1998. 'Navigating in Tropical Waters: British Maritime Views of Rio de Janeiro.' *Imago Mundi* no. 50: 141–55.
- 2001. *O Rio de Janeiro dos Viajantes: O Olhar Britanico (1800–1850)*. Rio de Janeiro: Jorge Zahar Editores.

Masquelier, Adeline. 2000. 'Of Headhunters and Cannibals: Migrancy, Labor, and Consumption in the Mawri Imagination.' *Cultural Anthropology* 15, no. 1: 84–126.
- 2001. *Prayer Has Spoiled Everything: Possession, Power, and Identity in Niger*. Durham and London: Duke University Press.

Massaquoi, Hans. 1999. *Destined to Witness: Growing Up Black in Nazi Germany*. New York: Morrow.

Matsubayashi, Kazuo. 1991. 'Spirit of Place: The Modern Relevance of an Ancient Concept.' In *The Power of Place*, ed. James A. Swan, 334–46. Wheaton, IL: Quest Books.

Mbembe, Achille. 2001. *On the Postcolony*. Berkeley: University of California Press.

McIntosh, Peggy. 1998. 'White Privilege: Unpacking the Invisible Knapsack.' In *Race, Class, and Gender in the United States: An Integrated Study*, 4th ed., ed. Paula S. Rothenberg, 165–69. New York: St. Martin's Press.

McKenzie, Peter. 1999. 'Swimming in and out of Focus: Second Contact, Vietnamese Migrant Others, and Australian Selves.' *Australian Journal of Anthropology* 10, no. 3: 271–94.

Mercer, Kobena. 1990. 'Welcome to the Jungle: Identity and Diversity in Postmodern Politics.' In *Identity: Community, Culture, Difference*, ed. Jonathan Rutherford, 43–71. London: Lawrence and Wishart.

Merleau-Ponty, Maurice. 1964. *Sense and Non-Sense*, trans. Hubert L. Dreyfus and Patricia Allen Dreyfus. Evanston, IL: Northwestern University Press.

Miles, Ann. 2004. *From Cuenca to Queens: An Anthropological Story of Transnational Migration*. Austin: University of Texas Press.

Moffitt, John, and Santiago Sebastian. 1998. *O Brave New People: The European Invention of the American Indian*. Albuquerque: University of New Mexico Press.

Mohanty, Chandra Talpade. 2003. *Feminism without Borders: Decolonizing Theory, Practicing Solidarity*. Durham and London: Duke University Press.

Moon, Seungsook. 2003. 'Immigration and Mothering: Case Studies from Two Generations of Korean Immigrant Women.' *Gender and Society* 17, no. 6: 840–60.

Morrison, Toni. 1998. 'The Site of Memory.' In *Inventing the Truth: The Art and Craft of Memoir*, ed. William Zinsser, 185–200. Boston: Houghton Mifflin.

Nagar, Richa, Victoria Lawson, Linda McDowell, and Susan Hanson. 2002. 'Locating Globalization: Feminism (Re)readings of the Subjects and Spaces of Globalization.' *Economic Geography* 78, no. 3: 257–84.

Narayan, Uma, and Sandra Harding, eds. 2000. *Decentering the Center: Philosophy for a Multicultural, Postcolonial, and Feminist World*. Indianapolis: Indiana University Press.

Nasta, Susheila. 1995. 'Setting up Home in a City of Words: Sam Selvon's London Novels.' In *Other Britain: Other British Contemporary Multicultural Fiction*, ed. Robert Lee, 48–68. London: Pluto Press.

– 2002. *Home Truths Fictions of the South Asian Diaspora in Britain*. Hampshire: Palgrave.

– 2004. 'Introduction.' In *Writing across Worlds: Contemporary Writers Talk*, ed. Susheila Nasta, 1–11. London and New York: Routledge.

Neidorf, Robin M. 1995. 'Two Jews, Three Opinions.' In *Listen Up: Voices from the Next Feminist Generation*, ed. Barbara Findlen, 212–20. Seattle: Seal Press.

Nenadić, Diana. 2006. 'Što je muškarac bez brkova.' Prikaz. *Hrvatski filmski ljetopis* 45: 96–7.

Noah, Eliza. 2003. 'Problematics of Transnational Feminism for Asian American Women.' *The New Centennial Review* 3, no. 3: 131–49.

Okihiro, Gary Y. 1991. 'African and Asian American Studies: A Comparative Analysis and Commentary.' In *Asian Americans: Comparative and Global Perspectives*, ed. Shirley Hune, Hyung-chan Kim, Stephen S. Fugita, and Amy Ling, 17–28. Pullman: Washington State University Press.

Ong, Aihwa. 1999. *Flexible Citizenship: The Cultural Logics of Transnationalism*. Durham and London: Duke University Press.

Orfalea, Gregory. 2006. 'The Arab American Novel.' *Multi-Ethnic Literature of the United States* 31, no. 4: 115–33.

Orfalea, Gregory, and Sharif Elmusa, eds. 1988. *Grape Leaves: A Century of Arab-American Poetry*. New York: Interlink Books.

Pally, Marcia. 1986. 'Kureishi Like a Fox,' *Film Comment* 22, no. 5: 50–53.

Panagakos, Anastasia N. 2003. 'Romancing the Homeland: Transnational Lifestyles and Gender in the Greek Diaspora.' PhD diss., University of California.

Parawansa, Khofifah Indar. 2002. 'Institution Building: An Effort to Improve Indonesian Women's Role and Status.' In *Women in Indonesia: Gender, Equity and Development*, ed. Kathryn Robinson and Sharon Bessel, 68–77. Singapore: Institute of Southeast Asian Studies.

Parreñas, Rhacel Salazar. 2005. *Children of Global Migration: Transnational Families and Gendered Woes*. Stanford: Stanford University Press.

Partridge, Jeffrey F.L. 2005. 'Review Essay. Adoption, Interracial Marriage, and Mixed-Race Babies: The New America in Recent Asian American Fiction.' *Multi-Ethnic Literature of the United States* 30, no. 2: 242–51.

Pavičić, Jurica. 2006. 'Što je Jović bez brkova.' *JutarnjiList* (27 January), www.jutarnji.hr.

Phelan, Peggy. 1993. *Unmarked: The Ontology of Performance*. London and New York: Routledge.

Pines, Jim. 2001. 'Rituals and Representations of Black "Britishness."' In *British Cultural Studies Geography, Nationality and Identity*, ed. David Morley and Kevin Robins, 57–66. Oxford: Oxford University Press.

Piot, Charles. 2007. 'Representing Africa in the Kasinga Asylum Case.' In *Transcultural Bodies: Female Genital Cutting in Global Context*, ed. Bettina

Shell-Duncan and Ylva Hernlund, 157–66. New Brunswick, NJ: Rutgers University Press.

Piper, Nicola. 2004. 'Rights of Foreign Workers and the Politics of Migration in South-east and East Asia.' *International Migration* 42: 71–97.

Plaskow, Judith. 1991. *Standing again at Sinai: Judaism from a Feminist Perspective*. San Francisco: Harper.

Polimac, Nenad. 2006. 'Hrvatski filmski preporod: Postali smo zanimljiva europska kinematografija.' *JutarnjiList* (25 February), www.jutarnji.hr.

Portes, Alejandro, Luis Eduardo Guarnizo, and Patricia Landolt. 1999. 'The Study of Transnationalism: Pitfalls and Promise of an Emergent Field.' *Ethnic and Racial Studies* 22, no. 2: 217–37.

Prazak, Miroslavia. 2004. 'Talking about Sex: Contemporary Construction of Sexuality in Rural Kenya.' *Africa Today* 47, no. 3: 82–97.

Procter, James. 2003. *Dwelling Places: Postwar Black British Writing*. Manchester: Manchester University Press.

Raben, Dale. 2004. 'A Typical American Family.' *Library Journal* 129, no. 12: 68.

Raharto, A., G. Hugo, H. Romdiati, and S. Bandiyono. 1999. *Migrasi dan Pembangunan di Kawasan Timur Indonesia: Isu Ketenagakerjaan* (Migration and Development in Eastern Indonesia: Labour/Human Resource Issues). Jakarta: PPT-LIPI.

Rajiva, Mythili. 2006. 'Brown Girls, White Worlds: Adolescence and the Making of Racialized Selves.' *Canadian Review of Sociology and Anthropology* 43, no. 2: 165–83.

Reinharz, Shulamit. 1992. *Feminist Methods in Social Research*. New York: Oxford University Press.

Rhode, Deborah L. 1997. *Speaking of Sex: The Denial of Gender Inequality*. Cambridge, MA: Harvard University Press.

Rich, Adrienne. 1986. *Blood, Bread and Poetry: Selected Prose, 1979–1985*. New York: W.W. Norton.

Riesman, Paul. 1986. 'The Person and the Life Cycle in African Social Life and Thought.' *African Studies Review* 29, no. 2: 71–138.

Rothman, Chana. 1997. 'On Being a Jewish Dyke at Oberlin College.' *Fireweed: A Feminist Quarterly* 59–60: 31–2.

Rouse, Roger. 1995. 'Questions of Identity: Personhood and Collectivity in Transnational Migration to the United States.' *Critique of Anthropology* 15, no. 4: 351–80.

Safran, William. 1991. 'Diasporas in Modern Societies: Myths of Homeland and Return.' *Diaspora* 1 (Spring): 83–99.

Said, Edward W. 1983. *The World, the Text, and the Critic*. Cambridge, MA: Harvard University Press.

– 1993. *Culture and Imperialism*. New York: Vintage Press.

Saldívar, José David. 1997. *Border Matters: Remapping American Cultural Studies.* Berkeley: University of California Press.

Saptari, Ratna. 2000. 'Networks of Reproduction among Cigarette Factory Women in East Java.' In *Women and Households in Indonesia: Cultural Notions and Social Practices*, ed. Juliette Koning, Marleen Nolten, Janet Rodenburg, and Ratna Saptari, 281–98. Richmond, UK: Curzon Press.

Sassen, Saskia. 1998. *Globalization and Its Discontents*. New York: New Press.

Schaeffer, Denise. 2001. 'Feminism and Liberalism Reconsidered: The Case of Catherine MacKinnon.' *American Political Science Review* 95: 699–708.

Schiller, Nina Glick, Linda Basch, and Christina Blanc-Szanton, eds. 1992. *Towards a Transnational Perspective on Migration: Race, Class, Ethnicity and Nationalism Reconsidered*. New York: New York Academy of Sciences.

Schultermandl, Silvia. 2009. *Transnational Matrilineage: Mother–Daughter Conflicts in Asian American Literature*. Münster: LIT Verlag.

Schwartz-Nobel, Loretta. 2002. *Growing Up Empty: The Hunger Epidemic in America*. New York: HarperCollins.

Selvon, Samuel. 1956. *The Lonely Londoners*. New York: Longman.

Sen, Krishna. 1998. 'Indonesian Women at Work: Reframing the Subject.' In *Gender and Power in Affluent Asia*, ed. Krishna Sen and Maila Stivens, 35–62. London and New York: Routledge.

Shell-Duncan, Bettina, and Ylva Hernlund. 2001. 'Female "Circumcision" in Africa: Dimensions of Practice and Debates.' In *Female 'Circumcision' in Africa: Culture, Controversy and Change*, ed. Bettina Shell-Duncan and Ylva Hernlund, 1–40. Boulder, CO: Lynne Rienner Publishers.

– 2007. *Transcultural Bodies: Female Genital Cutting in Global Context*. New Brunswick, NJ: Rutgers University Press.

Shohat, Ella. 2003. 'Reflections of an Arab Jew.' *Solidarity*. May–June. www.solidarity-us.org/node/626.

– 2006. *Taboo Memories, Diasporic Voices*. Durham and London: Duke University Press.

Shohat, Ella, ed. 1998. *Talking Visions: Multicultural Feminism in a Transnational Age*. New York: MIT Press.

Shohat, Ella, and Robert Stam. 1994. *Unthinking Eurocentrism: Multiculturalism and the Media*. London and New York: Routledge.

Silvey, Rachel. 2005. 'Borders, Embodiment, and Mobility: Feminist Migration Studies in Geography.' In *A Feminist Companion to Geography*, ed. Lise Nelson and Joni Seager. Oxford and Malden, MA: Blackwell.

Singh, Amritjit, and Peter Schmidt. 2000. 'On the Borders between U.S. Studies and Postcolonial Theory.' In *Postcolonial Theory and the United States: Race,*

Ethnicity, and Literature, ed. Amritjit Singh and Peter Schmidt, 3–69. Jackson: University of Mississippi Press.

Škrabalo, Ivo. 2008. 'Revitalizacija hrvatskog filma.' Intervju, Razgovarala Lana Gjurić. *Vijenac* 16, no. 370 (8 May): 27.

Smith, Linda Tuhiwai. 1999. *Decolonizing Methodologies: Research and Indigenous Peoples*. Dunedin, NZ: University of Otago Press.

Smith, Michael Peter. 2001. *Transnational Urbanism: Locating Globalization*. Oxford and Malden, MA: Blackwell.

Smith, Sidonie, and Julia Watson, eds. 1992. *De/Colonizing the Subject: Politics and Gender in Women's Autobiographical Practice*. Minneapolis: University of Minnesota Press.

Smith, Susan. J. 1989. *The Politics of 'Race' and Residence*. Cambridge: Polity Press.

Smith-Rosenberg, Carroll. 1986. *Disorderly Conduct: Visions of Gender in Victorian America*. New York: Oxford University Press.

Sollors, Werner. 1986. *Beyond Ethnicity: Consent and Descent in American Culture*. Oxford: Oxford University Press.

Sontag, Susan. 1989. *AIDS and Its Metaphors*. New York: Farrar, Straus and Giroux.

Spivak, Gayatri Chakravorty. 1988. 'Can the Subaltern Speak?' In *Marxism and the Interpretation of Culture*, ed. Cary Nelson and Lawrence Grossberg, 271–311. Urbana: University of Illinois Press.

Stavans, Ilan, and Harold Augenbraum, eds. 1993. *Growing Up Latino: Reflections on Life in the United States*. New York: Mariner Books.

Steedman, Carolyn Kay. 1991. *Landscape for a Good Woman: A Story of Two Lives*. New Brunswick, NJ: Rutgers University Press.

Stone, Linda. 2006. *Kinship and Gender: An Introduction*. Boulder, CO: Westpoint Press.

Sunindyo, Saraswati. 1996. 'Murder, Gender and the Media: Sexualizing Politics and Violence.' In *Fantasizing the Feminine in Indonesia*, ed. Laurie Jo Sears, 120–39. Durham and London: Duke University Press.

Talle, Aud. 2007. 'Female Circumcision in Africa and Beyond: The Anthropology of a Difficult Issue.' In *Transcultural Bodies: Female Genital Cutting in Global Context*, ed. Bettina Shell-Duncan and Ylva Hernlund, 91–106. New Brunswick, NJ: Rutgers University Press.

Taussig, Michael. 1993. *Mimesis and Alterity*. London and New York: Routledge.

Thomas, Lynn. 2001. '*Ngaitana* (I Will Circumcise Myself): Lessons from Colonial Campaigns to Ban Excision in Meru, Kenya.' In *Female 'Circumcision' in Africa: Culture, Controversy and Change*, ed. Bettina Shell-Duncan and Ylva Hernlund, 129–50. Boulder, CO: Lynne Rienner Publishers.

Thorpe, Jocelyn. 2005. 'Indigeneity and Transnationality? An Interview with Bonita Lawrence.' *Women & Environments International Magazine* (Fall/winter): 6–8.

Tostan. 2009. 'Abandoning Female Genital Cutting.' www.tostan.org/web/page/586/sectionid/547/pagelevel/3/interior.asp.

Trinh, T. Minh-ha. 1989. *Woman, Native, Other: Writing Postcoloniality and Feminism.* Bloomington: Indiana University Press.

Tsolidis, Georgina. 2001. 'The Role of the Maternal in Diasporic Cultural Reproduction – Australia, Canada and Greece.' *Social Semiotics* 11, no. 2: 193–208.

Tuan, Yi-Fu. 1974. *Topophilia: A Study of Environmental Perception, Attitudes, and Values.* Englewood Cliffs, NJ: Prentice-Hall.

– 1977. *Space and Place: The Perspective of Experience.* Minneapolis: University of Minnesota Press.

Turković, Hrvoje i Vjekoslav Majcen. 2001. 'Kinematografija u hrvatskoj: Izvještaj o stanju.' *Hrvatski filmski ljetopis* 27–8: 53–95.

Tyyskä, Vappu. 2003. 'Solidarity and Conflict: Teen–Parent Relationships in Iranian Immigrant Families in Toronto.' In *Voices: Essays on Canadian Families*, 2nd ed, ed. Marion Lynn, 312–31. Toronto: Nelson Thomson Learning.

UNESCAP (United Nations Economic and Social Commission for Asia and the Pacific). 2008. *Key Trends and Challenges on International Migration and Development in Asia and the Pacific.* Expert Group Meeting on International Migration and Development in Asia and the Pacific, Population Division, Department of Economic and Social Affairs, Bangkok, Thailand, 18 September.

US Department of State. 2001. *Report on Female Genital Mutilation as Required by Conference Report (H. Rept. 106–997) to Public Law 106–429 (Foreign Operations, Export Financing, and Related Programs Appropriations Act, 2001).* www.state.gov/documents/organization/9424.pdf.

Van Wolputte, Steven. 2004. 'Hang on to Your Self: Of Bodies, Embodiment, and Selves.' *Annual Review of Anthropology* 33: 251–69.

Vertovec, Steven. 1999. 'Conceiving and Researching Transnationalism.' *Ethnic and Racial Studies* 22, no. 2, www.transcomm.ox.ac.uk/working%20papers/conceiving.PDF.

Waters, Mary C. 1999. *Black Identities: West Indian Immigrant Dreams and American Realities.* Cambridge, MA: Harvard University Press.

Weiss, Brad. 1996. *The Making and Unmaking of the Haya Lived World: Consumption, Commoditization and Everyday Practice.* Durham and London: Duke University Press.

White, Luise. 1993. 'Cars out of Place: Vampires, Technology and Labor in East and Central Africa.' *Representations* 43: 27–50.

Wilkie, Richard W. 2003. 'Sense of Place and Selected Conceptual Approaches to Place.' *Journal of the American Institute of Architecture Students* 1, no. 55: 29–31.

Wojnarowicz, David. 1991. *Close to the Knives: A Memoir of Disintegration*. New York: Vintage Books.

Wolf, Diane. 1992. *Factory Daughters: Gender, Household Dynamics and Rural Industrialization in Java*. Berkeley: University of California Press.

– 2000. 'Beyond Women and the Household in Java: Re-examining the Boundaries.' In *Women and Households in Indonesia: Cultural Notions and Social Practices*, ed. Juliette Koning, Marleen Nolten, Janet Rodenburg, and Ratna Saptari, 85–101. Richmond, UK: Curzon Press.

Wright, John Kirtland. [1947] 1966. 'Terrae Incognitae: The Place of Imagination in Geography.' In *Human Nature in Geography: Fourteen Papers, 1925–1965*, ed. John Kirtland Wright, 68–88. Cambridge, MA: Harvard University Press.

Yamada, Mitsuye. 2003. 'Invisibility as Unnatural Disaster: Reflections of an Asian American Woman.' In *Feminist Theory Reader: Local and Global Perspectives*, ed. Carole R. McCann and Seung-Kyung Kim. 174–8. London and New York: Routledge.

Yeoh, Brenda S.A., Shirlena Huang, and Theresa W. Devasahayam. 2004. 'Diasporic Subjects in the Nation: Foreign Domestic Workers, the Reach of the Law and Civil Society in Singapore.' *Asian Studies Review* 28: 7–23.

Yeoh, Brenda S.A., Katie D. Willis, and S.M. Abdul Khader Fakhri. 2003. 'Introduction: Transnationalism and Its Edges.' *Ethnic and Racial Studies* 26, no. 2: 207–17.

Yuval-Davis, Nira. 2003. 'Nationalist Projects and Gender Relations.' *Narodna umjetnost* 40, no. 1: 9–36.

Zinn, Maxine Baca, and D. Stanley Eitzen. 1987. *Diversity in American Families*. New York: Harper and Row.

Contributors

Noor Abdul Rahman is a visiting fellow at the Department of Geography, National University of Singapore. Her research interests are labour migration, women, and work in Southeast Asia, in particular Indonesian transnational domestic workers. She is the co-editor of *Asian Women as Transnational Domestic Workers* (2005). She has been exploring housing issues faced by male migrant workers in Singapore and will embark on a comparative research project that examines the cultural knowledge of Indonesian and Thai migrants. She is also an executive member of Transient Workers Count Too (TWC2), an NGO concerned with the welfare of foreign workers in Singapore.

Theresa W. Devasahayam is a senior researcher in the Institute of Policy Development at the Civil Service College in Singapore. Holding a PhD in cultural anthropology and an MA in public administration from Syracuse University, New York, her main research areas are income inequality, social inclusion, and multiculturalism in Singapore. She has held research positions in the Centre for Asia Pacific Social Transformation Studies (CAPSTRANS) at the University of Wollongong in Australia and the Asia Research Institute (ARI) at the National University of Singapore. She has conducted research on globalization and the status of women, migration of unskilled female labour in Southeast Asia, aging and its implications for working female caregivers, and women's fertility and reproductive health and rights and has published in these areas in international journals.

Lan Dong is an assistant professor of English at the University of Illinois at Springfield. She holds a PhD in comparative literature and is the author of *Reading Amy Tan* (2009) and several journal articles and book chapters on Asian American literature and films, children's literature, and popular culture. Currently she is finishing a book manuscript for Temple University Press, entitled 'Mulan's Legacy and Legend in China and the United States.'

May Friedman lives in Toronto with her partner and children. As an academic and social worker, May spends much time thinking, writing, and teaching about motherhood. May's most recent project is an anthology, edited with Shana Calixte, entitled *Mothering and Blogging: The Radical Act of the MommyBlog* (2009). May's children continue to challenge her to consider the complexities of identity by interrogating the nuances of everyday life as only four- and seven-year-olds are able to.

Erin Kenny received her PhD in anthropology from the University of Kentucky in 2005. Her research interests are West Africa and the Caribbean; household economics; kinship and the family; and cultural constructions of personhood, including rites of passage, gender, and life course. Having recently written journal articles on intergenerational gifting and belly dancing, Erin is at work on a longer, autoethnographic project about transnational childhoods. She teaches in the Interdisciplinary Studies Center at Drury University in Springfield, Missouri.

Katrin Križ, who hails from Austria, earned a PhD in sociology at Brandeis University, Massachusetts. Katrin is an assistant professor in the Department of Sociology at Emmanuel College in Boston. Her research interests are families and comparative social policy. With Uday Manandhar, she has a four-year-old daughter.

Uday Manandhar, who was born and raised in Nepal, holds a Master of International Development degree from Clark University, Maine. Uday works as an information technology manager with an IT company in the Boston area. With Katrin Križ, he has a four-year-old daughter.

Alan P. Marcus is an assistant professor in the Department of Geography and Environmental Planning at Towson University, Maryland. Originally from Brazil, he now lives in Baltimore. He completed his graduate studies in the United States and received his BA in anthropology from Northeastern University, Boston, and his MSc (geography) and PhD (geosciences) from the University of Massachusetts, Amherst.

Noula Papayiannis is a PhD candidate in Canadian history at the University of Toronto. She holds a BA in history and philosophy from the University of Western Ontario and an MA in immigration and settlement studies from Ryerson University. Noula is currently working on her doctoral dissertation, which explores the memories and commemorative rituals of Greek immigrants in Canada.

Lea Povozhaev is a writer and writing instructor at Lakeland Community College in northeastern Ohio. She earned BA degrees at Malone University in English and secondary education. After teaching high school English for two years, she earned an MA in composition at the University of Akron and then an MFA in creative writing from Northeast Ohio Consortium. She is studying composition and rhetoric in the PhD program at Kent State University. She has published excerpts from *When Russia Came to Stay* in *Ohio Teachers Write* and *YACK* and the memoir is forthcoming with Conciliar Press. She writes a column in a Cleveland multicultural magazine, *Vindicator*, and other essays appear in *America*, *Spiritual Life* and *Sightlines*, among other spiritual and literary journals. She lives with her husband and two young sons in Stow, Ohio.

Silvia Schultermandl is assistant professor of American studies at the University of Graz, where she teaches courses in American literature and culture studies. Her research interests lie in multi-ethnic American literatures and transnational feminism. She is the author of *Transnational Matrilineage: Mother–Daughter Relationships in Asian American Literature* (2009). She has published widely on contemporary American literature including ethnic American literature, canonicity, and 9/11. She recently put together a special issue for *Interactions* on Asian American and British Asian culture. She is currently at work on a collection of essays (co-edited with Şebnem Toplu) on narratives of transnational identity politics.

Jelena Šesnić is an assistant professor in the Department of English at the University of Zagreb, Croatia. She teaches American literature and culture, with special emphasis on nineteenth-century and U.S. ethnic literature. She is the author of *From Shadow to Presence: Representations of Ethnicity in Contemporary American Literature* (2007). Jelena has participated at several international American and ethnic studies conferences, has been awarded short- and long-term grants (Fulbright, European

Association of American Studies, John F. Kennedy Institute library grant), and has contributed articles to English-language literary journals. Her research interests focus on ethnic and transnational American studies, feminist and gender theory, and psychoanalytic and postcolonial approaches.

Şebnem Toplu received her PhD from Ege University, Izmir, Turkey, where she is an associate professor. She is the author of two books: *Cultural Materialism: Text and Context Relation in Jane Austen's Works* (2001) and *Diverse Aspects of Italy and Italians in Contemporary British Literature* (2001). Şebnem worked as visiting professor at Modena University, Italy, in 2000–1 and 2004–6. Since 2002 she has been the editor of *Interactions*, published semi-annually by Ege University.

Samuel Veissière earned his PhD from McGill University in 2007. He is an assistant professor of anthropology and chair of social sciences at the University College of the North in Thompson, Manitoba. He has conducted ethnographic fieldwork on subaltern agency, street livelihoods, and transnational sex and violence in Salvador da Bahia, Brazil. Samuel is currently working on a book manuscript entitled 'The Ghosts of Empire: Race, Performance, and Violence in the Transatlantic Cultural Economy of Desire,' which combines his Bahian fieldwork with follow-up studies of Brazilian sex workers in Europe. He is also involved with First Nations education in Canada/Turtle Island on an ongoing basis.

Julian Vigo is an assistant professor of comparative literature at the Université de Montréal, where she teaches comparative literature, performance studies, ethnography, cultural theory, theories of modernity and postmodernity, and gender studies. In addition to her academic research and pedagogy, Julian Vigo is a dj and an installation and video artist and has been making ethnographic film and video in Latin America, the Middle East, the Maghreb, Europe, and the United States since 1988.